WOMEN'S CITIZENSHIP IN PERU

WOMEN'S CITIZENSHIP IN PERU
THE PARADOXES OF NEOPOPULISM IN LATIN AMERICA

Stéphanie Rousseau

WOMEN'S CITIZENSHIP IN PERU
Copyright © Stéphanie Rousseau, 2009.
Softcover reprint of the hardcover 1st edition 2009 978-0-230-61815-2
All rights reserved.

First published in 2009 by PALGRAVE MACMILLAN® in the United States—a division of St. Martin's Press LLC, 175 Fifth Avenue, New York, NY 10010.

Where this book is distributed in the UK, Europe and the rest of the world, this is by Palgrave Macmillan, a division of Macmillan Publishers Limited, registered in England, company number 785998, of Houndmills, Basingstoke, Hampshire RG21 6XS.

Palgrave Macmillan is the global academic imprint of the above companies and has companies and representatives throughout the world.

Palgrave® and Macmillan® are registered trademarks in the United States, the United Kingdom, Europe and other countries.

ISBN 978-1-349-38081-7   ISBN 978-0-230-10143-2 (eBook)
DOI 10.1057/9780230101432

Library of Congress Cataloging-in-Publication Data

Rousseau, Stéphanie.
  Women's citizenship in Peru : the paradoxes of neopopulism in Latin America / Stéphanie Rousseau.
    p. cm.
  Includes bibliographical references and index.

  1. Women in politics—Peru. 2. Citizenship—Peru. 3. Populism—Latin America. 4. Democracy—Latin America. 5. Latin America—Politics and government—21st century. I. Title.

HQ1236.5.P4R68 2009
320.985082—dc22   2009017449

A catalogue record of the book is available from the British Library.

Design by Scribe Inc.

First edition: November 2009

10 9 8 7 6 5 4 3 2 1

To Simone and Flore, my grandmothers

Contents

Acknowledgments	ix
Introduction	1
1 Neopopulism and Women's Citizenship in Latin America	11
2 Fujimori's Peru: State and Society	35
3 Feminist Activism: Engendering State Policy through NGO Work	67
4 Women Organizing in Shantytowns: State Co-optation and the Exhaustion of Solidarity	97
5 Entering the Mainstream Political Sphere: Women as Elected Representatives	129
Conclusion: The Paradoxes of Constructing Women's Citizenship under Neopopulism	157
Appendix: List of Interviews	179
Notes	183
References	195
Index	217

Acknowledgments

While the work involved in writing a book can be quite solitary at times, the contribution of many individuals to this enterprise not only enriched the quality of the research but also made the whole experience much more pleasant and stimulating. This project started as a PhD dissertation and grew more mature as I was turning it into a book. I want to express my wholehearted gratitude to Philip Oxhorn who acted as a superb advisor for my dissertation. Phil provided constant support, encouragement, and fine intellectual guidance. His high spirits and our shared interest for Latin America made the arduous tasks involved in the different steps of the research project not only more worthwhile but also gratifying. Elisabeth Friedman generously accepted to be the external evaluator of my dissertation and encouraged me to reflect critically upon several issues to write this book. I also want to thank the anonymous reviewers for their criticisms and suggestions, without which the final product would be much different. Also crucial was Cynthia Kelly's editing work.

My learning process of Peruvian politics included spending over a year in the country at a particularly difficult but interesting moment of its history: the last months of the Fujimori government and the beginning of what Peruvians were calling the "transition to democracy." Cecilia Blondet opened me the doors of the *Instituto de Estudios Peruanos* (IEP) where I spent six months as a visiting fellow, and commented on several drafts of this book. Martín Tanaka also shared his thoughts and provided feedback. The IEP was a great research environment due to the high quality and friendliness of its staff and research associates.

Of course, the many women working in the women's movement organizations that I interviewed for the purpose of this book, or with whom I had many informal conversations, were also a great source of inspiration. I want to thank those who made a special effort to assist me in carrying out my research project: Rosario Bustamante, Patricia Carrillo, Gloria Cubas, Cecilia Olea, Roxana Vásquez, and Ana-María Yañez.

Many other individuals helped me, willingly or without knowing it, in the discovery of Peru's multiple layers of complexity. I want to thank all these people, and in particular Erika Bocanegra, Jorge Valladares, Stephanie Boyd, Omar Pereyra, Nosa Luna, Sofía Macher, Rafael Roncagliolo, Guillermo Salas, Cynthia Sanborn, Pancho Soberón, and Julio Villanueva Chang.

Financial resources are always an essential component of academic research, and due acknowledgment is made of the following agencies' support: *Fonds Concerté d'Aide à la Recherche du Québec* (FCAR, now FQRSC), Social Sciences and Humanities Research Council of Canada, McGill University's Faculty of Graduate Studies and Research, and McGill University Centre for Research and Teaching on Women. Since I started as Assistant Professor at the Department of Sociology of Université Laval, the Faculty of Social Sciences has provided me valuable research grants, some of which facilitated the completion of this book.

Finally, I want to thank Marie-Diane, Louis, and Elisabeth for making me who I am and Rémi for his love and support.

INTRODUCTION

Studying democratic politics from the point of view of women's rights and status leads to unexpected paradoxes. Women's mobilization and participation have dynamics of their own that entertain a complex relationship with patterns of democratization, especially when one considers the differing social, economic, and cultural context of different groups of women within the same nation-state (Yuval-Davis 1997). While apparently women as a social category should and have benefited from enhanced public freedoms and more accountable state institutions, historically varied and sometimes contradictory situations have been found (Melzer and Rabine 1993; Jaquette and Wolchik 1998; Waylen 2007).

For example, the degree of women's involvement in democratic movements does not always correspond to enhanced recognition of their human rights as individuals or to solid institutionalization of their new won rights after the first few years of new democratic regimes. Important parallels with socialist or other revolutionary processes have been made where radical changes did not necessarily carry forward women's demands, although they often have unleashed new women's movements (Moghadam 1995; Kampwirth 2004 and 2006). After three decades of relatively unchallenged democratic rule in Latin America, have women gained greater space in public life, moved towards greater gender equity, and improved their economic and social status? How has the turn to democracy been compromised by the radical restructuring of Latin American societies in the era of neoliberalism and how have organized women fared under this new emerging "socio-political matrix?" (Garretón 2003).

The early enthusiasm generated by the "third-wave democracies" of the late 1980s and early 1990s has been gradually replaced by a more nuanced and historically specific program of research on the variety of democratic regimes and experiences. Consolidation of democratic rule continues to be a challenge in many Latin American democracies such as Peru's. But at a deeper level, what was conceived by scholars as a cohesive system of rights, rules, institutions, and practices, before the expansion of democracy beyond Europe and North America to Latin America and other regions, is now being treated as a collection of separate pieces in a democratic puzzle. For each piece of the puzzle there seems to be contingent and historical dynamics.

Any substantial discussion of democratic politics must take into consideration the social–legal order upon which it is founded. In Peru, the case I address in this book, over half of the population lives in poverty, the State is still highly "politicized,"[1] and social inequalities are strongly structured along ethnic and racial axes. Yet ethnicity is a complex system in Peru where it was largely absent as an explicitly politicized issue up to the 2000s. Class-based politics has been more important from the 1970s onwards through the formation of relatively strong left-wing parties, although these crumbled rather suddenly as a result of the debt crisis, the impasse of guerrilla-state conflict, and the election of Alberto Fujimori in 1990. The latter marked the beginning of a neoliberal restructuring of state-society relations in Peru.

Fujimori's rule in many ways revived what had been a key feature of Peruvian politics throughout most of the twentieth century (i.e., populism). While populism changed in shape, mobilization, and organizational patterns, from its early manifestation in the 1920s with the formation of the Alianza Popular Revolucionaria Americana (American Popular Revolutionary Alliance—APRA) party to its neopopulist incarnation under Fujimori, it also paradoxically evolved towards a much less threatening phenomenon for most Peruvian economic elites in the 1990s. However, this statement only makes sense if each cycle of populism is contextualized and proper definitions of what are to be considered "economic elites" and the "popular masses" are given for a particular period of history. Populism evolves in accordance with historical transformations of the social structure and political regime.

In this book, I understand (neo)populism as a specific mode of political articulation that emanates from and consolidates in contexts of highly unstable institutional order. Populist rule is based on the use of frustrated social demands that become subsumed under a new unifying category, the "people." Instead of being processed "individually" through the normal workings of political institutions, these claims coalesce in the populist leader's discourse, which is fundamentally negative, that is, opposed to the dominant political order. Populism is inherently based on the discursive formation of a "people" pitted against a common enemy: usually the oligarchy, imperialist forces, or the political elite. The "people" is created in the act of political representation (Laclau 2005). As a result, populism can be found in various historical contexts and the political ideologies of populist leaders can vary. Populist leaders usually seek to discredit political institutions that they claim to be inefficient or incapable of representing the "people." This explains the tendency of populist leaders to bypass established institutions and/or create new ones. Populism also requires the creation of a strong popular identification with a political leader, who comes to embody "the people" and whose discourse displays its symbolic unity. Once in power, populist leaders usually develop programs and policies that effectively channel resources to mobilized popular sectors or answer some of their demands in order to sustain their legitimacy (Roberts 1995; Weyland 2001).

Populism can best be seen as a recurrent cyclical phenomenon in Latin America, where institutional stability is weak in many countries and social inequalities among the highest in the world, thus leading to intense periods of political conflict, especially when new economic models are put in place (Oxhorn 1998; Roberts 2006). Neopopulism is the resurgence of populist politics in the contemporary period of neoliberal reform implementation throughout Latin America (mostly in the 1990s but not limited to that period). While not all cases exhibit neopopulist politics, Peru under Fujimori's rule is a notable case in point. As argued by Weyland (1996), neoliberalism and neopopulism have shown "unexpected affinities." Strong popular support to outsider leaders allowed them to adopt neoliberal reforms strongly opposed by entrenched elite and nonelite organized actors who benefited from corporatist and social protection schemes not enjoyed by the majority. Democratic elections provide legitimacy to neopopulist leaders who use or contribute to political institutions' popular discredit to concentrate powers and, in the case of Fujimori, shut them down and renew them through questionable procedures, to say the least. This being said, if there are indeed affinities between neopopulism and neoliberalism, the relationship is sometimes not mutually supportive. As shown by the case of Hugo Chávez in Venezuela, opposition to neoliberalism can just as easily serve to launch and sustain neopopulist politics.

Neopopulism is a widespread phenomenon in post-1980s politics in Latin America. Yet very little attention has been devoted to studying its impact on women's movement dynamics and women's citizenship. This book proposes to fill this gap by studying the case of Peru. Fujimori's rule (1990–2000) is one of the most cited cases of neopopulism in Latin America, building on a history of populist politics in Peru that started in the early twentieth century (Roberts 1995; Stein 1999; Weyland 1996, 1999). This case study is thus well placed to illustrate the complex relationship between democratic politics, populism, and women's citizenship construction.

WOMEN'S CITIZENSHIP IN PERU

One of the first academic contributions on contemporary women's movements in Latin America, published in the early 1990s, claimed that "there [is] very little in the theory of social movements or the practice of women's organizations that recognizes the need for a strong State or gives groups a role to play in establishing political accountability" (Jaquette 1994, 233). Today, the impact of the macropolitical context on Latin American women's mobilization and their capacity to influence political institutions and citizenship regimes is the subject of a growing literature.[2] This book offers a new perspective by exploring the case of Peru where neopopulism overshadowed democratic politics in the 1990s. What is the impact of neopopulist politics on the configuration of the state's relation to the women's movement, and how does gender fit into the analysis of neopopulist mobilization?

As will be showed throughout the book, neopopulism defies common dichotomous treatment of politics along the democratic/authoritarian axis. Under Fujimori, electoral legitimacy and multiparty politics combined with severe limits on democratic accountability and the separation of powers. Moreover, neopopulism meant the controlled mobilization of popular sectors by Fujimori and strong attacks on civil society's autonomy. How did organized Peruvian women adapt to this context and how can we explain the gains and losses made in women's citizenship rights in the 1990s?

This book will argue that neopopulism had the most negative impact on women from the popular classes who were paradoxically also the most mobilized by Fujimori himself. I will also show that the gains made by other sectors of the women's movement—mainly feminist NGOs—were in part possible because of the concentration of power in the hands of Fujimori. Yet the price to pay was also high in that the use of a purportedly women-friendly discourse by the president was set in the context of a highly polarized political context where human rights abuses and attacks on democratic accountability ultimately hurt the whole women's movement. Citizenship construction is a paradoxical process.

Citizenship is widely held to be "defined as a personal status consisting of a body of universal rights (i.e., legal claims on the State) and duties held equally by all legal members of a nation-State" (Somers 1993, 588). Debates abound regarding the historical patterns of citizenship development in different parts of the world, as it pertains to distinct categories of individuals and groups. My own perspective on citizenship emphasizes its gendered social construction, inspired by the seminal work of T. H. Marshall and his critical followers, in particular the feminist literature on citizenship (Marshall 1950; Pateman 1988; Turner 1992; Walby 1994; Yuval-Davis 1997; Lister 1997; Oxhorn 1998a; Siim 2000).

Central behind the notion of the social construction of citizenship is the socially and politically contingent nature of the particular set of rights and freedoms that come to define the essence of being a citizen under a given political regime and a particular social formation. In Latin America, social rights have long been synonymous with the received image of citizenship. These rights, usually enjoyed by a minority of organized workers and the middle class, were drastically undermined in Latin America in the 1980s and 1990s (Franco 1994; Fleury 1997; Pérez 1997). In truth, civil rights have been the most underdeveloped aspect of Latin American polities throughout their postcolonial history, apart from the protections afforded to the right to private property and related commercial rights (once again, the privileges of a minority; Lopez 1997; Mendez, Pinheiro, and O'Donnell 1999). As for political rights, the most basic components of political democracy, they were only granted in their most complete form in post-1970s democractic regimes, while still being circumscribed in indirect but compelling ways in some cases including Peru (Transparencia 2000b).

Feminist attempts to deconstruct and reconstruct the notion of citizenship in order to include women and, for that matter, all individuals, have all faced a central problem, best expressed by Kathleen Jones, which is "how to recognise the political relevance of sexual differences and how to include these differences within definitions of political action and civic virtue without constructing sexually segregated norms of citizenship [?]" (Jones 1988, 18, quoted in Lister 1995, 12). Indeed, sexual and gender differences are to be taken into account in an egalitarian vision of citizenship, but without reifying these differences as permanent, natural, or universal gender essence.[3] In that respect, it is important to note that Latin American women's aspirations to gender equality are diverse in their orientations and normative basis. For example, motherhood is widely asserted as a core women's identity, and what is challenged by several organized women's groups is the social hierarchy that derives from women's traditional gender role rather than gender differences arising from these roles per se (Friedman 2000, 47–49). There exists a variety of feminisms in Latin America, some of course that directly question women's traditional primary identity as mothers, and an LGBT movement that struggles for sexual freedom and challenges established gender boundaries.

As will be shown in the following chapters, the politics of women's citizenship is also strongly articulated along class and ethnic lines, leading women's mobilization to be fragmented into various political identities. This is part of the reasons why the relationship between political regime types and the institutionalization of women's citizenship remains ambiguous. In theory, political democracy facilitates participation and, as a result, women who participate more freely in politics will see their rights improve. Yet only a disaggregated analysis of different aspects of women's citizenship and their development within a specific political context can explain the dynamics behind gains and losses in citizenship rights. Women's mobilization and access to the institutional sphere is mediated by the social structure.

Moreover, institutions themselves can account for a great part of the dynamics. It is a fact, for example, that some aspects of women's citizenship rights have been (and may continue to be) improved under authoritarian regimes throughout the world. The phenomenon of "State feminism,"[4] whereby reforms granting more rights to women are initiated principally within the state apparatus, often defying dominant gendered patterns, can occur in a democracy just as well as under an authoritarian regime.[5] Regardless of their political stripes, governments can see that it is in their political interest (or it may fit the ideology they promote) to grant certain rights to women.

Different aspects of citizenship may be emphasized by state leaders. For example, a populist reformist military regime may promote social and economic rights such as housing subsidy or labour rights while disregarding civil and political rights such as freedom of expression or suffrage. A democratic regime governed by a neoliberal government may likely emphasize some political and civil rights, while curtailing social and economic rights. As Veronica Schild compellingly demonstrates in the case of post-transition Chile, the ability of the State to impose a definition of citizenship predicated upon neoliberal market-based reform has led to an increasing "clientelization" of women in state policies, and the exclusion of working-class and poor women's organizations from any residual reform benefits. By contrast, middle-class, professional women's organizations have had greater capacities to reap the benefits of neoliberal policy schemes. Schild observed that "paradoxically, these cleavages are manifested through what seems like a common language of rights" (Schild 1998, 111).

Therefore, only by disaggregating the category "women" as political actors with differing capacities to exercise power, different needs, and claims, can we analyze the political processes leading to the multiple and nonlinear transformation of women's citizenship rights. Understanding the nature of the political forces that have the power to dominate the political scene is key to assessing the potential opportunities and obstacles organized women may face. How States and governing coalitions are constituted (state identity) and what they aspire to achieve (state priorities) structures the parameters for the inclusion and transformation of women's citizenship claims. In the case of Peru in the 1990s, Fujimori's neopopulism was an unwieldy hybrid of authoritarian State-building and democratic facade, or what some have called a "competitive authoritarian regime" (Levitsky and Way 2002). Did Fujimori have a stake in mobilizing women and what kind of gender politics did he pursue to sustain his neopopulist appeal? Did his rule have an impact on different women's citizenship claims?

In order to answer these questions, different features of neopopulism need to be considered to understand how issues pertaining to women's citizenship become politicized. Neopopulism means the mobilization of a multiclass mass support against an elite by a political leader who seeks to pursue an important transformation of society. Are women involved as a distinct category in the leader's mobilization strategy? This book shows that this was the case in Fujimori's Peru. Part of Fujimori's neopopulist discourse addressed women as a specific political clientele and as an object of public policy. Is the transformation of society addressing key aspects of women's citizenship such as their right to contraceptive choice, their right to organize autonomously, their right to social protection, and their right to participate equally in the political sphere? Again, this book looks at the relationship between different sectors of the Peruvian women's movement and the State under Fujimori. It shows that neopopulism provided opportunities for some of their citizenship claims to be addressed while others were severely curtailed. The concentration of powers in the hands of the president facilitated by his neopopulist appeal allowed him to adopt some controversial policies that were contrary to some elites' positions—for example, on issues such as contraceptive choice or gender election quotas. Yet at the same time, his need to control popular sector mobilization led to important attacks against some women's organizations, ultimately leading to their co-optation.

METHODOLOGY AND STRUCTURE OF THE BOOK

This book brings the discussion of neopopulism to center stage by focusing on some of its unexplored facets: that is, its relationship to gender politics and its impact on women's citizenship. In the first chapter, I draw from the main literature on populism and neopopulism to highlight key questions regarding women's citizenship and women's mobilization under current Latin American democratic regimes. In Chapter 2, I discuss contemporary Peruvian politics with an emphasis on Fujimori's neopopulist rule in the 1990s as a background to understand the changing political opportunity structure that women have been presented with, and that they have also partly shaped during that period.

The core of the book is then devoted to three studies of different sectors where Peruvian women have organized and put forward citizenship claims in recent decades. Again, more space is devoted to analyzing the dynamics under Fujimori's rule, although each sector is treated from a historical perspective to situate the particularities of this period. These three sectors are, in the order in which they will be addressed, the feminist women's movement, the urban popular sector women's movement in metropolitan Lima, and the women active in the realm of formal politics at the national and local levels, that is, political parties and representative institutions. This categorization follows the one developed by the main Peruvian analysts of the women's movement (Barrig 1994; Blondet 1995; Vargas and Villanueva 1994). Rural-based movements are not covered in this study, mainly because of their more limited relevance in the Peruvian national political scene during the 1990s.[6] Human rights groups are also not addressed because, contrary to some well-known cases such as Argentina, in Peru the human rights movement is not part of the women's movement as such. Each sector under study in this book is approached from the point of view of how it contributed to defining politically salient women's citizenship issues, how it managed or not to translate these claims into actual institutional and legal changes, and through which mechanisms, strategies, and relationships with the State.

In the conclusion, I draw on these three studies and what they reveal about organized women's relation to Fujimori's neopopulist politics to propose a mapping of Peruvian women's citizenship gains and losses, together with an assessment of the role of state policies, institutional factors, and women's strategies in these developments. This also leads me to propose new understandings of women's mobilization patterns under post-1970s democratic frameworks, as I show that the case of Peru differs from other well-studied cases of the literature on Latin American women's movements. The contrast that is often drawn between authoritarian and democratic frameworks becomes much less obvious when addressing the case of Peru and considering what neopopulism represents.

In addition to a thorough review of the Spanish and English literature, research for this book included one year of field presence in Peru spanned over the period between February 2000 and June 2001. This period was particularly intense in Peru as Fujimori was in his last months of rule and then flew in exile. I held over forty formal semi-structured interviews and many informal conversations with a broad range of women's rights advocates, leaders of popular sector women's organizations, professionals from nongovernmental organizations, politicians, civil servants, academics, and journalists (a list of formal interviews is provided in the appendix). To complement this rich material, I also collected current and old pamphlets and publications by women's organizations to learn about their activities and discourse. Some official documents (Congress and State) were also selected for analysis. The written material and the interviews allowed me to identify the key building blocks and tensions within each sector under study, the role of organized women in Peruvian citizenship construction, and their perceptions of constraints and opportunities under Fujimori's rule.

CHAPTER 1

NEOPOPULISM AND WOMEN'S CITIZENSHIP IN LATIN AMERICA

The study of Peruvian women's movements' interaction with a neo-populist state needs to be contextualized in relation to what we already know about populism and women's participation in democratization processes in Latin America. In this chapter, I will first review existing accounts of populist and neopopulist political dynamics to define these key terms. I will then proceed to discuss how the gendered dimensions of (neo)populism have been described in a limited number of academic works, and finally connect these issues with the broadest questions of women's relationship with existing democracies in contemporary Latin America. In these different sections, I will highlight the specificities of the Peruvian case.

NEOPOPULISM AND ITS IMPACT ON STATE–SOCIETY RELATIONS

How States are built and how state elites articulate their national identity within society are central variables in understanding how citizenship gets constructed. The processes of claims formation established under successive governments determine the kinds of opportunities, resources, incentives, and mechanisms of political representation available to citizens, and structure their relationship with the State. For instance, building welfare States in the majority of West and North European countries, North America, and Australia has significantly expanded social rights and established a range of public institutions in these areas. With the rise of corporatism in the twentieth century as a dominant mode of interest representation in some industrialized and developing countries, the rights formation patterns have also come to reflect more evidently the identity of the collective actors who are included in corporatist systems. The institutional characteristics of Latin American political systems have been shaped by both of these two currents, but in a fragmented and partial fashion. Some of the most powerful political trends to shape these State–society relations over the past century in Latin America have been populism and neopopulism.

Populism and Neopopulism in Latin America

Populist politics have been a recurrent phenomenon in Latin America. In its first, classic phase, roughly between the 1930s and 1970s, populism was associated with the effects of late and dependent capitalist development. When a small but mobilized working class aspired to political inclusion (thus threatening the stability of the political system), charismatic leaders rallied to include some popular sectors in the political process and stimulate national development. Their efforts were typically pursued through nationalist industrialization programs, based on import substitution, price controls, and some redistributive measures targeted to organized workers. In the late 1980s and 1990s, during a second phase of populism in countries such as Brazil, Argentina, Ecuador, and Peru, some leaders adopted neoliberal, export-based development models. As a result, during the 1990s, the notion of populism was revised by scholars, and no longer reflected a particular set of economic policies, leading some to use the term "neopopulism" or to broaden significantly their theoretical understanding of populism (Roberts 1995; Weyland 1996; Knight 1998; de la Torre 2000; Mayorga 2002).

Early scholarly conceptualizations of Latin American populism described it as a nationalist movement characterized by urban, multiclass mobilization. This mobilization was channeled through the formation of mass-based parties, led by charismatic leaders. Populist ideology, as evidenced by the etymology of the word, relies on an evocation of the people (*el Pueblo* in Spanish), both as the source of mobilization and a political project to be completed. Those who "belong to the people" are thus considered to be united in an organic whole, opposed to the oligarchy or imperialist forces. In post-World War I and post-World War II social contexts, populism was associated with new national development projects based on the political integration of the middle and working classes. It was usually associated with redistributive policies in the form of social security for some organized sectors of the population, usually through labor unions. It stood to reason that in Latin American countries that had suffered the dislocations of dependent capitalist development, the fragmentation of the national social body would invite initiatives to build a more integrated

Nation-State through various redistributive policies, anti-imperialism, and cultural affirmation (Canovan 1981; Conniff 1982).

According to Ernesto Laclau, among others, populism tends to emerge during periods of crisis and leads to the formation of new hegemonic projects based on alliances between leaders, popular sectors, and other strata of society, like the intelligentsia or the middle class. Early populist projects in Latin America gave a voice to the public's moral rejection of increasingly irrelevant, closed, oligarchical political systems. This process had deep repercussions on the body politic and in some cases the very challenges that were made to established privilege and authority actually stemmed the growth of more radical revolutionary forces (Laclau 1977). Authors analyzing these transformations underscore the resulting strong emotional bonds that grow between the masses and their defiant leaders. Indeed, this bond is one of the central features of populist politics, and is usually enhanced through the strategic use of popular culture in the discourse and symbolism of populist parties or movements (particularly by their leaders) with the goal of creating a deep sense of national belonging.

Economic and political crises, even if recurrent in Latin American history, cannot alone account for the rise of populism, since it is not, as de la Torre and Knight argue forcefully, a temporary phenomenon waiting to be replaced by more "normal" circumstances (Knight 1998; de la Torre 2000). Rather, populism in its classic and new forms can be understood as a particular form of political representation, leadership, and rule corresponding to central features of Latin American political experiences. As Laclau aptly summarized it in a more recent piece, populism is a specific mode of political articulation that emanates from and consolidates in contexts of highly unstable institutional order. Instead of being processed "individually" through the workings of political institutions, frustrated and unattended social demands become subsumed under a new unifying category, the "people," whose identity is fundamentally negative, that is, opposed to the political order (Laclau 2005).

Laclau posits that in order for different social demands, carried forward by distinct actors, to develop a common political identity, there is a need to build a "chain of equivalences" between the groups' diverse interests or claims (Laclau 2005). "The equivalences are only such in terms of a lack pervading them all, and this requires the identification of the source of social negativity. Equivalential popular discourses divide, in this way, the social into two camps: power and the underdog" (Laclau 2005, 37–38). Therefore, major crises can precipitate the formation of a populist movement, but not all crises lead to populism or to a populist leader's rise to state power. Moreover, populist politics can actually be considered as the norm rather than the exception in many countries.

Peru has particular theoretical resonance in this area, since it has been cited as a central case in the literature on populism and neopopulism. Tracing the development of both political phenomena in Peru will provide some insight into their particular significance and clarify how I use the term neopopulism to characterize Fujimori's rule.

Peruvian Populism

Populism first emerged in Peru during the 1920s with the formation of the Alianza Popular Revolucionaria Americana (American Popular Revolutionary Alliance—APRA), the country's oldest political party, earliest mass-based populist initiative and the driving force behind the major pan-Latin American *Aprista* movement. In many ways, the Apristas would establish the tone and content for the discourses of Peruvian and other Latin American populist leaders to come. Founded in 1924 by the charismatic Victor Raúl Haya de la Torre, APRA's early platform was socialist, nationalist, resolutely anti-imperialist, and advocated a strong interventionist role for the State in the economy to foster national integration and better living conditions for the popular classes. APRA was a party that represented some sectors of the peasantry, the working class, and the middle class, and fought for the end of oligarchic domination. Not surprisingly, this very vocal populist party was the subject of substantial controversy with the established, colonial, land-owning oligarchy and was sporadically outlawed as an official political party, which hindered its political reach. During the 1950s, in a bid to obtain full legal party status, APRA began to collaborate with the oligarchy and abandoned many of its socialist ideals, a move that somewhat changed the party's historic reputation but kept it in the running to seize political power. In 1979, Haya de la Torre became the president of the constitutional assembly, which drafted a new constitution for Peru.[1] And in 1985, after decades of political activism and sitting as legislative opposition, the party was voted into office (Stein 1999; Rousseau 2005).[2]

Haya de la Torre was the first in an influential line of populist politicians in Peru. In 1931, Luis Sánchez Cerro ran against Haya de la Torre (then leader of the main opposition party) in the presidential elections, and became Peru's first populist head of State to be elected with the support of the literate popular sectors. Sánchez Cerro was a high-ranking *Mestizo* military leader who successfully ousted the dictator Augusto Leguía in 1930 and managed to build a multiclass coalition. His goal was to oppose APRA, which was perceived as too radical by the oligarchy and the military. Sánchez Cerro came from humble beginnings and captured the popular imagination for his bravery against the dictatorship and his noteworthy battle scars. He was affectionately nicknamed *El Cholo* (man of indigenous descent). The Sánchez Cerro's regime legalized divorce in 1930 and outlawed APRA in 1931. Sanchez Cerro's fight against the suppressed APRA party ended in violence when he was assassinated by an APRA member in 1933 in the context of a civil war between the North Peruvian *Apristas* and the State (Contreras and Cueto 1999, 200–208).

General Juan Velasco Alvarado, also of *Mestizo* origin, was another populist leader with whom the masses could identify. In 1968, after Velasco seized power through a coup, no elections were allowed and civilian politicians had little influence. Nonetheless, the junta respected most civil liberties, the press continued to function, and Velasco attempted to appeal to the masses through a system of broad, full, popular participation. APRA's founding principles figured prominently in his discourse. They also formed the backbone of many of his policies. Initiatives long advocated by APRA came to fruition as the reformist government gave new entitlements to labor unions such as a labor code and collective bargaining, introduced a policy for import substituting to build national industries, and nationalized foreign interests in oil, mining, telecommunications, the fishing industry, and other sectors. Velasco proclaimed the Quechua tongue of Peru's aboriginal people to be a coequal national language with Spanish and promoted equality for women. Perhaps the most striking accomplishment of his regime was its sweeping agrarian reform, which actually managed to crush what remained of the oligarchy's *latifundio* (high concentration of agricultural land ownership). Mismanagement, ill-conceived programs and austerity measures ultimately led to a fall from grace for the regime. Velasco was removed from power in a bloodless coup by Peru's more conservative military factions in 1975.

By the time APRA finally acceded to State power in 1985, it presided over (and precipitated, according to some analysts) the deepest political and economic crisis of Peru's history. To many, APRA's poor performance in the halls of power revealed the impossibility of pursuing traditional-style populism.[3] Based on the political vocabulary of populism inherited from past Peruvian patterns of representation and rule, Alberto Fujimori developed a neopopulist response to Peru's political and democratic crisis.

Fujimori: The Beginning of Neopopulism in Peru

Alberto Fujimori, elected president in 1990, has been described as a neopopulist leader because of his broad appeal to popular sectors and his critical discourse regarding Peru's political and economic elites (Roberts 1995; Weyland 1996). Clearly, his leadership represented a new type of populist politics, mainly because he did not rely on an appeal to organized workers, and because he put in place a set of policies contrary to classic populism's protectionist and corporatist tendencies. While the Fujimori regime based its legitimacy on winning democratic elections, the government's leadership style severely circumscribed the public sphere by working to eliminate intermediary channels of political representation between citizens and the State. Moreover, the new intensive concentration of power and authority in the hands of the president (deriving both from Fujimori's military "self-coup" in 1992, which suspended democratic institutions, and from his subsequent lack of respect for the new constitution he drafted in 1993) exacerbated the domination of the executive over legislative power in Peru. Fujimori imposed a draconian structural adjustment program, a spate of neoliberal reforms, and an approach to social programs focused on the uneven delivery of material goods to the poorest sectors within a paternalistic and clientelistic framework. Facing a tide of mounting corruption scandal, criticism over human rights abuses (including a controversial sterilization program for women) and growing political instability, Fujimori resigned in exile in 2000.

Populism vs. Neopopulism

Was Fujimori a populist or neopopulist? Some have questioned the use of the concept of "populism" to describe Fujimori's rule, since his political power was not founded on a mass-based party or on an appeal to organized working classes, as was the case for most previous populist leaders in Peru and Latin America (Lynch 1999; Stein 1999; Cotler and Grompone 2000). Moreover, Fujimori's economic policy was at the extreme opposite of the import-substitution industrialization model historically associated with populism (Weyland 2001). Kenneth M. Roberts contributed to the debate by proposing a "radial" definition of populism.[4] He focuses on five core properties of populism, namely 1.) A personalistic and paternalistic, though not necessarily charismatic, pattern of political leadership; 2.) A heterogeneous, multiclass political coalition concentrated in the subaltern sectors of society; 3.) A top-down process of political mobilization that either bypasses institutionalized forms of mediation or subordinates them to more direct linkages between the leader and the masses; 4.) An amorphous or eclectic ideology, characterized by a discourse that exalts subaltern sectors or is antielitist and/or antiestablishment; and 5.) An economic project that utilizes widespread redistributive or clientelistic methods to create a material foundation for popular sector support (Roberts 1995, 88).

Roberts's definition has the merit of broadening the *spatio-temporality of populism* beyond its classic phase (from the 1930s to the 1970s). He underscores the fact that populist social policies may not necessarily be redistributive but do deliver some goods necessary for the survival of the poor (e.g., targeted poverty-reduction programs implemented from the 1990s onwards). He also emphasizes the material basis upon which popular adhesion to a populist project is constructed in an era when import-substitution industrialization and interventionist state policy are no longer the basis of a country's development model. In other words, Roberts holds that the concept of populism should not be tied to economic policy associated with a specific phase of economic development (e.g., import-substitution industrialization), or to social policies with clear redistributive-corporatist characteristics.

For Kurt Weyland, comparing the limited set of policies included in the poverty-alleviation programs such as those implemented by Fujimori with broad-based programs of State intervention in the economy and redistributive policies amounts to conceptual stretching, which ultimately leads to confusion (Weyland 2001, 10). To understand current forms of populism, he calls for a *classical definition* of the concept as located exclusively in the political domain (Weyland 2001). For Weyland, the political strategy of a leader who wins and exercises power through the rallying of popular support that bypasses established political institutions represents the main plank in populist rule. Personalistic leadership, charisma, and an uninstitutionalized or loosely institutionalized endorsement from the masses are the core attributes of both historical populism and neopopulism (Weyland 2001). Depending upon the historical circumstances and whether the masses that are being mobilized by a given leader have been previously partaken in political organizing, a populist leader will seek to incorporate the masses, through more formal channels like populist parties, or adopt a more clearly anti-organizational strategy. The case of Peru in which there was an abundance of political parties and organizations throughout the 1980s (in a context of growing discontent with the economic and political state of affairs) certainly fits Weyland's description of the attack on organized civil society as a means to create a new state hegemony. In point of fact, Fujimori built his regime on an anti-organizational strategy of attacking established political actors and institutions.

Philip Oxhorn's approach is based on *popular class formation problems*. He also breaks with the economic policy prescription of older definitions of populism to focus on two kinds of populism, "popular sector ascendant," and "popular sector defensive." The two terms refer to two different sets of circumstances. The "popular sector ascendant" circumstances include situations in which political pressure is brought to bear to incorporate popular sectors politically. The "popular sector defendant" circumstances occur once popular sectors have been formally included (e.g., through universal suffrage) but continue to be both economically and politically marginalized—spurring their reaction against the political system. In both of these contexts, characterized by what Oxhorn defines as "the populist mode of interest intermediation," the political leader portrays him/her as the great defender of popular sectors from further marginalization (Oxhorn 1998b, 222).

Oxhorn's approach, while relying like Weyland on a political definition of populism, adds a *structural-historical* dimension that offers a causal explanation for the recurrence of populism in Latin America. The fragmentation of Latin American popular classes (in different sectors with contradicting interests) and the weakness of their organization at different political conjunctures create a regular need for populist leaders. Oxhorn stresses the potency of the promises populist leaders make to break with the dominance of economic or political elites. Based on his contextual analysis, he prefers to retain the term "populism" and qualify it with adjectives (*popular sector ascendant/ defensive*) to distinguish between two different manifestations of populism in Latin America. While Fujimori's rule could be termed a popular sector defensive expression of populist politics, I retain the term "neopopulist" to describe the new historical manifestation of populism in the case of Fujimori's Peru. As elsewhere in Latin America, neopopulism contrasts with the populism that preceded it while retaining significant basic features.

Joining in theoretical debate, I am compelled to return to Roberts' aforementioned five-fold spatio-temporal definition of populism. Weyland rejected the validity of the similarities pointed out by Roberts between 1.) contemporary social programs that provide goods to the poorest unorganized sectors; and 2.) past redistributive policies framed in the development model of import-substituting industrialization. But I would argue that while the substance and scope of both initiatives differ significantly from economic and developmental points of view, from a strictly political vantage point, neopopulist government leaders ultimately adopt such policies for comparable strategic reasons. In other words, if a leader wants to ground his or her clientelistic links to designated social sectors on some material basis, these policies can be equally instrumental. As for differences in the nature and consequences of these programs, in social-structural terms these are more easily explained based on preceding history, fiscal circumstances, and other policy constraints than based on essentially different political phenomena.

This point is echoed by Fernando Mayorga in his incisive analysis of the link between neopopulism and the new role of the State in Latin America under neoliberalism and democracy. On the one hand, neoliberal reforms since the late 1980s have led to the weakening and near-disappearance of many organized actors in society (such as labor unions) and the rise of other forms of collective action due to an increasingly informal labor market. On the other hand, the State has retreated from many spheres of the economy that are now deeply liberalized. In the current context, it therefore follows that a neopopulist appeal to highly marginalized sectors cannot reasonably expect to succeed by relying on the same old corporatist channels or the same mechanisms to establish clientelistic ties. These seismic socioeconomic changes also affect how populist appeals are made to the masses of people who (due to a decline of labor union strength and collective action) are no longer easily reachable through labor organizations. In the context of the turn to representative democracy, one alternative pursued by neopopulist leaders has been to address the masses as individual voters (Mayorga 2002). As de la Torre shows in his comparative analysis of Ecuadorian populism, the same language of popular inclusion is deployed in the context of increasingly informalized labor and policies going against national industrial bourgeoisie (de la Torre 2000).

One of the paradoxes of neopopulism is the extraordinary ability of neopopulist state leaders to rally popular support while implementing macroeconomic reforms that actually further impoverish the masses of marginalized urban and rural poor—their main political supporters. Weyland shows how neopopulist leaders go about carrying through on politically thorny neoliberal reforms without risking losing power by "isolating" themselves from the rest of the political system (Weyland 1996). They act against the institutions that could hold them accountable, instead relying on the legitimacy provided by democratic electoral success to ensure their power. In fact, neopopulist leaders bypass established political channels (such as parties and unions) to facilitate the adoption of neoliberal reforms that are unpopular among the social groups previously protected by past populist policies. Of course emphasizing the fiscal distress and crisis in which reforms are implemented facilitates the popular endorsement of neoliberal policies. But it is the new discourse on the state's role in development that ultimately persuades non-organized, poor citizens. The government simply purports that it is attacking corporatist privileges, and at that point neopopulist, neoliberal reforms come to represent a new popular hegemonic project. To spread their anti-corporatist message and ensure the support of the masses, neopopulists spin their populist appeals through a variety of mass media (Waisbord 2003). More recently, a new wave of neopopulism led by Hugo Chavez in Venezuela goes against the elites created by neoliberalism and the policies that were pursued in that name for over a decade in Latin America.

Alan Knight raises the important point that the followers of a populist movement or leader may be as rational as the followers of non-populist leaders or parties, even though the style of leader–mass interaction would lead us to believe that it is mainly based on emotional, affective connections (Knight 1998, 228). However, we should bear in mind that the goods—material and immaterial—that a populist leader grants or promises to designated sectors are central in this relationship. A strong sense of identity grows between the masses (or individual citizens) and the leader, and clientelistic bonds based on material exchange are the vehicle for political representation (e.g., using price controls on basic staples as a symbolic political gesture with strong material consequences). However, both neopopulist and populist State-society relations do not empower popular sectors to the point of transforming class hierarchies, even though the government may work hard to actually (re)distribute resources.

The concentration of political authority in a single person, to the detriment of democratic institutions and intermediary channels of political representation, is a central defining characteristic of both neopopulist and populist politics. In all of these respects, the Fujimori regime was a textbook example of neopopulism. Relatively unconcerned with upholding democratic institutionalization and the rule of law, it opted to champion short-term benefits (albeit arbitrary and unequal), and preferred to bypass democratic debate. Fujimori was a neopopulist leader in that, in his discourse, he claimed to put "the people's interests" first, promoting so-called "real democracy" as opposed to "democracy for the privileged," which the majority of the people had supposedly experienced in the past. Symbols of order, modernity, and pragmatism, coupled with some direct provision of material goods to selected social sectors (mainly the popular, unorganized classes) were used to justify most of Fujimori's severe neoliberal adjustment policies, state reforms, and flagrant disregard for human rights (Degregori 2001).

Neopopulism, Democracy, and Citizenship

The implications of neopopulism for democracy and citizenship are also a matter of debate in the literature. Authors like René Antonio Mayorga posit that neopopulism arises from a crisis of democratic institutions. The case of Bolivia, where neopopulist parties such as *Conciencia de Patria* (Nation's Conscience—CONDEPA) and *Unidad Cívica Solidaridad* ((Civic Unity Solidarity—UCS) emerged in the late 1980s in a context where the political party system was relatively stable, may seem to contradict this assertion. But R. A. Mayorga contends that these neopopulist parties have failed to win in national elections precisely because no crisis has been successfully declared (Mayorga 1995). The subsequent victory of the *Movimiento al Socialismo* (Movement Towards Socialism—MAS) led by Evo Morales in 2005, after a decade of intense street protests and the decline of the traditional party system, can be analyzed as Bolivia's evolution towards neopopulism (Rousseau 2010). In this case, the crisis of democratic institutions was very much created by the very actors that later rose to state power. Whether or not a crisis of democratic institutions is necessary for neopopulist leadership patterns to emerge is therefore a question of context and interpretation.

This said, neopopulist rule has sometimes proven to be detrimental to the consolidation of democracy in Latin America. The reason is clear: while neopopulist parties have claimed to be responding to a lack of representation for popular interests, they have followed a centralizing trend of political deinstitutionalization that has weakened and severed democratic accountability. Latin American presidential systems have typically been prone to concentrate undue power in the executive, but neopopulist leaders have exacerbated this tendency, severely encroaching upon the autonomy of other spheres, such as the legislature or judiciary. Furthermore, the personalization of politics has led to severe curtailments in the rule of law (Mayorga 1995). In the long run, neopopulism is also prone to be violently opposed, thereby leading to a new wave of institutional instability. The case of Argentina under Carlos Menem's presidency is paradigmatic in that respect, as shown by several authors (Levitsky and Murillo 2005). The 2001 crisis experienced by that country seriously questioned democratic institutions in the face of deep popular resentment against the whole political class including the Peronist party previously led by Menem.

In a contrasting view of the relationship between populism and democracy, Carlos de la Torre and Fernando Mayorga argue that neopopulism acts as a vehicle for the integration of excluded sectors that may be tempted to reject political democracy in the long run (de la Torre 2000; Mayorga 2002). What is at play is the legitimacy of democratic institutions as representative of the voices and interests of the majority of the population, which explains the rise of neopopulist projects in the midst of intense crises such as the one that was experienced in Peru in 1990. There is therefore a tension between the particular kind of inclusionary appeal under neopopulism, and the consequences on democratic institutions that may be very negative when neopopulist projects enter the State and dismantle some of the procedural components of democracy. This tension is present throughout my analysis of neopopulism and gender politics in Peru.

Gendered Populism and Neopopulism

Remarkably few theoretical and empirical works have analyzed the discourse and political strategies of populist leaders in Latin America from a gendered perspective, or the direct impact of populist rule on gendered citizenship rights. Neopopulism has not been addressed systematically from a gendered perspective either.[5] From the historical perspective of older cases, populism seems rather ambiguous in its impact on the social construction of women's citizenship.

One of the well-documented cases is that of Eva Perón (1919–52), the popular wife of Argentinian President Juán Perón, who was key to the success of his form of populist politics later labeled Peronism. Eva Perón has been held up as an example of the role that gender can play in Latin American populist politics, illustrating how a populist government can initiate groundbreaking gains for women's civil and political rights (Patroni 1999; Navarro 1999). In Argentina in the late 1940s through the early 1950s, Eva Perón took an active role as First Lady and was the only woman to be part of the Superior Board of the Peronist Party. She also founded the Peronist Women's Party. She created her own foundation, devoted to the social welfare of workers' families and played a key role in the lobby for women's suffrage granted in 1951 (Navarro 1999). In the elections that followed the victory for women's right to vote, not only were several women elected but Argentina could claim the first female Congressperson in the world to be named President of Congress. Eva Perón was also a pioneer in creating feminist civic centers throughout the country and her image as a wholesome, maternal, patriotic figure has endured in many quarters (Taylor 1979).

Eva devoted herself to numerous causes among the poor in general and for women in particular. Most importantly from the point of view of Perón's populist political success, as argued by Patroni, Eva Perón was a key politician acting for the consolidation of the Peronista party because of the intermediary role that Perón asked her to perform between organized labor and the State. Eva was an excellent speaker and came to embody the feelings and values of the Argentine working class who identified strongly with her. She was depicted as a very beautiful and model wife, dedicated entirely to the cause of the most vulnerable, and for this reason, associated with the values of motherhood even though she was not a mother herself. The symbol of the working class' aspirations that she came to represent was crucial in Perón's quest to squash organized labor's autonomy. Eva called herself the "bridge of love" between Perón's government and workers (Patroni 1999).

In Argentina, Eva Perón has created a culture of gendered populism. Through field-research among poor urban neighborhoods, Javier Auyero shows that today's Peronist clientelistic networks function according to a gendered division of labor, whereby policy-making is made by men and goods are delivered to the grassroots by women, who see their role as "naturally" emanating from their identity and experience as mothers. Working with the poor in grassroots survival activities is described by the very women involved in these networks as a special gift they have as women to feel and know what the needs of the poor are. Political action is closely entwined in a discourse on mothers' duties (Auyero 2000, 127; 136–39).

In her study of gendered populism in Puerto Rico, Ann S. Macpherson discusses how the populist colonial reform undertaken in the 1930s and 1940s addressed an already enfranchised and highly mobilized female labor movement. Minimum wage and new birth control policies were adopted in response to some of the basic daily grievances of working class women. Macpherson argues that the inclusion of women in the populist reform coalition facilitated the formation of a new hegemonic project, thereby allowing the State to "renegotiate its colonial compact." In reality, women's citizenship claims were only partially addressed, women themselves were treated as second-class citizens within the coalition, and the paternalistic control of political prerogatives on the part of male political leaders persisted (Macpherson 2003).

These two examples of the literature on gendered Latin American populism reveal a combined double register of national female identity, predicated on the reification in populist discourse of traditional gender roles. At the same time, it contributed to raising women's active involvement in spheres traditionally reserved to men such as politics or the workplace. Populist politics, particularly in the case of Eva Perón, was used strategically to valorize conventional feminine characteristics like motherhood, the submission of wives to their husbands, and the altruistic practice of self-denial for the good of the community. It must be said that both Peronism and the female leaders associated with the populist coalition in Puerto Rico have won better living conditions and new civil and political rights for women.

Likewise, in Peru traditional feminine identity was evoked in relatively similar ways by both Fujimori and some organized women. Fujimori exploited the same two registers of national female identity. He not only extolled the virtues of conventional gender roles in a neopopulist, essentialist discourse, but would also trumpet the unconventional new rights being accorded to women by virtue of their participation in the public and formal political spheres. Women's movements were challenged to varying degrees by the drastic shrinking of the public sphere, the centralization of political authority in the hands of the president, and the Fujimori regime's use of fear and selective repression. Indeed, State–society relations under Peruvian neopopulism meant an intensive restructuring of the political sphere and a weakening of civil society. At the same time however, in a paradoxical fashion, the 1990s were a watershed of opening for women's political participation in the state and party politics. When women's citizenship claims could penetrate state institutions in a way that could potentially boost the President's image as a modernizing, woman-friendly leader, these claims generally prospered.

In contrast to most cases of classic populism, neopopulism under Fujimori involved many women in high political positions, thus transforming public perception of the gendered frontiers of politics. So on one hand, apart from implementing unpopular neoliberal reforms that negatively affected women's material living conditions, it could be said that Peruvian neopopulism had the merit of applying reforms to some key women's rights issues. On the other hand, in as much as neopopulist initiatives deliberately crushed intermediary channels of political representation or disregarded the basic social and economic policy framework of past populist era, women's citizenship claims fared poorly under Fujimori's neopopulist rule, as will be shown in the following chapters. Understanding the opportunities and limits of women's movement politics under neopopulism contributes to shedding light on women's political experience under contemporary democratic regimes in Latin America.

Democracy and Women's Citizenship

Many of the Latin American countries that initiated transitions to democratic regimes in the 1980s have not seen their democracies consolidated, despite two decades of passably resilient democratic rule.[6] This "low-intensity democracy" has had numerous repercussions on both the political and social orders in Latin America, where political institutions remain unstable and citizens' rights are unequal and underdeveloped (O'Donnell 1999a, 1999b).

Most early analysts of gender relations since the 1980s agree that democratic politics under Latin American regimes have had unexpected exclusionary effects on women. The first wave of literature on Latin American women's political participation in transitional democratization (during the period of regime change in the 1980s), and the second wave literature on the post-transitional dynamics that followed both focus on patterns in women's mobilization and their entry into new democratic institutions.

The first wave of literature on the involvement of Latin American women in politics began to come out in the early 1990s, exploring women's political participation and the power struggles involved in processes of regime change (Alvarez 1990; Jelin 1990; Jaquette 1994; Jaquette and Wolchik 1998; Rodríguez 1998; Waylen 1994, Friedman 2000). Many of the first-wave authors who strove to broaden our understanding of the different levels and areas in which women were vital political actors concluded that a critical mass of Latin American women had mobilized to take their place at the forefront of civil society's struggle against authoritarian regimes. The central role of organized women in this struggle was explained by the minor threat women represented for authoritarian leaders who perceived them as unpolitical. Enduring a much lower level of repression than their male or mixed counterparts, women's organizations were therefore able to perform key resistance strategies and expose authoritarian abuses. This was key in initiating the fall of authoritarian power blocs. The first-wave authors observed that during the transition periods that followed, women's organizations wanted to redefine women's citizenship based on robust, equal, and nondiscriminatory terms. Despite the best efforts of Latin American women, first-wave authors concluded that their initiatives within post-transition legal and political frameworks yielded mixed results.

A second wave of literature on women in the new Latin American democratic regimes emphasizes that women continue to be underrepresented in political institutions and political parties (as is the case in the vast majority of older democratic and nondemocratic regimes throughout the world). Nonetheless, progress has been made when electoral or party gender quotas have been established and were effective (Htun and Jones 2002; Waylen 2007). Moreover, women's mobilization, which was often critical in initiating and sustaining civil society's demands for political liberalization and regime change under authoritarian regimes, has undergone major organizational and political transformations under the new regimes. The consequences of these shifts are multiple and still unfolding. They include a professionalization and formalization of feminist organizations through the formation of nongovernmental organizations (NGOs), the increasing prominence of issue networks rallying different sectors of organized women, and the relative marginalization of popular sectors' women's organizations (Schild 1998; Alvarez 1999; Craske and Molyneux 2002; Lind 2004 and 2005; Franceschet 2005; Waylen 2007).

The second wave of literature also makes the point that Latin American women lost their short-lived central role in politics when civil society demobilized or retreated, and male-dominated political parties took over under democratic regimes (Waylen 2000, 2007; Molyneux 2001; Craske and Molyneux 2002; Lind 2004 and 2005). Whereas many authoritarian States tolerated civil mobilization and claims for regime change on the part of women, democratic regimes reorganized and refocused the political sphere in the 1980s around male politicians. Having made the most of their respective countries' transition periods (at least in the cases of Brazil, Chile, and Argentina) through negotiating and winning certain rights in the new democratic constitutions, and having successfully lobbied for the creation of specialized state women's machineries (institutions mandated to integrate gender into State policy) organized women lost a great deal of this momentum during the post-transition period in Latin America in the 1990s (Waylen 2000, 2007; Franceschet 2005).

Once democracy had been achieved and political parties reemerged as central political actors, many politically active Latin American women found themselves marginalized from central spheres of power. Faced with this loss of political traction, many women were faced with a difficult choice: they could join the new male-dominated parties, remain in women's organizations, or try to reconcile both and get caught in a "double activism" dilemma, as emphasized by Franceschet (2005) among others. Besides, once social welfare services were cut under the strident structural adjustment programs embraced by many of these regimes, the dye was cast for countless Latin American women. As ever, they were expected to pick up the social welfare slack and shoulder the heavy workload of providing family and community services. Their compensatory social services saved the State a tidy sum under many of Latin America's post-transition neoliberal economic models, but the socioeconomic cost to women can be felt to this day (Craske 1998; Lind 2005; Waylen 2007).

Peruvian Women's Mobilization in the Transition and Beyond

Peru differs in several respects from most cases in the literature examining Latin American women's mobilization during transitions to democratic regimes and beyond. Let us begin by examining Peru's authoritarian regime in the late 1960s and early 1970s. One of the country's distinguishing features during this period was its reformist and anti-oligarchic tendencies. Popular mobilization in civil society was actually encouraged, and the government provided institutional vehicles to channel civil society's initiatives. The growing vocal left- and right-wing opposition to authoritarian rule was subjected to far less repression in Peru than under the conservative and highly repressive military regimes in Argentina, Chile, and Brazil. And it was from within the largely unoppressed, mainly legal, left-wing movements and parties that emerged during the period of authoritarian rule that women began to mobilize in earnest in Peru. Peruvian women did not lead the charge in demanding regime change any more than any other sector of civil society. They were simply part of a moderate anti-authoritarian movement. The relatively open political climate paradoxically led to a regime change that has been called a "conservative transition" to democracy (Mauceri 1997). Peru's democracy was not ushered in by organized popular actors, left-wing parties, or women's groups. Indeed, in the late 1970s, when the transition to democratic rule was initiated in Peru (before most other countries in the region), the women's movement that we know today was still in its infancy.

Later, in the 1980s and 1990s, Peru's political landscape changed substantially for civil organizations and political parties. The democratic regime installed in 1980 kept a tenuous hold on power until the early 1990s, contending with widespread political violence from armed groups who destabilized various regions of the country. It was the weakness of the democratic project in place and this ongoing violence that hastened the crystallization of a neopopulist regime in the 1990s. In 1992, elected neopopulist President Fujimori instigated a military coup in his own country to make some major institutional changes. One of the most notable traits of this new political landscape was the radical transformation of the party system that had been in place since the transition to democracy in 1980. This drastic reconfiguration, or *ruptura* (to borrow O'Donnell and Schmitter's term from 1986), of the party system broke many of the ties between civil society and political parties that had been relatively strong in the 1980s (at least from the point of view of the Left). These ties continued to fade away with the rise of Fujimori's neopopulist politics in the 1990s.

Peruvian democracy was severely circumscribed in the 1990s due to the decay of autonomous civil society organizations, the lack of accountability of state actors, and the concentration of powers in the executive. This had clear implications for women's movements as well as other political actors. The neopopulist appeal of Fujimori relied on democratic legitimacy brought by electoral success—contested only by an elite minority up to the end of the 1990s. Yet in practice, democratic institutions were strongly undermined.

Nevertheless, the Peruvian government's institutionalization of women's citizenship rights did follow two major trends that resembled those seen elsewhere in Latin America during the 1990s: on one hand modest advances were made in civil and political rights, while on the other hand social and economic rights saw some serious setbacks. Indeed, it is both the progress and the renunciation of Peruvian women's rights as citizens on a number of fronts that precludes us from formulating easy conclusions about the relationship between political regime type, the State, women's movements, and women's citizenship rights. We can say with certainty that any comparison between the trajectories of women's movements in Peru under Fujimori and other contemporaneous Latin American countries must be viewed through the lens of Fujimori's authoritarian reshaping of democratic institutions, which brought about an institutionalization of some women's citizenship rights and weakened national democracy. Overall, what also comes out strikingly is Fujimori's strategy to use gender politics to boost his neopopulist appeal. In this context, some women found a particularly fertile ground to advance their goals.

This brings us back to a central claim of the literature on women and democracy in Latin America: Latin American women's involvement in politics declined after their countries made transitions to democracy in the 1980s. In examining the reasons for declining political protagonism among Latin American women following transitions to democracy, some literature pointed to regime type as a vital determinant, associating democracy with the hegemony of male party politics. In point of fact, most of the literature shows that due to their gender, women were given more latitude than men to organize under military regimes. A host of women used the latitude afforded them under many of these regimes to develop new forms of mobilization, and went on to become key actors in the transitions. Once a return to democracy had been achieved, many Latin American women opted for a "return to hearth and home," and the ensuing displacement of civil society movements to State and party politics marginalized both Latin American women and their demands (Alvarez 1990; Jaquette 1989; Jaquette 1994; Waylen 1994).

However, to say that the overall role of Latin American women necessarily diminished under democracy is debatable. In Peru, the pattern was different. Women's mobilization and participation under authoritarianism was not followed by marginalization under democracy. The contemporary women's movement may have been born during the years of the military regime in the 1970s, but its growth and consolidation occurred under the subsequent elected democratic governments. Peruvian women were not leaders of the anti-authoritarian struggle and therefore were not especially marginalized under democracy. And while the mobilizing capacity of women's movements did decline in the 1990s (particularly among popular movements as will be showed), it was after a decade of living under a democratic regime and at a time when democracy became seriously challenged by Fujimori's authoritarian actions. Besides, important gains were made in women's civil and political rights in the 1990s. These gains represented some of the central demands of the feminist movement and of women politicians, who had gradually armed themselves with a new political arsenal to see that those demands were met.

This brings a new perspective on the factors accounting for women's mobilization and the resulting pattern of their citizenship construction. Latin American women are not merely *responding* to the opportunities that present themselves within the political structure such as change in political regimes. Rather, women's organizing is in constant interaction with various dimensions of the public sphere. This said, there are many characteristics of a political regime that can influence whether or not women are marginalized and what kind of opportunities they will have to mobilize. The most effective methodology for understanding women's mobilization patterns in post-transition regimes is therefore qualitative assessment conducted from a broad spectrum of perspectives.

In Peru, both after the democratic transition and throughout the years of controversy over the legitimacy of the Fujimori government, strategy was of primary importance to women's organizing efforts. Their strategies were crafted in great part in relation to neopopulism, in the context of a formally democratic regime. Of course, the classic question in this area is whether greater freedom under democratic regimes necessarily leads to a more robust civil society. Neopopulism tends to undermine autonomous organizations that present challenges to the state. Depending on the social basis of neopopulist power, one sector of civil society will be affected differently than another. Organized labor was typically most directly connected to classic populist power blocs and therefore often formed the privileged clientele. Labor's autonomy was often compromised as a result, as under Peron's rule in Argentina. Similarly, when Fujimori targeted popular sector women for his neopopulist base of power, it had the effect of marginalizing autonomous popular women's organizations.

Patterns in women's citizenship claims and strategies provide additional qualitative insight into the limits of collective action under Latin American democracies. While democracy has meant the return of political parties to the center-stage of politics in many countries, in Peru, the 1990s were marked by the breakdown of the party system. This paradoxically broadened the space available for some women to organize and has significantly altered the relationship that the Peruvian women's movements entertained with the State. This echoes the findings of some literature on women organizing in post-war Central American countries and in post-authoritarian South American countries, where "radical," diametrically opposed left-and right-wing women united to champion shared gender-based concerns, overcoming considerable political and class-based obstacles (González and Kampwirth 2001). When these unlikely coalitions of women joined forces, they carried the day on a host of issues. It must be said that none of these issues contradicted any of the Catholic Church's precepts, nor did they challenge the dominant neoliberal economic order. Rather, these coalitions chose to collectively pursue issues like paternal responsibility or domestic violence in the new political context (Gonzalez and Kampwirth 2001). Their initiatives changed the nature of women's organizing, producing unforeseen new alliances and incentives for greater autonomy for some women's organizations that were previously linked to political parties. However, both the political opportunity structure and the identity of women's organizations limited the type of issues that could be successfully pursued. The many political stalemates regarding reproductive rights or gay and lesbian rights remain as apt cases in point.

This brings me to another central question in the study of women's movements under Latin American democracies: beyond changing patterns of civil mobilization, what accounts for the changes in the institutionalization of women's citizenship? In my research on Peruvian women's citizenship from the mid-1980s to 2000, I wanted to determine whether the gains and losses in women's citizenship are primarily attributable to the agency of the women participating in the public sphere (organized women in different sectors), or whether these gains and losses might be explained by other aspects of the political process. The political agenda of State leaders, political institutional factors, or the possibility of stakeholder–State convergence are alternative variables to be considered. The neopopulist character of the Fujimori regime throughout the 1990s is at the core of this puzzle.

Looking at the ways in which organized women's objectives were pursued by the distinct components of their movements at specific historical junctures, we see how relationships with the State, civil society, and political parties were structured. We also see how various aspects of women's citizenship came to be institutionalized or not. Patterns of State–society relations are key to understanding how such opportunities to assert women's citizenship claims were structured and why they led in very different directions, to varying degrees of success.

Mala Htun (2003) draws on this State–society relations approach in her work on abortion, divorce, and family law reforms in three South American countries, in which she develops a "disaggregated analysis of gender policies." She demonstrates that gender equality reforms that coincidentally or intentionally promoted gender equality were initiated under various political regimes (authoritarian or democratic) in which the opportunities for advancing a reform agenda depended significantly on the kind of relationship that existed between the Catholic Church and government leaders. Political issues were categorized by Htun as "absolutist" or "technical," according to whether they relied on moral arguments or not. This categorization was emphasized by Htun as being a crucial variable in elucidating the success or failure of reforms. Several actors in civil society and the State, constrained by the nature of political institutions and the rules governing legal reforms, acted as facilitating or negative factors in explaining the fate of reform proposals. While Htun did not ground her analysis in an examination of the dynamics between the State and women's movements as such, her work constitutes a rare attempt to develop a comparative framework of State–society relations within the processes of legal reforms affecting women's citizenship in Latin America.[7]

My argument relies essentially on the dynamics between different sectors of the women's movement and the State. To shed light on how women's citizenship is constructed, the claim I am making is that under Alberto Fujimori's neopopulist regime, gains made in women's citizenship have been a response to two converging phenomena. The first phenomenon was the presence and demands of a feminist movement that forged strategic alliances with key politicians and civil servants who were willing to promote an agenda of specific civil and political rights reforms. The second phenomenon is the decision by President Fujimori himself to use a discourse promoting some women's rights in order to sustain his "modernization" project and ensure support for his regime from women (and, arguably, men) at various levels of Peruvian society. These two phenomena were the linchpins in the gains made in Peruvian women's citizenship during the 1990s. Moreover, these gains were integrally linked to the agendas of some key international organizations, acting under pressure from the international women's movement. The international context provided incentives and resources both to Fujimori as state leader and to Peruvian women's movements to legitimize their policies and claims.

On the negative side, I argue that the weakening or stagnating social and economic rights in the 1990s may be attributed to the disintegration of the popular sector women's movement throughout the 1990s. In turn, the latter largely resulted from the interest of Fujimori in co-opting this movement through the creation of institutional tools to manipulate these sectors based on material daily needs. In the 1990s, the adoption of a neoliberal framework by the Peruvian government, accompanied by the prescriptions of international agencies to develop compensation schemes and state assistance programs for the poorest sectors (most affected by the radical reshaping of the economy), guided the Fujimori regime's policy toward women in the popular sectors, the poorest in Peru. Its economic policy and its political foundations (a coalition of the business elite and some members of the military that legitimized its power based on an unmediated appeal to the popular sectors) were inimical to social and economic entitlements demanded by many organized sectors in civil society.

The emphasis that middle and upper class women placed on civil and political rights, relative to the emphasis of women from popular sectors on social and economic rights, exposed substantial differences in priorities for the various sectors of the women's movement. This rift in priorities would yield widely variable results under the Fujimori regime in the 1990s. More fundamentally, neopopulist politics both revealed and enhanced the weakness of intermediary organizations in civil society. These organizations provide the channels through which representation could be made to political interests within the political party system and state institutions. This weakness affected all sectors of the women's movement and hampered women's citizenship rights from moving beyond formal gains in the legal and institutional spheres.

In the following chapters, I will analyze the evolution of different sectors of the women's movement and their interaction with the State, particularly under neopopulism in the 1990s. I will show that, paradoxically, the sectors that were most directly targeted by Fujimori's gendered populist mobilization—poor women in popular neighborhoods—ended up losing the most from his decade-long rule in terms of organizational strengthening and claims-recognition. More privileged sectors of the women's movement, struggling to maintain their autonomy from the State, had relatively greater success in pushing through a number of their agenda items into the institutional arena. All in all, the most significant gendered dynamics in the 1990s was the rise of a number of women from varied social strata to the electoral sphere and to state bureaucracy. Let us start by situating Fujimori's neopopulism in contemporary Peruvian politics.

CHAPTER 2

FUJIMORI'S PERU

STATE AND SOCIETY

A few months after being elected in 1990, President Alberto Fujimori declared 1991 to be the "Year of Austerity and Family-Planning" for the Peruvian State, at a time when Peru experienced its worst crisis of the century. Central to his policy goals was stabilizing the economy and addressing poverty. Women's role would be emphasized as key to the state's strategies, particularly in dealing with the social impact of adjustment. Facing enduring hyperinflation, a war with deadly insurgent forces that resulted in more than half the territory being under a state of emergency, a deeply shaken political party system, and a state on the verge of collapse, Fujimori and his allies significantly reshaped Peru's political institutions and state-society relations. In this process, women were the first to ask for authoritative and efficient state action to reduce the daily sources of insecurity. However, what at first seemed to the majority to be a "strong" government ended up in the second half of the 1990s to be increasingly seen as corrupt, self-serving, and authoritarian. Over and above the evolution of public opinion on the government's legitimacy, the persistence of a "culture of fear" and the use of special so-called antiterrorist laws, human rights violations and lack of guarantees for civil rights were some of the tools used and instilled by Fujimori to demobilize civil society (Burt 2006).

The 1990 elections marked a historical turning point in the country's politics. All the actors who had previously been central to Peruvian politics and who had led the different waves of popular mobilization in the twentieth century disappeared or receded in the early 1990s—with the notable exception of the military. Fujimori, a political outsider, managed to rule Peru with very few institutional safeguards throughout the 1990s. The *Alianza Popular Revolucionaria*

Americana (American Popular Revolutionary Alliance—APRA), a populist party that had fought the battle for the inclusion of popular sectors from the early 1920s, won its legal status in the 1940s but later collaborated with the very oligarchy it had opposed in its first decades of existence. When finally in power from 1985 to 1990, it precipitated the crisis that would lead to Fujimori's election. The new Left parties that had emerged in the 1960s and 1970s against and in parallel to the reformist military regime of General Juan Velasco—who enacted the most radical reforms to break the power of the oligarchy and develop an interventionist state—had a brief but important period of electoral success in the 1980s. Faced with the sustained war launched by insurgent guerrillas in 1980, the democratic Left collapsed at the end of the 1980s under the weight of its internal divisions and its ambivalence regarding democratic rule and revolutionary insurrection.

The Right, which regained strength and popularity in the late 1980s due to the hegemonic rise of neoliberal economic policy in Latin America, still represented a political elite that the majority of the Peruvian population was no longer willing to tolerate in power, as demonstrated in the 1985 elections where around 75 percent of the electorate voted either for the APRA or the United Left (Cotler 1995; Lynch 1999; Contreras and Cueto 1999). While the new economic elite associated with the right-wing coalition *Frente Democrático* (Democratic Front—FREDEMO) led by world-famous writer Mario Vargas Llosa was different from the old landed oligarchy and consisted mainly of modern business sectors, the image it projected to the Peruvian voters was that of a white, privileged and corrupt political class.

To understand the success of Fujimori, a number of elements need to be brought to light. First are the elements of continuity: populism and authoritarianism are key features of Peruvian politics in the modern period. Governance was achieved either through civilian power-holders elected under limited suffrage or through the military directly intervening at key junctures in political and social crises to "accomplish" reforms that the civilian authorities, be they conservative political parties or oligarchs, were incapable of implementing. In parallel, popular mobilization was channeled mostly through the APRA, a populist, anti-imperialist, nationalist party relying on the working and middle classes.

Electoral democracy as a pluralist, free competition between parties with solid institutional checks and balances, has never consolidated throughout Peruvian history. The ten-year period of democratic rule with universal suffrage after 1980 was seriously affected by the insurgent war launched by the *Sendero Luminoso* (Shining Path) and the *Movimiento Revolucionario Tupac Amaru* (Tupac Amaru

Revolutionary Movement—MRTA) against the state. The lack of democratic consolidation thus accounts in part for the ease with which Fujimori was able to dismantle existing democratic institutions and reshape the constitutional order in the early 1990s.[1]

The weakness of democratic politics can be explained by the specific pattern of citizenship construction in modern Peru (Franco 1994; López 1997; Lynch 1995). The period when most social rights were granted by the state was associated with the reformist military regime of General Juan Velasco (1968–75). Yet, the transition to democracy with universal suffrage in 1980, paradoxically, was preceded by waves of repression against the social actors who had recently been empowered by these rights. The economic crisis that built up during the 1980s, with only exceptional periods of partial recuperation, maintained the process of erosion and negation of social rights and caused further deterioration of the living conditions of Peruvians. For the majority, democratic governance was, therefore, not synonymous with social justice, and instead was interpreted as coterminous with social chaos and dramatic economic decline.

When Fujimori dismantled democratic institutions through a "self-coup" (from the Spanish "*autogolpe*") in 1992, the majority accepted and supported his decision. The context of multiple crises had placed the state in a situation of near breakdown, and Fujimori and his allies resorted to old patterns that characterized Peruvian politics, such as personalism, clientelism, and authoritarianism. As Burt argues, the "remaking of the state," which took place in the first part of the 1990s, and the corruption web of unprecedented magnitude that accompanied it, were marked by authoritarian political rule inimical to democracy-building (Burt 2004).

Under international pressure to do so, Fujimori reestablished democratic institutions few months after his self-coup. The post-1992 regime has been alternatively described as a "degenerate delegative democracy" (O'Donnell 1994; Cameron and Mauceri 1997), a "formal democracy" (Stokes 1996), a "semi-democracy" (Levitsky 1999), a "pseudo-democracy" (Diamond 1996), as a form of "competitive authoritarianism" (Levitsky and Way 2002) or, as most Peruvian analysts have termed it, an increasingly authoritarian regime (Cotler 1995, Carrión 2001). This chapter will argue that Fujimori's government can best be understood from the perspective of neopopulist politics rather than along the continuum going from authoritarianism to democracy. Retaining the legitimacy of an elected leader, Fujimori was seen by many as the solution to the ills of the country's democratic system. The president and his allies carefully constructed a neopopulist discourse pointing to all opposition forces and parties as potential terrorists or as corrupted, self-serving elites. Peruvians were called in to support the "only" political leader who could save the country from its past failures. At the same time, though, this legitimacy relied on several undemocratic practices filled with selective repression against opposition figures and the media, severe human rights violations, control over several of the key print and electronic media, the use of special antiterrorist laws and control of judicial and electoral bodies (Conaghan 2005; Burt 2006).

In order to understand the origins of his political regime as it was reconfigured by Fujimori in the early 1990s, a brief discussion of the transition period between the military regimes of the 1970s and the establishment of democratic rule with universal suffrage in 1980 will first be presented. The multiple crises building up in the 1980s will then be explained, so as to understand the role of the main political actors. Following this, I will examine the 1990 elections and the subsequent formation of a governing coalition around Fujimori as president, to form the particular regime sometimes referred to as *Fujimorismo*[2].

At the core of this chapter, I will discuss Fujimori's neopopulism— a combination of some features of classical populism in a neoliberal policy framework with universal suffrage and democratic elections. The final section will argue that previously excluded actors and issues that did not challenge the neopopulist and neoliberal project of his government did find some space in a political context that had eliminated other alternative political options, from the radical Left to traditional right-wing. Such was the case for a limited interpretation of some feminist demands and the inclusion of more women in politics, but not for the empowerment of organized lower class women. I will introduce one of the book's main arguments that Fujimori's regime was strongly articulated around a neopopulist appeal to women, with negative and positive consequences on women's political space and the success of their citizenship claims.

From a Military to a Democratic Regime

When General Juan Velasco seized state power through a coup in 1968, he legitimized the military's intervention by asserting the country's need for a vast reform program to end the enduring crisis prompted by peasant mobilization. He sought to bypass the obstruction presented by the country's elites against the modernization of the state and the economy. The classic study by Alfred Stepan (1978) defines the spirit of the project that animated the "inclusionary corporatist organist-statist" regime as contrasting importantly with the other military regimes that ruled at the same time in neighboring countries, the so-called "bureaucratic authoritarian regimes" (O'Donnell 1979). The latter's primary "function" was to repress working classes' demands that had built up as a result of import-substitution industrialization programs.

In Peru, instead, the military was seeking to develop the state apparatus in order to achieve what the populist parties such as APRA, who had never governed by then, and *Acción Popular* (Popular Action—AP), who had governed from 1963 to 1968, had not achieved (i.e., imposing major structural reforms). These were deemed essential by a group of reformers within the military, among others, who identified the need to include the urban popular sectors that mobilized increasingly, and respond to the claims of the burgeoning peasant movement demanding a redistributive land reform. The extremely high level of dependency of the Peruvian economy on foreign capital and raw material exports, combined with the small size of the state and its incapacity to implement policies to accelerate national integration and the modernization of the country, were all used to justify a radically new model of governance (Stepan 1978; McClintock and Lowenthal 1983; Wise 2003).

The reformist program built over time after the military assumed power, including land reform, nationalization of some key natural resource industries and the promotion of peasant and worker cooperatives. As such, it was meant to crush the power base of the oligarchy. The need to compensate for years of delay in industrializing Peru, in comparison with its neighbors, also formed part of the consensus reached by the high ranks of the military, as well as most of the intellectual elites of the country. As a result, there was little opposition to the military taking power in 1968 (Stepan 1978; Contreras and Cueto 1999).

In terms of the gains made in citizenship rights, as noted in the introduction, the Velasco regime represented the most fruitful period for the extension of social rights. The national state for the first time introduced a series of reforms aimed at creating new entitlements and recognizing new collective subjects such as peasants, workers, and urban slum dwellers. The right to collective land ownership was extended and a much more ambitious land reform was implemented, Quechua was recognized as a national official language, a number of new labor rights were granted, and the strengthening of a number of ministries in the areas of education, health, and social security was meant to reflect the priority given by the new regime to social development. Economic innovations such as worker participation in the management of industries through "industrial workers' communities," as well as the granting of property rights in Lima's popular settlements were also meant to enhance the power of the lower classes. Just as well, the advancements in the field of civil rights were connected first and foremost to extending the protection of the right to strike and freedom of association (López 1997).

Women also benefited from the reformist regime in several ways. Through the enlargement of the state apparatus, the first university-educated women entered the public bureaucracy in greater numbers. Their presence influenced some policy areas such as the education sector. A special commission was set up for the "revaluing of women," and special programs were implemented with new vocational training for women in male-dominated sectors (Anderson 1985, 107). Importantly, the first National Commission on the Peruvian Woman (*Comisión Nacional de la Mujer Peruana*—CONAMUP) was created in 1974, mostly prompted by the government's desire to show some results at the first United Nations' World Conference on Women held in Mexico in 1975, which opened the first Women's Decade (Anderson 1985). These efforts instilled a modest, new dynamics within the state to address women's status in policies and programs. If anything, however, the commission planted the seeds for professional progressive women to continue the work outside the state once the Velasco regime crumbled in 1975.

On the political front, the new model of state-society relations implemented under *velasquismo* included the promotion of popular mobilization and participation, notably through a state agency created for this purpose, the *Sistema Nacional de Apoyo a la Movilización Social* (National Social Mobilization Support System—SINAMOS). SINAMOS devoted itself mostly to organizing the lower classes of Lima's shantytowns on a territorial basis. The regime also created corporatist organizations for peasants and workers in an attempt to control these sectors. As analyzed by Cotler (1983) and Stokes (1995) among others, this generated one of the contradictions embedded in the Velasco regime: maintaining its own corporatist system at the same time that it tolerated civil society organizations and left-wing parties, thus generating a situation leading to the radicalization of important sectors of the population who refused to be co-opted by the state and who benefited from the openness of the public sphere to develop their autonomous strength (Cotler 1983, 34; Stokes 1995, 113). The growth of a number of Marxist parties such as the *Partido Comunista Peruano* (Peruvian Communist Party—PCP) or the *Partido Socialista Revolucionario* (Socialist Revolutionary Party—PSR), and their involvement in union organizing was one of the unintended results of the Velasco regime.

The Velasco regime entered into crisis in the mid-1970s for a set of reasons including the difficulties in sustaining its economic model based on the nationalization of key industries, the development of agricultural cooperatives, and heavy foreign borrowing. Growing political opposition and internal military infighting added to the material difficulty of coping with declining export prices (Contreras and Cueto 1999). Conservative sectors within the military prompted a coup and installed General Morales Bermúdez in power. The policy orientations of the government changed gradually with the replacement of pro-reform military and civilian officials. The increasing labor unrest and broad-based popular mobilizations incited repression by state authorities, which in turn only increased the pace of strikes and protests throughout the second half of the 1970s. The abrupt end to the Velasco regime notwithstanding, analysts of the so-called "Peruvian Experiment" concluded that by and large "the core program of nationalist affirmation, economic modernization, anti-oligarchical reform, and systematic state-building supported institutionally by the armed forces . . . was implemented to an impressive degree" (Lowenthal 1983, 419).

When it became clear that the popular pressure for an end to military rule had become unmanageable in the long run, and in light of the fact that the military felt it lacked other credible alternative models to *velasquismo*, the regime began discussing with a select group of political parties the return to democratic civilian rule. The coalition involved actively in leading the transition was made of a sector of the military together with two parties, the APRA and the right-wing *Partido Popular Cristiano* (Christian Popular Party—PPC; Lynch 1995). The other parties were either excluded from the discussions, like most of the parties of the Left, or self-excluded themselves, like *Acción Popular* (AP) whose leader Fernando Belaúnde had been deposed in 1968. AP also abstained itself from participating in the elections for the Constituent Assembly held in 1978, whereas the leftist parties that did participate used the opportunity afforded by the relatively important presence they won in the Assembly to raise their radical political platforms and salvage the gains made in social rights under the regime of Velasco.[3]

The transition to democracy was marked by an increasing gap between political parties and Peruvian social movements, a gap that preceded even the Velasco regime according to Bernales (1995). Most of the debates inside and between the parties of the Left and the APRA emphasized early on ideological questions such as the nature of the State, the relation between nationalism and economic policy, and the kind of class alliance necessary to confront imperialism. In contrast, the burgeoning social mobilization, which increased during the military regime, was motivated by concrete issues of economic redistribution and participatory democracy (Bernales 1995, 156).

Mauceri also describes the transition to democratic rule in Peru as "politically conservative," leading to the "restoration of a restrictive political democracy." According to him, it was elite-led and did not reflect the major changes that had occurred in civil society as a result of the Velasco regime and the mobilization of numerous social forces (Mauceri 1997, 14–15). However, the constitution drafted by the Constituent Assembly and adopted in 1979 guaranteed a number of the gains made under the Velasco regime in terms of social rights and structural reforms. It was indeed one of the conditions imposed by the military upon creating the Constituent Assembly: the constitution should "include the regulations which institutionalize the structural transformations" that occurred under the military regime (Mauceri 1997, 22).

The best way to describe the transition process is probably to say that it revealed a strong contrast between street politics and institutional negotiation. Much social protest was repressed and strikes continued, but a progressive Constitution emerged from the Constituent Assembly, which recognized the land reform, industrial communities, union rights, gender equality, a clause allowing for affirmative action in order to end discrimination, and universal suffrage for all Peruvians above the age of eighteen. In a highly symbolic gesture, the leftist parties elected at the Assembly did not sign the new constitution, thus indicating their refusal of the new democratic regime. Mauceri interprets this move as caused by the fact that "for Peru's left, civilian rule was identified with the conservative governments of the 1940s and 1960s" (Mauceri 1997, 25).

The Crisis Building Up to the 1990 Elections

It may not be an exaggeration to say that the profound crisis that built up during the 1980s was primarily due to a crisis of the political system, if we define the latter to include not only state institutions but key political actors such as parties. The transition to democracy did not provide the foundations for a renovated political order that could carry within the sphere of political institutions the vast expectations that social reforms and mobilization in civil society contained. Even if, formally speaking, the constitution expressed the kind of society that reformists had envisaged, and aside from the novelty represented by the electoral performance of left-wing parties, the other parties continued to act as if nothing had changed during the 1970s (Bernales 1995, 157–58). In the context of weak parliamentary institutions, the *caudillo* style of political rule was maintained, especially as the first president elected through democratic, universal suffrage was Fernando Belaúnde, still heading the old *Acción Popular* party.

On the side of the left-wing parties, the same ambivalence regarding the democratic regime they had exhibited during the transition remained throughout the 1980s, combined with the phenomenon that Bernales describes as the "*parlamentarización de los partidos*" (parliamentarization of parties), a problem affecting all parties during the 1980s. Parties lost their function of articulating and representing the demands of society as well as provide channels for the mobilization of citizens, focusing their attention on the number of seats they were able to win and how to gain benefits in parliament in between the elections (Bernales 1995, 163).

The division of the Left along ideological and personalistic lines made it difficult to efficiently represent popular sectors and carry their demands within the state. Two phenomena were at play here, the second being much more problematic for the consolidation of democracy. First, the internal unity of *Izquierda Unida* (United Left—IU), the coalition of the majority of left-wing parties that formed after the 1980 elections, was constantly challenged by ideological differences and competition between party leaders. The compromise reached through the choice of Alfonso Barrantes as presidential candidate of IU as of the mid-1980s reflected the tensions within the coalition. Barrantes was in fact much closer, ideologically speaking, to the social democratic platform of the APRA government under Alan García's leadership than to most of the Marxist parties of the Left (Reyna 2000, 68). The personal popularity of Barrantes explained the choice made by the leadership of the IU, yet his personalistic style and ideological distancing from the more radical wings meant that, overall, the IU was not a sustainable coalition of parties.

Second, the rise of more extremist sectors within the Left such as the *Partido Comunista del Perú Sendero Luminoso* (Communist Party of Peru Shining Path), more commonly known as *Sendero Luminoso* (the Shining Path), and the *Movimiento Revolucionario Túpac Amarú* (Revolutionary Movement Tupac Amaru—MRTA) led to the unleashing of a low-intensity war in numerous regions of the country as of 1980, the year when the democratic regime was reinstated. These guerrillas launched their warfare activities first in the south-central Andes and Amazon and then in Lima in the late 1980s, the Shining Path being the strongest and most deadly of the two groups.[4] Some of the democratic left-wing parties such as *Partido Unificado*

Mariátegui (Unified Mariategui Party—PUM) often expressed their sympathy toward *Sendero Luminoso* and the MRTA while continuing to function within the sphere of democratic electoral politics. This ambivalent stance generated distrust among the population, especially those affected by the armed struggle between guerrillas and security forces, while increasing the risk for leftist militants of being targeted by security forces. Ultimately, this also meant that the attachment of left-wing parties to the democratic regime was on shaky grounds.

As mentioned above, the old populist parties regained the upper hand in the democratic context of the 1980s, yet without having renewed their platforms and ruling style. *Acción Popular*, with former President Fernando Belaúnde still leading, benefited from its distancing from the military during the transition phase to win the first inclusive democratic elections in 1980. However, his government quickly faced major crises on both the economic and security fronts. The economic situation that had drastically deteriorated at the end of the 1970s continued to decline. Belaúnde pursued the liberalization of the economy started by General Bermúdez's government, but the growing debt and rising inflation, combined with the mistrust of the economic elite after years of state intervention and nationalization, impeded economic renewal.[5] The lack of sustained investment in agriculture and the heavy rains associated with the phenomenon of *El Niño* led to a deteriorating agricultural production (Contreras and Cueto 1999). Finally, the rapid growth of guerrilla activities in the Central Andes was not foreseen by Belaúnde, who reacted late and then granted full authority to the military to take control of the areas under guerrilla influence beginning in 1983. The number of emergency zones under military control started to grow from then on.

The numerous failures of the Belaúnde government opened the way for an easy victory of the APRA under the leadership of the young and charismatic Alan García in 1985. His ruling style was personalistic, resonating with traditional populist style. The heterodox economic program implemented by García amounted to a late version of import-substitution industrialization. His attempt to nationalize the banking system unleashed a strong opposition movement among the elite and galvanized the Right. With an explosive rise of the foreign debt, his government's refusal to continue abiding by its financial obligations vis-à-vis international financial institutions was justified by García as an anti-imperialist policy that he tried to use to build an international third world movement. While he largely failed in this endeavor, since no country followed his path of opposing up front the international orthodoxy at the end of the 1980s, the net result for

Peru was also dramatic: no further credit could be lent to the country and it became more and more isolated from the international system.[6]

The high degree of centralization of power inherited from the Belaúnde period was maintained during García's rule, except that the latter pledged to decentralize the country and indeed created regional governments in 1989. Generally speaking, García reinforced the tendency of the Peruvian presidency to be overly autonomous and omnipresent vis-à-vis the elected chambers and even his own cabinet. This "*presidencialismo*," coupled with García's own political charisma, generated a strong current of admiration in the population in the first year of his rule, when the first measures aimed at supporting the national economy were giving some immediate—but short-term—returns.[7] García even proposed the idea of reforming the constitution to allow for presidential reelection, which did not prosper.

García's populist "*caudillo*" style, combined with his economic populism, meant a substantial increase in the number of state employees—the new jobs often being offered to APRA supporters—and a strategic use of subsidies and tax exemptions to sustain clientelistic networks. García's economic program led to fiscal and financial crises, prompting the first set of adjustment measures to be adopted in Peru in September 1988. But the latter did not lead to an improved situation. On the contrary, the inflation rate soared from 115 percent in 1987 to 1723 percent in 1988 and continued to climb up to 7650 percent in 1990 (Cotler 1995b, 129). The informalization of the economy progressed at a rapid rate.[8] This deteriorating situation was compounded by the spread of guerrilla activities to Lima in the late 1980s, creating an explosive situation in most of the capital's shantytowns and a high level of insecurity for all Lima residents as car bombs and power failures became a periodic threat. Human rights abuses by security forces and insurgents increased substantially (Cotler 1995; Reyna 2000).

The rule of García thus ended with the country left in a state of chaos, the popular sector movement decomposing itself in fear and division, the democratic Left also divided and the Right regaining strength. The APRA government had antagonized most of the economic elites who perceived a threat of socialist take-over either by the government or by the insurgent groups. While the nationalization of the banking system was halted by the courts, the APRA experienced serious internal divisions due to García's lack of consultation with his own party.

At the same time, the Left's ideological differences reached an unsustainable level of polarization in 1989. The more radical parties of the IU were seeking to prepare for popular insurrection as they felt that the situation was ripe for revolution due to the progress of *Sendero Luminoso* and the economic and political chaos that the country was experiencing (Tanaka 2002, 8). The more reformist parties, led by Barrantes, were eager to remove the radicals from the IU. The increasing tension led to the disintegration of the Front and the creation of *Izquierda Socialista* by Barrantes. The Left would again run divided in the 1990 elections.

Political organizing for the 1990 elections changed course when García attempted to nationalize the banking system. The reaction from business sectors came rapidly in the form of denunciations that Peru was on the road to becoming a totalitarian state that curtails fundamental freedoms. Mario Vargas Llosa, one of the most vocal critics, soon transformed into the leader of a new political "movement," the first of a kind that would later become the norm in the way Peruvian politics restructured at this time. United around a neoliberal discourse proposing a radical shift in the Peruvian development model, Vargas Llosa's *Movimiento Libertad* also launched its leader as the first "political independent," a "new" brand of politician emerging primarily because of his (or her) personal qualities and with the virtue of not being related to any existing political party.[9]

The 1989 municipal elections confirmed that this trend was a potentially rewarding one for ambitious political entrepreneurs when Ricardo Belmont, the owner of a radio-broadcasting enterprise, won the mayorship of Metropolitan Lima under an independent ticket. The broad coalition of business, media, and higher middle classes that gathered around Vargas Llosa and Hernando de Soto, a prominent economist defending a strong version of Washington Consensus economics, called for a new type of political leadership as the only way out of the multidimensional crisis.

With the elite business sector for the first time getting directly involved in politics through the *Movimiento Libertad* (ML), the old political parties that had traditionally been closer to their interests, AP and the PPC, eventually made an alliance with ML to form the *Frente Democrático* (FREDEMO) as the general elections were approaching. This move, according to many analysts, was probably responsible for Vargas Llosa's defeat at the 1990 elections. As Bernales explains, this corresponded to a contradiction between ML's discourse that sought to create a new political style and its decision to ally with two of Peru's old political class representatives (Bernales 1995, 175).

Other analysts emphasize the fact that this alliance did not facilitate Vargas Llosa's already difficult efforts to convince popular classes that he could adequately represent their interests and project an image of a modern, inclusionary Peru. Cameron underlined the fact that "the FREDEMO list read like a who's who of the Peruvian political establishment" and that "by failing to position himself near the majority of the electorate, Vargas Llosa created an opportunity for a new competitor to enter the political marketplace" (Cameron 1997, 43). Aside from his elite origins, another major factor accounting for Vargas Llosa's defeat was his unequivocal electoral promise to implement a shock-type structural adjustment program that was rejected by the majority of the population.

The greatest surprise of the 1990 electoral campaign was the rise of Alberto Fujimori, the son of Japanese immigrants and Dean of the Agrarian University, who entered the electoral race with his own political movement, *Cambio 90* (Change 90), made up of political unknowns, a good proportion of them coming from the Evangelical Church. With little apparent political charisma, carrying no solid political program and lacking a credible team of advisors, Fujimori nonetheless managed to attract increasing public attention in the weeks before the first electoral round. He simply represented the ideal political "independent" or "outsider" from a modest social origin that makes his way on his own. Moreover, Fujimori explicitly stated during his campaign that he would not undertake a structural adjustment program of the kind proposed by FREDEMO, although his own policy orientations remained vague.

While Vargas Llosa won 32.6 percent of the vote and Fujimori 29 percent in the first round, the latter won with 62.5 percent in the second round, and FREDEMO obtained 37.5 percent. These results confirmed that the votes of the APRA and IU had almost all shifted in favor of Fujimori, while the elite-based nature of FREDEMO's vote remained unchanged (official results reported in Lynch 1999, 137). Nonetheless, the vote for the Senate and the House of Representatives did not give Fujimori control over the Legislature, since *Cambio 90* was far from holding the majority of seats.[10]

In many ways, Fujimori went further than Vargas Llosa in representing the new kind of political leadership that *Movimiento Libertad* (Freedom Movement) was advocating so strongly. While the FREDEMO could not achieve the radical break with the traditional political system it had sought, such a break was the most appealing option for the majority of Peruvians faced with the failure of APRA's populism, as well as the division and radicalism of the Left. If Vargas Llosa made the idea of the "political independent" attractive, it was Fujimori who most benefited from it.

The major qualitative difference between Vargas Llosa and Fujimori, however, resided in the nature of the political alliances that the latter was willing to make in order to consolidate his regime. An important aspect of the political dynamics of the late 1980s was the reemergence, within the military, of the old doctrine placing the military at the core of new strategies to salvage the state from total collapse. Some sectors were indeed preparing for military intervention in reaction to the dramatic crisis. These sectors drew up a Government Plan, also referred to as the *Plan Verde* (Green Plan), whereby it would take over state power and resolve the crisis of governance that was threatening the integrity of the state in the late 1980s (Cotler 1994; Kenney 2004). In order to solve the dramatic economic crisis, the new regime envisaged by this plan would implement a neoliberal reform program similar to that of Chile's Pinochet government (Rospigliosi 1995; Cameron 1997; Cotler and Grompone 2000).

Designed in secret by the military, the Green Plan was ready before the 1990 elections. While the neoliberal reform strategy contained in the plan indicates that some business actors may have been consulted when it was designed, no solid evidence exists on business leaders' direct involvement (Kenney 2004). The way the plan was implemented following the electoral victory of Fujimori was also due essentially to the role of Vladimiro Montesinos, a former military officer who made his second career as a lawyer defending drug dealers. Montesinos started to advise Fujimori in the last months prior to the election, first by "negotiating" with the judiciary to erase charges of fraudulent real estate deals brought against the presidential candidate. Because of his links with the leadership of Intelligence Services, Montesinos was given the plan by some military officials, although some analysts argue that there is a possibility that Fujimori himself was informed of the existence of the plan and had been in touch with the military sectors promoting it before he assumed power in July 1990 (Rospigliosi 1995, 330).

In any case, negotiations between Montesinos, Fujimori, and the military resulted in a proposal for the establishment of a "*democracia dirigida*" (controlled democracy), that is, an authoritarian government with the appearance of a democracy (Rospigliosi 1995, 330; Cameron 1997, 51). This solution, which relied on the legitimacy of Fujimori as democratically elected president, had the advantage of preserving the civilian face of the government while ensuring that the military—or other actors such as Montesinos—would have a great share of actual control over the state. The fact that Fujimori did not have any solid team behind him or any credible party organization, as well as his own inexperience in politics, may explain why he was so prone to being drawn into the arms of the military. His own capacity to govern was dependent on his ability to form a powerful governing alliance and the military appeared as a "reliable" ally in the context of the extremely high polarization and volatility of political forces.

The absence in Fujimori's initial campaign platform of a coherent political program, combined with the growing influence of neoliberal orthodox thinkers such as Hernando de Soto, who became presidential advisor soon after the election, explains the other half of the governing coalition. Fujimori indeed embraced the policy prescriptions of multilateral financial institutions advocating a harsh adjustment program, thus negating his own campaign promises. With the help of the international contacts of de Soto and the Peruvian former United Nations Secretary General Javier Perez de Cuellar, Fujimori was able to meet rapidly with the International Monetary Fund, the World Bank and the Inter-American Development Bank, all of whom promised their support in exchange for the rapid implementation of a shock therapy structural adjustment (Gonzales de Olarte 1998, 22). The so-called "Fujishock" was implemented few weeks after Fujimori came to power. Thus, even the economic prescriptions of the military *Plan Verde* were realized.

Women from the popular sectors were generally supportive of Fujimori at the 1990 election. Seen as a candidate who would not implement a structural adjustment shock therapy on the economy, as he had promised, he represented an alternative to the discredited APRA, the fragmented Left, and the elite. By election time, the majority of poor women were looking for a savior who could terminate the constant fear and insecurity due to the insurgent war and hyperinflation. Few months after his victory, disillusion grew but at the same time, women were generally ready to give the regime the benefit of the doubt, especially as Fujimori's government initially recognized the role of popular sector women's organizations in finding solutions to poor neighborhoods' daily survival, as will be shown in Chapter 4.

Fujimori's Regime Post-1992

The military coup as envisaged in the *Plan Verde* was delayed until April 1992, and actually took the shape of a relatively rare phenomenon: an "*autogolpe*" (self-coup) led by President Fujimori himself. The elected president shut down the Legislature and suspended the Courts, with the open and active support of the military. Fujimori issued a decree creating the "Government of Emergency and National Reconstruction." Some elected legislators were placed under house arrest and the judicial system was purged. The new government was to rule through executive decrees.

The delay between the election of Fujimori and the *autogolpe* can be explained by various motives.[11] First was the need to forge greater consensus within the armed forces about the need to launch a coup. This was facilitated by the increasing violence due to the rising strength of *Sendero Luminoso* in Lima, which placed the military in the difficult position of being called to act forcefully while limited by the law. The perspective of being granted special powers to "terminate subversives," a proposal that the Congress opposed, was therefore very appealing. Another factor affecting the consensus within the military was the control that Fujimori managed to get as of 1991 over the nominations at the high ranks of the military, a control that he used to place loyal generals and admirals who endorsed the coup project (Cameron 1997, 51–52; Burt 2004, 259). Nicolás Bari de Hermoza was named head of the army and Commander in Chief of the armed forces in 1991. He remained in place until 1998, an unusually long mandate that went against the one-year term tradition (Burt 2004, 259).

The second motive was the building of a *rapport de force* between the Congress and President Fujimori that would render the coup acceptable to public opinion. As already mentioned, the president did not have a majority in either house of the Congress. This situation was particularly challenging in light of the extremely high level of crisis affecting the country that required prompt and potentially painful reforms. After initially adopting a generally collaborative stance, Congress started to discuss how to remove the president from office in February 1991. It also adopted a "Law of Parliamentary Control over the Normative Acts of the President" allowing Congress to veto important presidential decrees (Kenney 2004, 250–51). The conflict revolved around two axes: 1.) ideological differences regarding the restructuring of the economy and society according to neoliberal principles, a domain where the APRA and the Left raised their opposition, and 2.) the powers to be granted to security forces to fight insurgent violence, which could easily lead to severe civil rights curtailments.

Fujimori's arrogant attitude did not ease the conflict, and in fact he actively promoted it by recurring to an anti-establishment rhetoric accusing political parties of acting self-servingly without considering the crucial problems facing Peruvian society (Levitsky and Cameron 2001). At the heart of Fujimori's motivations for carrying a coup was his political survival as well as his capacity to run for a second mandate, impeded by the 1979 constitution. Over and above ideological or programmatic lines was therefore the intention to lengthen Fujimori's rule.

The coup found many supporters within the population and abroad. At the national level, the coup of April 1992 did not generate strong opposition that could have threatened its success, even though some sectors obviously protested vehemently against it. By focusing on the ills of the past García government, Fujimori made it easier to justify the self-coup (Cotler 1995a, 350–51). The lack of credibility affecting the political class since the 1990 elections had only been reinforced by Fujimori's daily attacks, and was compounded by the weakness of civil society and its incapacity to respond to the breakdown of democratic order. This weakness resulted from years of insurgent and counter-insurgent violence that had instilled fear, distrust, and ultimately led to the collapse of many popular sector organizations (Burt 2004). Moreover, the informalization and degradation of the labor market also precipitated the dissolution of traditional forms of organizing based on the workplace (Roberts 1996; Cameron 1997).

Two major dynamics can therefore be distinguished to explain the capacity of Fujimori to perpetrate a self-coup and terminate with the democratic regime established in 1980. On the one hand, the reorientation of the centrist and leftist vote toward the political outsider left the APRA and the Left without any credibility to oppose the new president afterwards. On the other hand, the fact that Fujimori basically endorsed the neoliberal economic platform of the FREDEMO also made the latter irrelevant in the context of the new government. Basically, Fujimori had neutralized the political parties on their own political terrain, even if this meant an extreme contradiction in the first months of his rule. Moreover, Fujimori used his autonomy to forge an undemocratic alliance with the military and international capital that gave him a solid backing to rule the country while maintaining his isolation from the rest of the political system. With a weak civil society and no other credible alternative for the population than to believe that a new type of political leadership might solve the country's dramatic problems, the coup was perpetrated with no major demonstration of opposition.

Panfichi raises two crucial points about popular sectors' support to Fujimori that are not directly related to the state of the political party system: first, the strong identification of popular sectors with the president as an individual who shared in the experience of ethnic discrimination and migration that characterized most of Lima's popular neighborhoods. As a son of Japanese immigrants, Fujimori had built his own success against the traditional monopoly of the elite. Most of Lima's shantytowns were populated by rural migrants who were predominantly indigenous and faced intense cultural shock and discrimination in the city. They looked to Fujimori as a symbol of promised success, particularly as the new president decidedly targeted his discourse to the poor and made unprecedented efforts to visit popular neighborhoods and rural areas.

The second element of popular identification with Fujimori resided in the fact that previous authoritarian rulers—such as Velasco—had acted more predominantly in the interests of the popular classes than had past and succeeding elected governments, which gave Fujimori some credibility in his opposing the "interests of the nation" to those of "privileged, egoistic" politicians connected to the 1980 democratic regime (Panfichi 1997). The "anti-establishment," neopopulist strategy of Fujimori received a favorable welcoming within popular sectors.

The more challenging opposition to the authoritarian bloc formed by Fujimori, Montesinos, and the military came from foreign governments and, to some extent, the same international financial institutions that had endorsed Fujimori's government on its promise to apply a strict formula of structural adjustment, liberalization, and privatization. Official condemnation arose from most governments of the Americas and the European Union. The unease of the international community can be explained principally by the timing of the coup in the early 1990s, in the midst of the initial enthusiasm of the West regarding the steps taken by many developing countries and the former Communist world to democratize their political system. In Latin America, most countries had gone through a transition to democracy. It just seemed too risky to accept a precedent such as the one that Fujimori was attempting to set, whereby democratic institutions could be shut down by or with the support of the military, even if a democratically elected president continued to govern. Diplomatic pressure was followed by the interruption of economic aid from Washington. The prospect of seeing Peru once again being isolated from the international financial system was strong enough to prompt Fujimori's governing coalition to design a unique institutional solution to end the threat posed by the lack of international recognition of his coup regime (Cameron 1997).

This "solution" came in the form of electing a Constituent Assembly, named *Congreso Constituyente Democrático* (Democratic Constituent Congress—CCD), to draft a new constitution. This corresponded to a dual objective of 1.) reestablishing a new "democratic" institutional framework, since the CCD would be elected through universal suffrage and would lead the way to new democratic elections in 1995; and 2.) drafting a new constitution that would consolidate the profound restructuring of the Peruvian social contract, including the nature of the State's role in the economy, its social obligations and citizens' rights and obligations that Fujimori had started to implement in the first two years of his rule. Most importantly, the new constitution would allow the president, according to Fujimori's plans, to run for a second mandate. The CCD was to function until the 1995 elections, acting as a legislative body in addition to drafting a new constitution (Cameron 1997). This solution had the advantage of satisfying foreign powers' requirements for a democratic regime to be reestablished in Peru, even if only superficially and after deciding to tolerate the maintenance in power of a president who had so obviously violated democratic principles. This showed that the international community generally had high stakes involved in ensuring that Fujimori remained in power since he appeared to be the only viable guarantee that the pace of economic reforms would continue as initially agreed with the IMF and other financial institutions.

The elections for the CCD were held in November 1992, a few months after the *autogolpe* and in a context of great uncertainty as to the rules and procedures. The opposition parties, as a result, had a hard time positioning themselves vis-à-vis the new regime that was being built by the president and a majority of them actually abstained from participating, such as APRA, AP, and the left-wing PUM. While the latter justified their abstention due to their opposition to the unconstitutional interruption of the democratic order, Cotler argues that "public opinion interpreted this as an indication of their irrelevance" (Cotler 1995a, 352). In any case, Levitsky and Cameron describe the political dynamics following the *autogolpe* as one whereby the political cleavages were reduced to one single dimension, that is, support or opposition to Fujimori. Opposition parties were strongly challenged when they attempted to defend democratic institutions *per se*, since it amounted, in the eyes of many Peruvians, to a rejection of Fujimori (Levitsky and Cameron 2001, 17).

Political support for Fujimori's new institutional framework was not as strong as it could have been in light of the weak popular opposition to his self-coup. The CCD elections gave a slight majority of forty-four seats out of eighty to Fujimori's coalition in a unicameral assembly dominated by "political movements" that did not exist three years before (Rospigliosi 1995, 324).[12] At the 1993 referendum to approve the new constitution, only 4 percent separated the two options, with 52 percent of the population allegedly endorsing the new fundamental law. The referendum set the stage for the kind of controversial electoral processes that would take place in the remaining of Fujimori's rule. It was the first since before 1980 where strong accusations of irregularities came out from different sectors of society rather than only from the losing party as had been the case previously.[13] Notwithstanding the contested legitimacy of the referendum's results, the new constitution was adopted and a unicameral Congress with a single electoral district was created,[14] thereby abolishing the representation of regional interests and reinforcing the traditional centralization of the Peruvian state and political system.

It is appropriate at this stage to discuss the extent to which the regime set in place by Fujimori as of 1993 could be termed democratic or authoritarian, or a particular combination of both. Three interrelated phenomena merit attention. First, Fujimori's numerous violations of the constitutional framework he himself put in place in 1993 constitute an irrefutable demonstration of his authoritarian tendencies, even if the regime remained nominally democratic. Second, the behavior of opposition political parties throughout the rest of the 1990s—key actors who could have challenged much more forcefully Fujimori's claim to have reconfigured Peruvian democracy in order for it to be "real," also seem highly problematic. Finally, public opinion polls showed that a majority of Peruvians from all social classes supported Fujimori's coup and the new regime he put in place, not because they preferred authoritarianism but rather in a belief that these changes would improve the democratic system, an important nuance underlined by Kenney (2004).

Referring to a minimal definition of democracy that focuses on the conditions for and occurrence of free and fair elections, Cynthia McClintock (1999) and Gregory Schmidt (2000) have both raised serious doubts about whether the Fujimori regime could qualify, considering the extent to which the executive actually controlled the judiciary, the electoral bodies and a large portion of the media. Fujimori also used state resources and agencies for the benefit of his electoral campaigns and resorted to all kinds of blackmail and threats against opponents. Moreover, through the use of special "anti-terrorist" laws and tribunals, the state was able to arrest and jail numerous opponents often associated with left-wing union or community organizations (Burt 2006).

The difficulty analysts—and political opponents—have faced, according to McClintock, is related to the lack of measurable criteria to define the threshold for qualifying elections as free and fair (McClintock 1999, 92). Most of the problems resided in the use of state resources for political campaigning and the manipulation of public opinion by the government through control of some of the main media. Moreover, solid indications built up on the lack of independence of both the technical and judicial electoral bodies. The extent of the fraud and irregularities committed on the day of the various elections that took place between 1992 and 2000 was a problem in itself, leading many not to consider the electoral context as free and fair. But the ability of the Fujimori government to use its popularity to side-track criticisms arising from national and international electoral observers—up to the 2000 elections—was facilitated by the lack of consensus within Peruvian opposition and international observers on what exactly was to be considered a threshold below which an election could not be deemed free, fair and transparent.

The 1995 election was an example of this confusion. The president won by a landslide over his major opponent, Javier Pérez de Cuellar, a former United Nations Secretary General who had created *Unión por el Perú* with leftist leaders from the IU, former leaders of *Movimiento Libertad*, and other personalities from various sectors who joined together around the theme of "bringing democratic institutions back to Peru." While Fujimori resorted to tactics like inaugurating public works during the electoral campaign, mobilizing state institutions including the military and municipal authorities to campaign in his favor, using the media to launch smear campaigns against his opponents and so on, his electoral victory did not raise much suspicion, as all observers acknowledged the high level of popularity enjoyed by Fujimori at the time. He was credited for the eradication of most of the insurgent threat with the capture of *Sendero luminoso*'s leader Abimael Guzman few months after the *autogolpe*, and for stabilizing the economy even if the majority of the population was far from finding a solution to their daily survival problems in the new neoliberal economy. The results of the elections, particularly at the Congress level, were questioned by the opposition and electoral observers, but without them being able to reverse the course of events.[15]

Aside from electoral issues, Fujimori's government violated several democratic principles, among which respect for civil and political liberties such as freedom of expression and the right to due process. Anti-terrorist laws adopted under Fujimori broadened the scope of military court jurisdiction and introduced vaguely defined criminal offenses as part of its counter-insurgent strategy, leading to the imprisonment of thousands of suspected terrorists, many of which were later shown to be innocent (Burt 2004, 262–63; Burt 2006). Moreover, the Colina Group, a paramilitary organization, carried out several extrajudicial executions such as the Cantuta University and Barrios Altos (in Lima's popular neighborhood) cases. No investigations were carried out during Fujimori's rule.

In the second half of the 1990s, Fujimori's popularity exhibited weaknesses. The positive feedback of the stabilization and relative pacification of the country was exhausting itself, and the regime was looking for new sources of legitimacy. Fujimori's desire to remain in power for a third mandate even though this was going against the rules of the constitution he himself had drafted led him to adopt new strategies that increasingly violated the rule of law. In August 1997, Congress adopted what became known as the "*Ley de interpretación auténtica*" (Authentic Interpretation Law), which stipulated that the constitutional provision allowing for a second presidential mandate could apply to Fujimori's electoral candidacy in 2000 because his first mandate had been the result of an election held under the previous constitution. Through a slight majority ruling, the Constitutional Tribunal declared the law constitutional but inapplicable to Fujimori's case. The judges who had ruled against the law were impeached and removed from office by Congress, who left the Tribunal without replacements for these judges until after the 2000 elections. Fujimori claimed that the *Ley de interpretación auténtica* represented the will of the people because it was adopted by a democratically elected Congress.

Congress also rejected in 1998 the demand by over a million Peruvians who had signed a petition calling for a referendum to decide whether or not the president should have the right to run for a third mandate. This constituted another violation of the 1993 Constitution, which mandated the state to organize such referendums when citizens collect a minimum number of required signatures. A coalition of civil society groups who had promoted the initiative had fulfilled all the legal requirements for the collection of signatures according to most independent opinions. When Congress voted against the possibility that Fujimori's right to run for a third mandate be submitted to popular opinion through a referendum, the last hopes of using the legal, constitutional framework to respond to Fujimori's authoritarianism disappeared (McClintock 1999, 81). By then, the regime had a firm control over the judiciary through the functioning of a Reform Commission on the Judiciary, a body selected by Fujimori who had oversight power over the nominations of judges.

Repression against independent media continued to increase, up to the point that the owner of a private television network was persecuted and deprived of his Peruvian citizenship, forcing him to go in exile and abandon his property (Cotler and Grompone 2000, 42). In preparation for the 2000 elections, Fujimori's new electoral machine *Perú 2000* hired a team of people to forge up to one million signatures of voters in order to be able to register as a legal political party. While this scandal was brought to light by some of the individuals who had been involved in the fraud and confirmed by testimonies gathered by respected independent media, no legal sanction was adopted against Fujimori or his supporters, all of whom were allowed to run in the elections.[16]

While the highly polarized context of the 2000 elections led to greater international scrutiny and a renewed mobilization of civil society, with the irregularities and fraud being denounced in a much more systematic fashion, Fujimori nonetheless managed to "win" the second round after his challenger, Alejandro Toledo, refused to participate under such irregular electoral conditions. The main issues at stake were the monopoly of *Perú 2000*'s advertising in the main broadcast media, as well as the generous use of state resources to finance its campaign. This third victory, however, was of a short duration. The degree to which Fujimori's regime had resorted to fraud, manipulation, and human rights abuses led the international community to force his new government to commit to implementing profound institutional reforms under international monitoring by the Organization of American States (OAS).[17] This international pressure was accompanied by increased divisions within Fujimori's governing coalition, leading to the regime's collapse in September 2000. The public release of a video showing Montesinos bribing a Congress member was the final blow and led to the flight of Montesinos followed by the self-exile of Fujimori in Japan.[18]

Based on this account of the Fujimori regime's manipulation and lack of respect for democratic laws and institutions, it can be claimed that it did not fulfill the requirements of free, fair, and transparent elections, therefore failing to meet the minimalist criteria defining a democracy (Schmitter and Karl 1993). If most North American analysts attempted to circumscribe the problem through conceptual innovations to grasp this particularly limited version of political democracy, Peruvian analysts were prompt to denounce the use of a legalistic façade with the appearance of democracy to legitimize a new form of authoritarianism.[19]

Besides the semantic debate on how to best express the circumscribed character of Peruvian democracy under Fujimori, one is pressed to answer the question of why most opposition political parties participated in the various electoral processes—with the partial exception of the 1992 elections for the CCD and the second round of the presidential elections in 2000. Indeed, this seems to be one of the most important factors lending legitimacy to Fujimori's claim about the democratic character of his regime (Levitsky and Cameron 2001). Even if the latter did not conform to the minimalist standards defining a democratic regime, the most significant actors of the political system, political parties, acted as if such a democracy existed, at least from the point of view of its electoral component, even if they resorted to all kinds of criticisms to denounce the regime's abuses.

Some explanation can be found in the near breakdown of the state when Fujimori was first elected (Burt 2004). The new President and his group implemented a specific strategy of delegitimizing the political class and democratic institutions, culminating in the *autogolpe*. The subsequent electoral marginalization of all the "traditional" parties,[20] paralleled by the confirmation of the "political outsider" and "political movements" as new norms in Peruvian politics, had very negative consequences for the capacity of the political system to exercise checks and balances on executive power. Ultimately, this also affected the reaction of most of the opposition and that of the average Peruvian to Fujimori's severe encroachments on democracy. The low level or absence of institutionalization of the new political movements reflected political independents' interest in elected office for personal benefit. This led to anarchical and unpredictable behavior on the part of most political forces. Aside from a general lack of incentives and collective action problems for defending the integrity of democratic institutions and the rule of law, there were numerous political defections within the opposition or from the opposition to the government side, supported by a widespread corruption fed by the regime (Levitsky and Cameron 2001). Instead of protesting as a unified bloc against the electoral conditions that were far from providing a framework for a free and democratic competition, opposition politicians chose to take advantage of the opportunity it offered them to win seats. Some opposition Congress members even decided to support the regime inside Congress in return for generous bribes.[21]

The final variable to consider, which in many ways explains both Fujimori's and opposition parties' behavior, is the considerable level of public support garnered by the president around the coup period and in the first years following the coup. Kenney's detailed survey of public opinion polls reveals that over 70 percent of the population approved the coup when it was carried out. Peruvians' preference for democratic over military or revolutionary Marxist regimes grew from 73 percent just one month before the coup to 83 percent one year after, when the new democratic framework was put in place. One month after the coup, 52 percent characterized the post-coup regime as democratic, 34 percent as dictatorial and 14 percent abstained (Kenney 2004, 228–31).[22] Even if less people found the post-coup regime democratic than the proportion who endorsed the coup, the fact that the general preference for democracy continued to grow indicates that among those who endorsed the coup, a majority believed that it was in the interest of democracy in the long term or that Peru was not in conditions to have a democratic regime even if it was preferable.

Neoliberalism and Neopopulism: New State-Society Relations

As described above, the governing coalition behind Fujimori was built in part on the basis of a common goal of leading Peru into a drastic turn to a neoliberal model of development. The international financial institutions that extended their support to the regime in the first months of Fujimori's rule, and the military factions who had promoted the coup and allied with the civilian president and Montesinos, had an interest in seeing the implementation of a structural adjustment program, the liberalization of the economy, and the privatization of key sectors such as mining and telecommunications.[23]

The majority of the population, especially in low-income sectors, was not initially favorable to such programs, and indeed had rejected Mario Vargas Llosa's presidential bid in large part for this reason. However, faced with rampant inflation, a GNP lower than ever in the preceding ten years, and the failure of García's state-led development model, most Peruvians had no other option but to wait patiently for the promised growth to emerge out of the dramatic decline of their living conditions that the initial adjustment shock therapy created.[24] The neoliberal model was further consolidated with the 1993 Constitution that abolished the social economy model inherited from the military regime's structural reforms. The role of the state as a regulator of capitalism and promoter of redistribution through social rights was displaced by a model emphasizing free market allocation of resources. Agricultural credit was abolished, mining was privatized, financial markets were liberalized, and so on.

Economic reforms led to renewed growth from 1992 to 1998, a normalization of the inflation rate, and a more balanced fiscal situation. This said, the impact of this growth on poverty reduction was limited, as shown by the fact that with a diminishing fertility rate, the percentage of the population living under the poverty line went from 37.9 percent in 1986 to 55.3 percent in 1991, 46.5 percent in 1994 and 49 percent in 1996 (Gonzales de Olarte 1998, 85–86). Another sign of deterioration in the living conditions of Peruvians in the 1990s was the continuing decline in formal employment. The employment rate for the economically active male population went from 77.4 percent in 1972 to 62.7 percent in 1986 and 53.2 percent in 1996, whereas for the female population the same decline in employment went from 48.1 percent in 1972 to 31.5 percent in 1986 and then a slight increase to 33.2 percent in 1996 (Ugarteche 1999, 188). Informal employment was the only form of employment that rose steadily throughout the 1990s, for both males and females, indeed becoming the predominant form of income-generation for a majority of Peruvians. For example, while in 1991, 52.7 percent of the Lima population worked in the informal sector, in 2000 this proportion had increased to 59.2 percent, encompassing respectively 67 percent and 53 percent of all economically active women and men living in metropolitan Lima (ILO Panorama Laboral 2001).

The net effect of liberalization and privatization policies was to transfer economic power from productive sectors to financial sectors—the banking and trade sectors—that amounted to, according to Efraín Gonzales de Olarte, a displacement of the national agricultural and industrial sectors. This, in turn, was facilitated by the favorable conditions that the Fujimori government offered to foreign private investors, to the detriment of national capital (Gonzales de Olarte 1998). Foreign investment was found primarily in natural resource exploitation and services. Even though the national bourgeoisie initially supported the neoliberal orientation of the regime, it never managed to institutionalize its relationship with the Fujimori government or to convince it to develop strategic sectoral intervention policies in order to stimulate national investment (Gonzales de Olarte 1998, 66; Durand 1999, 198–99).

With a middle class strongly affected by drastic cuts in public sector employment, the support of popular sectors appeared to be vital for Fujimori's political success. While the latter formed his main electoral base in 1990, the brunt of the negative impact of the adjustment was carried by the same popular sectors, with few possibilities to gain from the neoliberal economic model. Women from popular sectors were particularly numerous in supporting Fujimori in 1990, and continued to form a strong power base throughout the 1990s, even though their economic situation did not improve significantly.[25]

Three factors explain the relatively enduring support that popular sectors provided to Fujimori throughout the decade. They can be described as political, identity-related, and material, the latter encompassing economic and security dimensions. Their relative importance varied from one period to the other, and they were conditioned to a great extent by the regime's neopopulist strategies in targeting these sectors and establishing new state-society relations.

Politically speaking, it should be emphasized that Peruvian popular classes, be they rural or urban, experienced what Oxhorn refers to as Latin America's popular sectors' problems of class formation and collective action (Oxhorn 1998). This reflects the pattern of late, dependent and partial capitalist development that generated weak and fragmented lower classes with divergent interests in relation to the mode of production and the nature of state intervention in the economy (Oxhorn 1998). In the case of Peru, popular mobilization led by the APRA for most of the twentieth century was transformed as a result of the efforts by the state under the Velasco regime to include these classes in the political process. This corporatist inclusion was paralleled by the rise of new left-wing parties and autonomous popular organizations in the 1970s and 1980s.

Paradoxically, the transition to a civilian democratic regime was a response to mounting repression against organized popular sectors and left-wing parties. Later, party leadership within the APRA and the left-wing parties were not able to carry forward popular classes' aspirations for more profound social change, not to mention sustained economic growth. In fact, the only thing that grew during that period was political violence, which increasingly alienated most Peruvians from the public sphere and instilled a pervasive "culture of fear" (Burt 2006). Democratic rule became synonymous with a growing distance between the political system and popular sectors (Franco 1994). The breakdown of the oligarchic order produced by the Velasco government's policies, notably through the expansion of social and economic rights, was followed by universal suffrage in 1980 whose benefit was actually contradicted by the contraction of social and economic rights (Franco 1994; Lynch 1995; López 1997). Political rights were not sufficient to compensate for the weakness of the political system and the state in particular, which failed to provide the minimum level of stability and security.

In contrast, Fujimori provided a new phase of rupture with the political elite associated with the democratic regime of the 1980s. Even if the fundamental processes that had characterized the weakness of democracy were maintained and even worsened—personalistic rule, clientelism, absence of institutional checks and balances, centralization of power in the hands of the President—Fujimori's political "independence" and his ability to rebuild a new political order were welcomed by popular sectors who saw it as an alternative to the state of desperation they had been immersed in for some time.

The identity component of popular sectors' support is related to the high degree of personal identification that a majority developed vis-a-vis Fujimori. As alluded to above, aside from sharing in his experience of discrimination related to his Japanese roots, and his popular class background, Fujimori also used popular culture references in his language and the marketing images he created by wearing traditional clothing of the different regions of Peru he visited, and dancing on stage with techno-cumbia dancers, for instance (Degregori 2001). He also became famous for visiting the most remote villages to inaugurate public works, schools or clinics. Such extensive presidential contact with popular sectors was unseen in preceding Peruvian politics. At the same time, Fujimori also played on his Asian character, which was associated with business success and international networks. His neo-populist appeal to popular sectors was anchored in a peculiar mix of cultural references that resonated with many Peruvians and led them to develop a particularly strong bond with the president.

The identity and political components of popular sectors' support for Fujimori throughout most of the 1990s would probably not have held for long without the material benefits popular classes derived from his rule. Notwithstanding the difficult economic situation in which the majority of the population remained throughout Fujimori's rule, the fact that he began his presidency during an unprecedented crisis is important to consider. Indeed, three major achievements were acknowledged by Peruvians, and by popular class Peruvians in particular, as key improvements in their socioeconomic life. First, in terms of security, the government made impressive gains against insurgent groups, such as arresting Abimael Guzman, leader of *Sendero luminoso*, a few months after the April 1992 *autogolpe*, as already mentioned. While political violence would continue to haunt Peruvians throughout the decade, notably with a hostage crisis instigated by the MRTA at the Japanese Embassy in 1997, the number of insurgent attacks in Peru's major cities and most regions was drastically reduced as of 1994, and Fujimori claimed and received personal credit for this victory.

Two other material gains related to security were, first, the general improvement in the macroeconomic situation, with inflation stabilized and economic growth reinitiated in the early 1990s, and second, the social policies designed to target the poor implemented especially after 1993. After relying on emergency assistance programs that sought to mitigate some of the negative impacts of the initial adjustment shock on low-income sectors, Fujimori's government developed a whole range of social compensation programs with the support of international cooperation funds.[26] The centralization of most social programs under the umbrella of the Ministry of the Presidency, controlled by Fujimori, provided a direct link between the president and people's welfare. Social policy was oriented by a "poverty-reduction" approach corresponding to the dominant framework of multilateral lending agencies from the 1990s onwards. It consisted in the delivery of short-term benefits whereby aid recipients remained dependent on state assistance. State policy did not promote sustainable employment, nor provide productive resources or technical training.

Instead, clientelistic social programs corresponded to Fujimori's need to exercise direct political control over marginalized popular sectors, and indeed a number of sources have shown that social expenditures increased in a significant fashion in the months preceding electoral campaigns (Gonzales de Olarte 1998; Cotler and Grompone 2000). As will be explained in later chapters, women formed a "privileged" clientele of most of these social programs.

Thus, not only did social policy target the poor in a paternalistic fashion, it also created institutionalized clientelistic relations between popular sectors and the state. In the context where popular sector organizations were already weak and fragmented due to years of insurgent and counter-insurgency violence in shantytowns and rural areas, the massive entry of state agencies in the field of basic needs provision further debilitated their autonomous capacity. The president directly benefited from the new clientelistic networks because of the concentration of resources in the Ministry of the Presidency, which controlled most such programs, at least until 1996 when the Ministry for the Promotion of Women and Human Development (PROMUDEH) was created. PROMUDEH was the government's response to the critiques about the concentration of power in the Ministry of the Presidency, and while a number of poverty-reduction programs were transferred to it, it maintained the same basic policy orientations (Adrianzén 1999; Henriquez 1999; Portocarrero et al. 2000). PROMUDEH pursued the government's strategy of targeting popular sectors with the delivery of goods that were essential to the population's daily survival, as no other alternative existed.

This description of the foundations of popular classes' support to the Fujimori government substantiates the claim that the latter represented a new kind of populist rule pursuing the trends in political representation and governance that characterized Latin American politics for at least half of the twentieth century (Roberts 1995; Weyland 1996 and 1999; Oxhorn 1998). Fujimori, along with other Latin American neopopulist leaders who emerged in the 1990s, exhibited several of the traits associated with past populist rule such as personalistic leadership, the mobilization of heterogeneous mass support concentrated in the popular classes, and weak intermediary channels of representation between the leader and his followers.

Yet his economic policy was clearly opposed to past populist programs of import-substitution industrialization and corporatist redistributive measures. The lack of an identified core class support base also distinguished Fujimori's neopopulist rule from past, "classic" forms of populism relying predominantly on working classes. For while popular classes were especially targeted by Fujimori's policies and media, his political constituency was multi-class, including some sectors of the economic elite connected to foreign capital. Fujimori's neopopulism is best explained by the failure of the Left (IU) and center-Left (APRA) to develop sustainable forms of representation of popular class and middle class interests, as well as the incapacity of the Right to present them with a political party capable of winning their adhesion through elections. The Fujimori regime centered its strategy on an antiestablishment and anti-institutional discourse and exercise of power. In contrast to classic populism, such as with the early APRA relying on well organized and structured mass-based support, no attempt was made by Fujimori to develop a strong and institutionalized political party capable of mobilizing and disciplining followers. Instead, mass media were amply used to transmit Fujimori's propaganda through control, bribery, and repression against the independent press (Conaghan 2005).

Fujimori's neopopulism also comes out because of the particular use of political violence in his strategy of social control. Either as a pretext to justify repressive measures, or as a violent actor itself, the state under Fujimori exerted popular adhesion through a deadly mix of fear and longing for security. Fear of terrorism was manipulated by Fujimori to control and suppress all forms of autonomous political organizing, particularly on the Left. Special laws and the whole judicial apparatus were used to arrest and detain opponents. As Burt reports, Peruvians exhibited self-censorship and avoided protesting for most of the 1990s because of the fear of being targeted either by the Shining Path or the State (Burt 2006). The role of the military in the coalition and the use of Intelligence Services to control political opponents further guaranteed the possibility for Fujimori to rule unimpeded by the organized interests of society, as well as his capacity to undertake a radical reshaping of the economic and political order through the 1992 self-coup.

To understand further the social basis of Fujimori's neopopulism, his reliance on "outside" sources of support to build his governing coalition—such as international financial institutions (IFIs), among others, is also key. Empowered by transnational capital and IFIs' hegemonic discourse of neoliberal reform, Fujimori's regime was able to remain relatively autonomous from any significant national political organization or economic interests. To sustain the legitimacy of his regime, Fujimori did not need to develop extensive systems of corporatist benefits granted to national economic elite sectors, contrary to what was generally the case under past populist rule in Latin America. Instead, his government's policy opened the door to foreign capital and the financial sector was among the few to benefit from the privatization policies.[27]

Conclusion: Democracy and Citizenship under Fujimori

As the analysis presented in this chapter reveals, the multidimensional crisis of the late 1980s led to the near breakdown of the state and the profound transformation of the political party system that had presided over the transition to democracy. The democratic regime created in 1980 was replaced in 1993 by a new institutional framework corresponding nominally to a political democracy, yet used to display a particular form of "competitive or electoral authoritarianism." Respect for the rule of law was weak and rather amounted to a legalistic façade, while legislative, executive, and judicial institutions were controlled by Fujimori's governing coalition and used to selectively repress opponents.

Because of the deep crisis in which the country was found by Fujimori on the day of his first electoral victory, and the extent to which popular sectors in particular were prone to accept a profound reshaping of the political system, the legitimacy of Fujimori's rule could rely on a new form of populist politics combining an appeal to these marginalized sectors and a willingness to destroy the remnants of preceding political projects, be they from the Left or the Right.

The ease with which Fujimori pursued his neopopulist crusade against the political class and against the democratic institutions of the 1980s was facilitated by the fact that they were not associated with most of the past advances in citizenship rights that had been won by or granted to popular sectors be they workers or peasants. As described above, prior to the coming to power of Fujimori, the authoritarian regime of General Velasco was the historical reference for the first wave of recognition of popular sectors by the state through the creation of a set of social rights and innovative channels of political and economic inclusion. The parties of the Left that had grown in strength since then, while important as a support for popular sector organizing and with some electoral success, ultimately lost their power through ideological and personal infighting and the negative impact of the guerrilla war on the Left's image. With the failure of the archetypal populist party, the APRA, at the head of the state from 1985 to 1990, the space was left to be filled by a new political force that, potentially it seemed, could lead the country to more secure grounds under new political terms.

The coalition formed by Fujimori, Montesinos, the military and the business sector connected to international capital was then able to lay the roots of a new neopopulist model of state-society relations. The latter relied on a negation of past social rights—that had become largely obsolete because of concrete circumstances—and the extension of free market principles to most spheres of social and economic life. The role of the State shifted to providing short-term assistance to the poorest sectors that were left out of the formal productive sphere. In such a context, citizenship under Fujimori amounted to a formal political equality in a regime that legitimated itself on the basis of elections—of which the free and fair nature was sometimes highly questionable—and the use of opinion polls. With the party system dominated by the "model" of independent political entrepreneurs, the political sphere was left open to the manipulation of the democratic façade by the Fujimori government. This was made easier by the continuing participation of opposition parties in the various electoral processes up to the year 2000, since the government was thereby apparently fulfilling the minimalist requirements of political democracy.

In concluding this chapter and linking it to the following ones, it should be underlined that the disappearance of old patterns of party politics and the weakness of institutional checks and balances paradoxically opened up space for some actors or issues that had previously encountered great difficulties in penetrating the public sphere, not to mention their access to state power. Such is the case of the women's movement's claims for greater participation in formal party politics, as well as a set of reforms in legislation and policy aiming at enhancing women's status. Chapters 3 and 5 will detail my argument on this issue.

As will be shown throughout the rest of this book, the concentration of power in the hands of Fujimori gave him extraordinary capacity to impose some policies that were previously divisive inside and between the different political forces dominating Peruvian politics. On the other hand, as I have shown, his economic policy orientations seriously circumscribed the kind of reforms that could be implemented in favor of women's citizenship rights, especially in the field of social and economic rights, thus affecting negatively the prospects for the development of popular sector women's citizenship in particular.

More fundamentally, the neopopulist character of Fujimori's rule circumscribed and obstructed the development of intermediary organizations that could become the basis for stronger autonomous political action. This had a particularly detrimental impact on some sectors of the women's movement that were particularly vulnerable to government cooptation in the face of persistent poverty. Other sectors benefiting from foreign financial and political support had more capacity to resist and build a political balance of power favorable to the adoption of some of their rights claims by the Fujimori government. However, the lack of state accountability and the absence of clear institutional safeguards to ensure the implementation of state commitments was another clear limit to the institutionalization of women's citizenship rights under Fujimori.

Chapter 3

Feminist Activism

Engendering State Policy through NGO Work

When Fujimori assumed power in 1990, the second-generation feminist movement in Peru already had almost two decades of organizing behind its back. Faced with the task of pursuing its agenda in the context of institutional transformations and neoliberal economic reform, the movement also experienced severe stress as part of civil society's experience of neopopulist politics. Transnational and regional networking provided resources and strategies to Peruvian feminists building their power base and legitimacy against the all-mighty Fujimori. Tensions within the movement, however, revolved around the extent to which organized feminists should collaborate with the state and participate in electoral processes, thereby lending some support to the regime.

The first Peruvian feminist groups, instrumental for the construction of a women's liberation discourse in Peru, can be traced back to the early twentieth century, with the first feminist group *Evolución Femenina* formed in Lima in 1914 by María Jesús Alvarado (Villar 1994). The "second-wave" feminist movement emerged in its Peruvian version in the 1970s to address the causes and consequences of gender inequality as they unfolded in the country, borrowing from the models and discourses exhibited by European, North American, and other South American feminists. Going from a radical period of definition of its feminist identity in the 1970s to a decade-long period of intense collaboration with the popular sector women's movement in the 1980s, the Peruvian feminist movement has since shown an increasing interest in influencing policy-making at the core of political institutions and the bureaucracy. This move has been facilitated by the support of international donors and the consolidation of relatively powerful feminist nongovernmental organizations (NGOs). The latter dominate the politics of the feminist movement since the late 1980s in Peru and elsewhere in the region. They have been instrumental in pushing for most of the advances in women's citizenship rights that have occurred in the country in the 1990s.

In analyzing the Peruvian feminist movement's contribution to the construction of women's citizenship in the 1990s, some key international and national factors will be emphasized. First, the space and resources provided by the international women's movement around the cycle of United Nations International Conferences in the first half of the 1990s created an environment whereby incentives were greatest for both the State and feminist organizations to achieve progress in the institutionalization of women's citizenship. Second, the steps taken by the Fujimori regime to address some "women's issues" and promote women's access to political power went beyond the expectations generated by the international context. But as the goals of Fujimori and those pursued by feminist organizations coincided at times, they also clashed in the concrete implementation of various aspects of the feminist agenda.

This chapter will argue that the strong emphasis by the feminist movement on influencing state policy on a professional and technical basis, while leading to important advances, also had a negative corollary: the distancing of the movement from popular sectors that, coupled with the emphasis on civil and political rights, contributed to fragmenting the women's movement. Besides, aiming at engendering the State was particularly risky for the feminist movement in the context of Fujimori's neopopulist politics, because of the regime's blatant disregard for human rights and the rule of law. This generated an ambivalent stance in the movement towards the Fujimori regime, an ambivalence that can be explained both by fear of state repression and the movement's political objectives.

After a brief presentation of the contemporary feminist movement as it developed in Peru, I will analyze the opportunities and strategies around the consolidation of feminist NGOs and their emphasis on developing autonomous, professional expertise on women's issues. This expertise was used to sustain a new type of dynamics with the State, based on lobbying for legal and policy reforms, and providing professional human resources to implement these reforms. I will then explain how the international context shaped feminist organizations' demands and the State's incentives to innovate and create new state institutions devoted to women's status. The chapter will close with an assessment of feminist politics and the state in the context of neopopulism to highlight the limits of institutional work on behalf of women's citizenship under Fujimori.

FEMINISM IN PERU

Analysts of the women's movement in Peru generally agree on a typology of its different sectors that places the feminist movement in a distinct category, separate from the popular sector women's movement and the women involved in party politics (Villavicencio 1987; Palomino 1987; Vargas and Villanueva 1994; Blondet 1995; Anderson 1996b). Many of the feminists emerged out of the many left-wing parties that formed in the late 1960s and 1970s. After participating in the elaboration of the Left's platforms and struggling unsuccessfully for the recognition of gender oppression as a phenomenon not to be subsumed under class oppression, many leftist women decided to leave the parties to form feminist groups in order to address gender oppression in an autonomous fashion and as a central priority. Their split from the parties also responded to the need to break free from a second-class status as party members who did not have equal voice and access to power positions within party organizations (Ponce del Castillo 1984).

Also key for the formation of the feminist movement in the 1970s was the creation within the reformist military government of Velasco of an official space for reflection on the *"problemática de la mujer"* (woman's status) with the creation of *the Comisión Nacional de la Mujer Peruana* (National Commission on Peruvian Women—CONAMUP) in 1974. While the Commission was created mainly for opportunistic reasons, in light of the imminence of the first UN Conference on Women in 1975, it was abolished three years later without having done much else than producing working papers and funding small women's development projects (Anderson 1985). Nonetheless, it represented an opening for professional women who worked within CONAMUP. Some of them then went on to form private institutions working on women's issues (Ponce del Castillo 1984, 243–44; Anderson 1985).

The first International Decade on Women opened in 1975 and provided an additional framework within which Peruvian feminists derived legitimacy and discursive tools to articulate their first feminist groups. The first instances of feminist mobilization were articulated around the issue of abortion. Amidst the difficulties of the military government and the beginning of the economic crisis in the mid-1970s, the emergence of feminist ideas received little attention within left-wing parties, which gave further incentive for many women to form their own spaces for reflection on feminist identity and strategy.

In 1978 and 1979, that is, before the transition to democracy was completed, the first contemporary feminist groups were created, such as the *Movimiento Manuela Ramos* (Manuela Ramos Movement), the

Centro de la Mujer Peruana Flora Tristán (Peruvian Women's Centre Flora Tristan), the Socialist Front of Women, and *Mujeres en Lucha* (Women in Struggle). The first two remain up to this day the most powerful feminist institutions, having moved from their early status as small groups in the late 1970s to sophisticated nongovernmental organizations exercising leadership at the national, regional, and international levels as of the late 1980s.[1] Other feminist organizations, and women's organizations not necessarily defining themselves as feminist but dedicated to promoting women's equality in different spheres were formed in the 1980s and the 1990s, some of them staffed by women who had continued their party militancy for some years before turning to nonpartisan, women-focused civil society organizations.[2]

Feminism and Party Politics

As stated above, a number of feminist activists received their political education in the left-wing parties created in Peru in the 1960s and 1970s. The relationship between the feminist movement and the formal political sphere was therefore more sustained while these parties were strong in the late 1970s and 1980s. Yet this relationship did not impede the feminist movement from opting for an autonomous stance from political parties early on.

As Villavicencio explains, the incapacity of the feminist current to position itself as the leader of the women's movement in the early 1980s led it to retreat from the public sphere and consolidate its identity through the formation of groups, some of which would later become NGOs (Villavicencio 1987, 9). Palomino describes the early years of feminist self-definition as a period of "separation from the other sectors, where joint actions and dialogue are interrupted" (Palomino 1987, 22). She then refers to the subsequent "vanguard" project of the feminist movement that asserted itself as responsible for articulating women's consciousness of gender-based oppression.

However, organized feminists made a return to political life in the mid-1980s, claiming to be the vanguard of the women's movement and to represent Peruvian women as a whole in the 1985 general elections. Two feminist leaders launched themselves as candidates running under the banner of *Izquierda Unida* (United Left). The 1985 electoral experiment was relatively unsuccessful in great part because the feminist candidates could not legitimately claim to represent the whole women's movement or, even less, the Peruvian female population.[3] Following the electoral defeat of the two candidates, the feminist movement chose to consolidate its own institutional basis and continue to exercise its political influence through lobbying the state and political institutions rather than direct participation in electoral politics. This distanced it further from party politics at a time when the growing crisis of the Peruvian party system was reaching dramatic proportions in the late 1980s.

In the face of the rise of political "independents" and the instability of the party system, the core of the feminist movement, through a few NGOs such as *Movimiento Manuela Ramos* and *Centro de la Mujer Peruana Flora Tristán*, adopted a new posture toward the formal political sphere. Starting in the late 1980s, these NGOs maintained the same distance from partisan politics that had marked the formative years of feminist organizations, while they also broadened the range of their political interlocutors by moving away from an exclusive focus on politicians from the Left to include women politicians from all parties as well as presidential candidates (Vargas and Olea 1997).[4]

From the 1990s onwards, the new tactic of creating feminist NGO coalitions such as *Foro-Mujer* (Woman's Forum) provided flexible mechanisms to join forces and establish common feminist policy agendas. *Foro-Mujer* in particular served to channel the demands of the feminist movement toward the various political forces competing for state power. By presenting their agenda to all candidates and parties and trying to get their commitment to implement some of these demands, the feminist NGOs placed women's rights claims above the partisan debate and articulated it as a public affairs issue. This option was part of a communications strategy to universalize the feminist agenda into an agenda for women's citizenship. Yet as noted by Vargas and Olea, *Foro-Mujer* included only a few NGOs, whereas prior coordinating bodies such as the *Colectivo de Coordinación del Movimiento Feminista* (Feminist Movement Coordinating Collective) created in 1986 had a more inclusive character and did not rely exclusively on the power of NGOs (Vargas and Olea 1997, 22).

Feminism and the Popular Sector Women's Movement

The feminist movement in Peru was built on a strong consciousness of gender and class inequalities. The particular context for the emergence of Peruvian social movements, in a period of intense mobilization partly sponsored or encouraged by the Velasco government, accounted for the influence of socialist ideas on Peruvian feminism (Ponce del Castillo 1984). But the first years of feminist mobilization were marked by an emphasis on issues such as abortion and sexuality, which did not facilitate its links with the popular sector women's movement struggling for the construction of basic infrastructure in urban slums and building autonomous organizations around the need to find solutions to the problems of hunger and chronic unemployment.

Yet early on in the 1980s, feminist NGOs such as *Movimiento Manuela Ramos* and *Centro de la Mujer Peruana Flora Tristán* developed programs to provide advisory services to women in popular neighborhoods, working on such issues as women's health or violence against women. Feminist organizations used their daily work in the slums as a reference to articulate their understanding of gender oppression. They also used it to disseminate their platforms in popular neighbourhoods, even if according to some observers, feminist activists always questioned the potential of popular organizations to empower women (Palomino 1987).

Virginia Vargas, a key founder and member of *Centro de la Mujer Peruana Flora Tristán*, expressed the feminist movement's ambivalence vis-à-vis the popular women's movement based on survival organizations, in the following terms: "It is striking that women [in popular neighborhoods] have not struggled resolutely to be represented as organizations in the neighborhood committees; it is also striking that no serious questioning was made of the dominant interests, for example in relation to food provision. On the other hand, there is a lack of trust on the part of the rest of organizations vis-à-vis this movement: there is an explicit or implicit resistance to see them as valid, creative, or new" (Vargas 1988, 259; my translation).

Notwithstanding this critical distance, the feminist movement developed a sustained dialogue with the relatively strong popular sector women's movement in the 1980s and maintained an extensive presence in popular neighborhoods up to the beginning of the 1990s. After that, the relationship between feminist NGOs and popular women's organizations became more remote.[5] As key feminists Barrig and Vargas concluded in 2000, "The feminist movement has never been a mass movement, it never had social bases. The popular sector women's movement in the 1980s was not our social basis; they were our interlocutors, our equals with different agendas; we shared common elements and others were negotiated" (Barrig and Vargas 2000, 227; my translation).

This understanding of the two movements as equals independent from one another is contradicted by the reality of the discourse of the feminist movement, which often appeals to a terminology referring to "the Peruvian woman" or "Peruvian women" in the articulation of their analyses and proposals. While the self-positioning of feminist NGOs as representing the interests of all Peruvian women is grounded on years of research, networking, direct contact with and services provided to women from different sectors and areas of the country, politically speaking, the women's movement remained segmented, as in the majority of Latin American countries and elsewhere. This was manifest in the absence of a broad-based coalition including popular sector women's organizations and other branches of the women's movement such as union women. This failure to create a broader women's movement is even more notable in Peru because of the fact that the feminist movement was so involved for a decade in collaborating with popular sector women's organizations in the 1980s.

Feminist Political Mobilization in the 1990s

Feminist work in the late 1980s and 1990s was predominantly structured around nongovernmental organizations that formed coordinating bodies at specific conjunctures or around thematic issues. Yet at various moments in the 1990s, the feminist movement demonstrated its willingness to participate in opposition politics by launching initiatives that resolutely positioned it as a political actor. One such instance was formed around the 1993 referendum to approve the new constitution proposed by Alberto Fujimori. Feminists organized a "Women's Movement for a Vote of Conscience" (*Movimiento de Mujeres por un Voto Consciente*) to criticize the abolition, in the proposed constitution, of some articles concerning gender equality and explain the legal implications of the new constitution from a gender perspective. The Movement opposed the new constitution, rejecting both the text itself and the authoritarian context in which the 1979 constitution and democratic institutions had been abolished by Fujimori (Vargas and Olea 1997).

Similar opposition activities took place in the second half of the 1990s when Fujimori's willingness to remain in power at all costs became all too evident for some sectors of civil society, including some feminists. Two important initiatives arose from the feminist movement, adding to the political landscape of a reemerging civil society and giving a more active voice to women who sought to oppose the regime's authoritarian tendencies. The *Movimiento Amplio de Mujeres* (Women's Broad Movement—MAM) and the *Movimiento de Mujeres por la Democracia* (Women's Movement for Democracy—MUDE) emerged in 1996 and 1997, respectively. They both attracted public attention and positioned themselves as women in civil society opposed to Fujimori's authoritarianism.

The MAM grew out of the debate that unfolded around the creation of the Ministry for the Promotion of Women and Human

Development (PROMUDEH) that I discuss in the next section. Some feminists opted for maintaining distance from the state, while others welcomed the possibilities that this new institution could potentially provide for the advancement of women in Peru. The MAM, which defended the former posture, was created as a space for individual feminists who wanted to organize opposition to various instances of authoritarian abuse by the government. Moreover, it set for itself the task of bringing together in a flexible forum feminists and women from all sectors who shared the desire to rethink the relationship between the state and society, and develop a new vision of citizenship based on the principles of autonomy, horizontal and vertical democracy, and gender equality. As part of its activities, MAM took on difficult cases such as the defense of Leonora LaRosa, an ex-secret services agent who had allegedly been tortured by her colleagues. This case was extremely politically sensitive because it highlighted the authoritarian nature of the regime and involved a woman left handicapped by her torturers. The MAM also denounced abuses in the state family planning program that had led to cases of coerced sterilization, and publicly exposed the threats being made against the victims of these abuses who had brought their cases before the courts.[6]

The MUDE was formed a year later by other feminist activists who needed a space outside their respective NGOs to express their political opposition to the regime. It first launched its activities around the initiative of various civil society organizations to gather citizens' signatures to press for the holding of a referendum on the legality of Fujimori's intention to run for a third time for the presidency. The MUDE was one of the more active groups campaigning for the referendum and gathering signatures. As an informal group, it constituted a space for discussion and the expression of political opposition for important feminist leaders working in feminist or other types of NGOs, and for women leaders of social organizations as well as a few intellectuals.[7]

Both the MUDE and the MAM took an active role in the public mobilization against Fujimori's 2000 electoral campaign, mobilizing thousands of women and men to participate in their demonstrations against the regime.[8] Although the importance of these events resulted from a general process of popular mobilization occurring in Peru at the time, it also reflected a renewed political protagonism of the feminist movement. However, when such initiatives materialized, most of the nongovernmental organizations that dominated the feminist movement did not participate in their own institutional name. Rather, individual feminists, belonging to NGOs or not, mobilized on an individual basis to join these movements.

The fact that NGOs *per se* generally decided not to join in was connected to several factors. The control exercised by the Ministry of the Presidency over the transfer of funds coming from international donors to the NGOs, as well as the common practice of sending the State Taxation Agency, the SUNAT, to investigate the accounts of political opponents, were only two of the tools used by the regime to threaten and silence the opposition.[9] Moreover, most foreign funders were hesitant to support civil society organizations that acted as open political opponents, or even strictly forbade activities of a purely political nature as a condition for granting financial support. Lastly, the difficulty of resolving some internal political debates to generate a clear political stand on the part of the feminist NGOs made it easier to act in an individual fashion rather than as civil society organizations, even if in concrete terms the latter were often lending material and human resources to support these causes.

Institution-building in the 1990s: A Strategic Opportunity for Feminist NGOs

Notwithstanding the impact of these instances of political mobilization for raising public awareness of a few cases of grave women's rights violations and the need to oppose the regime's authoritarian tendencies, the fact that feminist NGOs as institutions generally pursued other strategies rather than oppositional politics conditioned the meaning of feminism in the 1990s in a significant way.

When observing the main patterns of feminist activities during this period, one can infer that a strategic decision was made to address the State and the legislature in a nonpartisan fashion to push the feminist agenda or at least parts of it. The most important contribution of the feminist movement to the construction of women's citizenship was therefore through the dissemination of some key feminist demands within the public institutional sphere, pressing for legal reforms and the creation, within the state apparatus, of mechanisms and agencies working to institutionalize a gender perspective in public policy. As will be shown later, this strategic decision of feminist NGOs led to important advances in some areas.

The main goals of feminist organizations in the 1990s were the institutionalization of state responsibility in promoting gender equality and the consolidation of their own institutional basis. Strengthening their power as feminist institutions allowed them to exercise greater influence through advocacy campaigns, publications, and intensive lobbying. In that regard, Rocío Palomino remarks that it would be unfair to say that the feminist movement has overly invested in developing a relationship with the State. Rather, she claims that it is through the few spaces granted by the State that feminist NGOs, as institutions, have developed and applied the technical expertise they had accumulated for the execution of major projects with the support of international funds (Palomino 2000, 67). In other words, the construction of solid feminist institutions occupied a great part of feminist activities, and the latter involved the State insofar as the projects implemented by feminist NGOs required state approval for the channelling of international funds and sometimes signing cooperation agreements with various state institutions.

A key element to underline in analyzing the dual process of institution-building within the feminist movement and within the state—to engender state institutions—is the broader political framework. The feminist movement adapted to an environment where political parties had no substantive platforms to adhere to and behaved in an anarchical, self-destructive fashion. The NGOs chose a strategy based on targeting individual politicians and the executive to convince them of adopting legal and policy reforms. They positioned their agenda above the partisan field by giving it a universal character, emphasizing that women's rights is a matter of state obligations and duties. By the same token, they established themselves as the vehicle representing "women's interests," using the discourse of women's human rights to legitimize their claims.[10]

Thus the main feminist NGOs reoriented their strategic behavior "from protesting to proposing" ("*de la protesta a la propuesta*"), as goes a famous phrase in the Latin American women's movement. The technical and specialized expertise they used to influence public policy formation and legislative reforms became their main asset in positioning themselves in the public sphere. This orientation meant that the politics of women's rights was played first and foremost through the development of a critical mass of knowledge and principled arguments in favour of key reform proposals.[11]

The international context of the UN Cycle of Conferences in the 1990s provided the financial and political tools needed for the feminist NGOs to perform particularly well in that period. Following on the progress made by feminist ideas and proposals throughout the 1980s, a relatively favorable international context testified to their success and opened new possibilities for alliances and strategies for women's empowerment, not to mention the financial resources that were made available by international donors in a highly competitive fashion.

Internal Dynamics of the Feminist Movement

Once the decision to build a feminist movement independent of other social forces or other sectors of the women's movement was confirmed around the second *Encuentro Feminista Latinoamericano y del Caribe* (Latin American and Caribbean Feminist Meeting) held in Lima in 1983, the consolidation of some feminist organizations and their increasing institutionalization became the dominant process, making the survival of less formal and more spontaneous expressions of feminism more difficult. An important step was the creation of a coordinating committee of the movement in 1986, whereby each member had to be officially registered in order to vote. This formalized the participatory process within the feminist movement and consolidated the leadership role of a few organizations. In 1991, this committee was abolished during a period when the concentration of financial and human resources within a few powerful NGOs led to further marginalization of the noninstitutionalized feminists groups (Barrig 2000a, 11).

A number of factors explain the evolution of the first feminist collectives into sophisticated and efficient NGOs. First is the need for professional women who had been the founders of the feminist movement to find greater stability and achievement in their work. Some of these professionals explained in interviews that the evolution of their organizations reflected in many ways the evolution of their own personal lives, which now required greater financial stability, greater security, and opportunities for professional development. Second, the availability of international financial support, with all the performance requirements this imposed, also encouraged the building of administrative structures and accountability procedures, as well as the development of work plans around specific thematic projects with measurable results. All of this required a degree of professionalization that only an institution investing in its own organizational capacity could achieve.

When Sonia Alvarez describes what she calls the "NGOization of Latin American feminisms," she refers to the increased specialization and professionalization of the feminist groups and the multiplication of feminist NGOs. A few elements of the feminist agenda have been incorporated in the dominant public policy discourse due to the role of feminist NGOs in the process of policy formation and public debate on legislative reform (Alvarez 1998, 306). In light of the increasing pressures coming from the international community, which reflect the success of the international women's movement, there was a coincidence of interests between feminist organizations seeking more access to the State and more influence on the policy process and, on the other hand, a State that needed expertise and resources to implement its new commitments.

This new mode of action for many feminist NGOs in the 1990s, including in Peru, is expressed quite clearly in a statement by the general coordinator of the NGO *Movimiento Manuela Ramos* in 2001 when she looked back on the 1990s and said "Manuela Ramos also transformed itself in the 1990s. From questioning and calling on the Peruvian State, we redefined our objectives towards a dialogical, critical and careful stance aiming at the implementation of public policies. This was done through taking into account the broad perspective of state policies, beyond the transitory conjuncture of successive governments" (V. Villanueva in Manuela Ramos 2001, 11; my translation).

Most feminist NGOs generally maintained a position similar to that expressed by Villanueva, in the sense of acting primarily as both a specialized executing agency and an advocate of women's rights. Alvarez suggests that the NGOization of the movement, coinciding with the application of neoliberal reforms that reduced the size of public service provision, led feminist organizations to replace the State in many spheres (Alvarez 1998, 307). While "filling the gap" left by a smaller public sector is often accompanied with memorandums of agreement between NGOs and the relevant public authorities to define how they will provide professional services in the domain of women's rights, communications channels go from official correspondence to ongoing consultations with public officials. Thus the state becomes a partner or even an "employer," which makes it difficult—although not impossible—to then criticize it publicly. The nonpartisan stance of the feminist movement also meant that it was left on its own when having to deal with the Fujimori regime's decisions regarding some components of the women's rights agenda they promoted.

International Context

The Peruvian feminist movement's strategies were deeply influenced by the international context. The important space occupied by the women's movement at the international level in the 1990s was due in great part to the activities, political profile, and resources devoted to preparing and attending the United Nations (UN) Fourth World Conference on Women held in Beijing in 1995. A growing network of women's organizations from various countries increased their lobbying and advocacy efforts. This network was empowered by the results of the Third World Conference on Women held in Nairobi in 1985—where it was recognized for the first time by an international forum of states that violence against women is a serious source of discrimination against women—and by the visibility women's rights activists obtained at the International Conference on Human Rights held in 1993, where it was recognized that "women's rights are human rights." What became known as the global women's movement managed to attract international attention on issues such as violence against women, sexual and reproductive rights, and the need to apply a gender-sensitive grid to human rights norms and mechanisms. The cycle of UN World Conferences in the early 1990s—including the World Conference on Population and Development in 1994—provided a unique opportunity to mobilize women and UN member states around key issues of the women's movement's agenda.[12]

The direct impact of this international context first consisted in concentrating foreign donor resources in supporting the elaboration and dissemination of the platforms of women's movements in the various regions of the world. In Peru, foreign donors set up a *Mesa de coordinación en género* (Gender Coordinating Body) to facilitate the participation of Peruvian women at the Beijing Conference. Although a strong debate took place in Peru and at the regional level on the political convenience of agreeing to allow the United States Agency for International Development (USAID) to finance the NGO regional preparatory process, because of the contradictions between USAID's orientations and some key feminist demands, it was finally accepted except by the Brazilian NGOs (Friedman, Hochstetler, and Clark 2001, 24).

The second impact to be underlined is the moral obligation it created for governments to come up with some kind of analysis of the situation of women's status in their country, as well as to consider various proposals for reform advanced by women's organizations and international agencies. In other words, the international agenda was set favorably for women's organizations to use this window of opportunity to raise the profile of their claims and perspectives at the national level, including in Peru. Of course, though, what allowed this context to actually benefit the women's organizations within Peru was the particular strategies and accumulation of forces displayed by some women's NGOs.

In December 1993, nine Peruvian women's NGOs joined together in the creation of the *Grupo Impulsor Nacional "Mujeres por la Igualdad Real"* (National Working Group "Women for Real Equality") to promote civil society's and women's organizations' participation in the preparation for the Beijing Conference. Starting in 1994 and up to the Conference in September 1995, the *Grupo Impulsor Nacional*

(National Gender Promotion Group) organized national and local consultative meetings to gather the points of view and demands of women throughout the country (Bermúdez 1995, 30). Following the conference, the coalition continued to function as a nongovernmental body to monitor the Peruvian State's performance in implementing policies and laws in line with the commitments made around the negotiation of the Beijing Conference's Platform of Action.

The government, through its *Comisión Permanente de los Derechos de la Mujer* (Permanent Commission on Women's Rights) at the Ministry of Justice, worked collaboratively with the *Grupo Impulsor Nacional* in formulating the Peruvian National Report to be submitted at the official Beijing Conference. Some consultants from the women's movement were hired by both the State and the *Grupo Impulsor Nacional* to produce their respective documents and syntheses (Olea and Vargas 2000, 63). However, feminist NGOs asked that some of their representatives be included in the official Peruvian delegation to the Beijing Conference. This demand was not accepted. The only instance of such inclusion had occurred in a Latin American Regional Preparatory Meeting for the World Conference on Population and Development, where a representative of *Movimiento Manuela Ramos* was part of the official delegation. Her presence within the official delegation at the World Conference itself was vetoed by conservative sectors in Peru (Olea and Vargas 2000, 52).

The profile of Peruvian feminist NGOs was nonetheless reflected at the regional and international levels through the nomination of Virginia Vargas, founder and leading member of the *Centro de la Mujer Peruana Flora Tristán*, as head of the Latin American and Caribbean NGO Coordinating Committee for the Beijing Conference. This allowed the Peruvian feminist NGOs to be directly in touch with the mobilization process and the negotiation of the NGO Platform throughout the region, as well as at the NGO Forum held in parallel with the World Conference on Women (Acosta et al. 2000).

All analysts concur in describing this period as exceptionally favorable to the visibility and mobilization of the women's movement, and of the feminist movement in particular since its leaders had more access to the regional and international meetings. However, the process through which the agenda of Peruvian civil society was set up did not mobilize a broad spectrum of social forces outside the women's movement. It essentially involved the different sectors of the women's movement, notably through the *Red nacional de promoción de la mujer*, a national network of women's organizations from the twenty-four regions of Peru that formed in 1990 at the instigation of a consultative process initiated by then President Alan García.

While the Peruvian state's presence was particularly noticed at the Beijing Conference because of the participation of President Fujimori himself—the only male head of state who addressed the Conference—the Peruvian delegation sided with conservative countries on many issues (Ewig 2006). In the list of reservations it adopted in reference to the Conference's Platform of Action, the Peruvian State affirmed that life begins at conception, opposed the legalization of abortion, and restricted the use of the notion of "sexual rights" to heterosexual relationships (Friedman, Hochstetler, and Clark 2001, 29). These went against the Peruvian feminist movement's platform on sexual and reproductive rights. Thus the efforts invested by the Peruvian women's movement in the Beijing Conference process did not necessarily translate into concrete gains in several fields of the feminist movement's agenda.

National Institutions and Areas of Advancement in Women's Citizenship

Contrary to other cases such as Brazil, Bolivia, or Chile, where the creation of high-level state institutions specialized on women's issues formed part of the demands emerging from social mobilizations during the transition to democracy and were the object of intense negotiations between political parties and women's organizations, in Peru it was essentially created from above (Pitanguy 1990; Chuchryk 1994; Palomino 2000, 63). The role of President Fujimori himself, and his interest in benefiting from the international momentum generated by the UN Conference on Women to derive greater political legitimacy, was central in the dynamics leading to this breakthrough in the Peruvian State.

The integration of some feminist demands within the State's reform agenda and the creation of high-level institutions addressing women's issues can be interpreted in great part as resulting from the Fujimori regime's willingness to benefit from a women-friendly image and hence attract international donor funds, rather than as a response to the political power exercised by the Peruvian feminist movement (Palomino 2000, 68). Other factors to consider in explaining these developments are the influence of some individual feminist leaders and a public opinion more favorable to promoting women's equality. The latter resulted in part from the feminist movement's public activities and the dissemination of its discourse. But the story behind the decision to create these institutions reveals that the initiatives of a few individuals were the determining factor in their creation, rather than a concerted strategy led by political parties, social sectors or the women's movement itself.

"Engendering" the State under Fujimori

Aside from a few incursions into the public institutional sphere, no high-level space was instituted to address women's issues or gender equality within the state before Fujimori came to power in the 1990s. Prior to this, the *Comisión Permanente de los Derechos de la Mujer*, under the authority of the Ministry of Justice, had been formed in 1974 but was limited in its actions. Only after completing his first mandate did President Fujimori open up the gates to some key demands of the feminist movement, such as electoral gender quotas or the creation of a Commission on Women within the Congress. Other institutional innovations, such as the Ministry for the Promotion of Women and Human Development (PROMUDEH) created in 1996, and the Specialized Women's Rights Section (SWRS) within the Ombudsman's Office, also established in 1996, allowed the Peruvian government to show it was abiding by the commitments made at the Beijing International Conference on Women.

The Ombudsman's Office was created by the 1993 constitution, but its installation got delayed a few years, probably due to the low priority accorded to it by the regime. Jorge Santistevan, who was a relatively progressive senior civil servant with international experience, was appointed Head of the Office by the Congress in 1996 and was granted wide latitude in setting up the institution. The SWRS was not included in the original mandate of the Ombudsman's office, but Santistevan had full latitude to innovate in establishing the institution's structure.

The SWRS was created mostly due to the influence that some feminist lawyers exercised on Santistevan. The direct access that they had during the process of creating the institution, in addition to the commitment of Santistevan himself, explains why the Ombudsman's Office became one of the most active state institutions documenting women's rights violations and developing proposals for legal and administrative reforms in favor of women's rights (Palomino 2000, 64). Its mandate included all the responsibilities shared with the other sections of the Ombudsman's office, that is, receiving complaints of human rights abuses committed by civil servants or state authorities, investigating them, making recommendations on public policies and the reform of legal norms, producing studies and reports, promoting debate and provide training to different entities of the state (Defensoría del Pueblo 2000, 8–9).

Once the decision to establish the SWRS was made, Rocío Villanueva, a feminist lawyer who had previously worked at *Movimiento Manuela Ramos* and other NGOs, was appointed to lead it. She was able to maintain a high degree of collaboration between the Ombudsman's Office and feminist NGOs as well as turn her unit into a reference point and ally of women's rights advocates, this time within the state. Because of the independence of the institution that the Ombudsman ably defended throughout his mandate from 1996 to 2000—an independence relying in practice on the support of international donors such as the Canadian International Development Agency—the SWRS became a central mechanism for the construction of state norms and accountability in matters related to women's rights.[13]

The creation of PROMUDEH in 1996 followed a different path. Various motives have been mentioned to explain Fujimori's strategy to promote women's issues and create a cabinet-level state institution on women's status. One such motive could have been the President's willingness to deal with the consequences of his marital difficulties exposed during his first mandate. His wife Susana Higuchi denounced the corruption in his government in 1992. As of 1994, the conflict in the presidential couple became public. Higuchi claimed to be victim of domestic violence. The couple divorced that year and she became an active member of the political opposition. Occurring a few months before the 1995 election, this complicated Fujimori's campaign, yet did not seem to affect his electoral performance. However, it may not be a coincidence that his pro-women discourse became more important just after the elections, in a probable attempt to recuperate his credibility at this level.[14]

Notwithstanding the detailed motivations behind his decision, Alberto Fujimori announced the creation of the ministry right after an official meeting with foreign donors in Germany. Since the news reached Peru through the press even before the President was back to the country, this announcement took everybody by surprise.[15] The elaboration of the ministry's mandate included the feminist movement only insofar as a few feminist leaders were consulted on an individual basis by the senior female civil servants close to Fujimori in charge of setting it up (Palomino 2000, 64). But this consultation occurred only after the decision to create the ministry was made. Hence the surprise was huge, more so considering that PROMUDEH was the first cabinet-level ministry on women's status not only in Peru, but in Latin America as a whole.

A few months before the presidential decision, in a book published in October 1995, Virginia Vargas from the *Centro de la Mujer Peruana*

Flora Tristán, had expressed the feminist movement's demand for the creation of state institutions addressing women's rights in these words: "it is necessary to modify state institutions through the creation or reinforcing of specialized agencies that will push forward the process of eliminating discrimination against women. These institutions should be high-level and benefit from sufficient financial resources coming from regular state budget, as well as have the power to dictate transversal policies" (Vargas 1995, 37; my translation). While Vargas did not explicitly call for the creation of a cabinet-level Ministry on Women's Affairs, her description of what was required to tackle the problem of discrimination against women, that is, high-level state agencies capable of exercising policy influence and benefiting from stable financial resources, could not be closer to what PROMUDEH represented when it was announced. Yet the decision by Fujimori to create the ministry was welcomed with ambivalence by the feminist movement. It could not condemn it for obvious strategic reasons and internal coherence, since it corresponded to the commitments they had lobbied their government to make before and during the Beijing Conference. But the process by which it was set up and the priorities it put forward were far from falling in line with the feminist movement's demands.

This gap was reflected partly in the choice made by Fujimori in appointing the successive heads of the ministry. The ministry's leadership did not come from the feminist movement. The first woman appointed in 1996 was Miriam Schenone, a lawyer who had served as Deputy-Minister of Justice and in that position had pushed ahead the work of the Permanent Commission on Women's Rights at the Ministry of Justice, the women's unit which preceded the creation of PROMUDEH. She was generally seen by the feminist movement as a bright, open-minded woman who deserved professional respect, until it was revealed that she had ties with Vladimiro Montesinos and collaborated in undermining the independence of the Judiciary. The second appointed minister, Luisa Maria Cuculiza, was a former mayor in one of Lima's middle class districts, and became a close presidential ally around the time of her nomination in 1999, when she was instrumental in Fujimori's bid for reelection in 2000. Cuculiza, a nurse and former local beauty contest winner in Huanuco, became famous for her demagogical use of the fear of terrorism in justifying many of the government's decisions.[16]

With no formal consultative process either with civil society or through the Congress prior to its creation, the ministry mainly served Fujimori's need to respond to the criticisms against the concentration of resources in the Ministry of the Presidency. A number of programs with very different objectives, such as the *Programa Nacional de Asistencia Alimentaria* (National Food Aid Program—PRONAA), *Cooperación Popular* (Popular Cooperation), the *Instituto Nacional de Bienestar Familiar* (National Institute for Family Welfare), the *Instituto Peruano de Deporte* (Peruvian Sports Institute), and the *Programa de Apoyo al Repoblamiento* (Resettlement Support Program), were transferred from the Ministry of the Presidency to PROMUDEH.

The latter adopted a poverty reduction rather than a gender equality framework to articulate its policies and strategies. This was made clear in the legislative decree creating the ministry, which stated that the latter was justified by the high level of efficiency that characterizes state investment in antipoverty programs targeting women (Grupo Impulsor Nacional 1997, 29). The Ministry followed the government's social compensation approach already in place through a number of major social programs targeting the poor. While pretending to carry the flag of "the promotion of women," few initiatives were taken by PROMUDEH under Fujimori in the field of structural reforms aiming at generating gender equality (Olea and Vargas 2000, 66). Indeed, the ministry primarily pursued the regime's strategy of consolidating a clientelist system designed for low-income women who depended on state support for daily survival, as explained in Chapter 4. Roxana Vasquez, from the feminist NGO DEMUS, also claimed that the decision to create PROMUDEH was strongly influenced by the willingness on the part of the executive to capture more funds from international cooperation agencies, the latter being eager to finance programs addressing gender-based poverty-reduction strategies.[17]

Aside from providing a venue for concentrating some of the state's targeted social assistance programs, PROMUDEH also allowed the Fujimori regime to pursue its claim of being a women-friendly government. This followed the trend whereby Fujimori made a number of senior nominations that indicated his support for women's role in the public service. Throughout the decade, in an unprecedented fashion, Fujimori appointed eight women as ministers and more than twenty women as deputy-ministers. Moreover, he named several women to head state agencies such as the Consumers Protection Institute (*Instituto de Defensa del Consumidor*—INDECOPI), the Office for the Promotion of Peru (*Oficina de Promoción del Perú*—PROMPERU), the National Customs Agency (*Superintendencia Nacional de Aduanas*—SUNAD), the Micro Credit Agency (*Proyecto de Fomento al Crédito para la Micro Empresa*—MIBANCO) and others. The position of Chief Public Prosecutor was filled by a woman during most of Fujimori's rule and a woman also headed the Reform Commission at the Public Prosecutor's Office (Blondet 2002, 21). The inclusion of more women in public institutions was overshadowed by the notoriously corrupt nature of state bureaucracy under Fujimori, particularly regarding judicial authorities.

Promoting women's access to important public positions served several strategic objectives from the point of view of Fujimori's regime. On the one hand, the loyalty that a number of highly skilled professional women could offer in return for high-level appointments or inclusion in party lists was manifest in the willingness of key female officials to be in the frontline defending the president, as will be shown in Chapter 5. Because the power that these positions gave to women depended on the President's will, in a context where the Peruvian political system in general was still relatively adverse to giving women access to powerful positions, the president could count on a number of absolutely loyal representatives (Blondet 2002; Schmidt 2003).

Another related factor is the evolution of Peruvian public opinion on women politicians that improved steadily throughout the 1990s, as revealed in numerous surveys (Blondet 1999a, Alfaro 1996 and 1998, Calandria 2000).[18] Schmidt notes that Fujimori's reliance on public opinion surveys as a technique of political management and his access to the National Intelligence Service's sophisticated public opinion survey infrastructure could have played into his decision to increase the number of women in his administration and political movements. The regime's centralized selection of candidates for political and bureaucratic positions was based, among other factors, on a rigorous set of screening tests that would, according to Schmidt, have played more favorably for women than the traditional selection method based on the "old-boys networks" (Schmidt 2003).

Citizenship Rights: Claims and Victories of the Feminist Movement

When analyzing the gains made in women's citizenship in the 1990s, an important component consisted in the setting up and performance of the SWRS within the Ombudsman's Office. By investigating cases and patterns of women's rights violations and making recommendations for legal redress and reform, the SWRS represented a reliable space within the state apparatus acting as a source of accountability and normative change.[19] Rocío Villanueva, the special representative on women's rights at the Ombudsman's Office, claims that the Fujimori government was generally open to her recommendations and arguments because women's issues were seemingly a much less "political" issue for the regime: "it was a theme on which they could yield. They would not give in on the issue of the judiciary, or the Constitutional Court, but on women's rights there was a lot of important progress made. Maybe because there is this perception that 'it's less political'. This was so until the electoral campaign [in 2000]! Because then we criticized the use of social programs to get women's vote."[20]

While Villanueva noted that the regime reacted much less positively when the SWRS entered the field of the 2000 electoral campaign with criticisms of the political use of social programs to buy popular sector women's vote, her comment as to the "less political" character of women's issues should be nuanced considering the extent to which the Fujimori regime used some key issues put forward by the feminist movement to build part of his political capital. Indeed, this was part of his neopopulist appeal strategy, especially as of 1995, as already mentioned.

Coming back to the achievements made in the 1990s from the point of view of the feminist movement's agenda, it should be underlined that its emphasis on the legalization of abortion was toned down for strategic reasons. After forming part of its key demands in the 1970s and 1980s, it was "put on the back burner" in the early 1990s, especially after the failure of the movement to advance on this issue during the important public debate on abortion in 1989 as part of the first reform of the Penal Code.[21] The incapacity of the feminist movement to win over public opinion on this issue, due to its extremely sensitive character and the strength of conservative sectors, was confirmed again in the 1993 constitution, where Article 2 granted legal personhood to the fetus from the moment of conception. Not surprisingly, the SWRS chose not to include the issue of abortion in its component work on reproductive rights, partly because of the fact that the Ombudsman's Head himself was not open to the issue.

Focusing instead on other aspects of reproductive rights, under the label of "reproductive health," the feminist NGOs managed to make impressive gains although several political objectives were pursued by the State that did not fit feminist prescriptions. For the first time priority was given to providing family planning information and access to contraceptive methods within public medical facilities free of charge throughout the country, as of 1995. The Reproductive Health and Family Planning Program 1996–2000, issued by the Ministry of Health, stated that "Women's right to reproductive health is a social right and a public good that the State should guarantee from within the perspective of gender equity" (cited in Grupo Impulsor Nacional 1997, 93; my translation).

As noted by the *Grupo Impulsor Nacional*, a coalition of NGOs, this recognition marks a profound change in perspective from the past policy frameworks when women were described as being in charge of human reproduction and, as a result, should be "taken care of in order for society to ensure that children were born and raised healthy" (Grupo Impulsor Nacional 1997, 93). Together with this program came the modification of the National Population Law in September 1995, when Congress made sterilization surgery legal. This allowed its integration into the range of state-provided family planning services. But the Reproductive Health and Family Planning Program 1996–2000 came under fire starting in 1997. By then, around a hundred cases of allegedly forced sterilization and the allegation that public health medical staff was required to fulfill quotas in performing sterilization surgery came to light as a result of an investigation by Giulia Tamayo, a feminist lawyer.

For the feminist movement, these cases showed the dangers of a government that adopted some elements of the feminist agenda but did not provide any guarantee for a transparent and democratic implementation of the new policies. The testimonies of the victims were gathered by Tamayo, and indicated patterns of misinformation and coercion of women, especially in poor rural communities, submitting them to sterilization surgery without informed consent and often with very deficient follow-up medical care (Tamayo 1999).

The use of family planning as a means to "reduce poverty," a government goal already stated by Fujimori in a presidential address in 1990 and in his speech at the Beijing Conference in 1995, was being exercised against respect for the basic human rights of women such as bodily integrity, the right to health care, and others. Aside these clearly abusive state practices, the *Grupo Impulsor Nacional* raised the fact that the state program aimed at attaining greater contraceptive coverage with a special priority given to promoting sterilization surgery, rather than a more holistic approach based on women's autonomy in reproductive choices (Grupo Impulsor Nacional 1997, 102).

Some women's organizations sitting on the *Mesa tripartita de seguimiento a la Conferencia sobre Población y Desarrollo* (Tripartite Follow-Up Working Group on the Population and Development Conference)—an ad-hoc tripartite consultative body on reproductive health composed of government representatives, nongovernmental organizations and international donor agencies—as well as most opposition Congresswomen, hesitated in condemning the government in a forceful fashion for these abuses, in part because of the risk of losing all of the gains made in the field of family planning (Barrig 2000a). Only in 1999 did the *Mesa Tripartita* issue a public statement acknowledging that there had been "certain problems in the quality of the health services performed in some cases" (cited in Barrig 2000a).

In 1998, before this statement, thirteen women's organizations, among which two of the three NGOs who were members of the *Mesa*, had sent an open letter to President Fujimori to demand the end of fertility rate reduction targets, the elimination of the priority given to sterilization within the range of available contraceptive methods, the revision of the procedures manual for medical staff performing sterilization surgery, the implementation of the Ombudsman's Office's recommendations on the issue, and the replacement of the Health Minister.

Fujimori attacked the critiques voiced by feminist NGOs and by the MAM—one of the strongest critics—in a discourse made at the United Nations during the June 1999 five-year review of the progress made in the implementation of the goals adopted at the World Conference on Population and Development. In a press statement following the President's speech, various nongovernmental organizations, both Peruvian and international, condemned his speech as filled with lies and hiding the truth. Only one of the three NGO members of the *Mesa tripartita* signed the statement. The others chose to remain within the parameters of political dialogue with the government (Barrig 2000a, 46).

While the nonconfrontational attitude of some feminist NGOs could be interpreted as indicative of a clientelistic relation between this sector of the women's movement and the state, it also amounted to a pragmatic, strategic stance in front of the fragile political backing behind the family planning program and the absence of institutionalized procedures that could guarantee the survival of the program's overall objectives if the criticisms were too strong.[22] Still, a more radical sector of the women's movement—through the *Movimiento Amplio de Mujeres* for example—took to the streets protesting the abuses and denouncing the threats made against Giulia Tamayo and some of the victims who had brought their case to the court. Only in 2001, after the fall of Fujimori, did the state create a special commission to investigate these abuses (Ewig 2006; Rousseau 2007).

Paradoxically, the issue of violence against women, central to the feminist movement's agenda, witnessed several advances in the 1990s, even though the terminology used in state legislation and programs was gender-neutral. The *Ley de protección frente a la violencia familiar* (Law on the protection against family violence) was approved in 1993 and improved in 1997. Domestic violence, including psychological violence, was now recognized as a matter of public policy and state responsibility, although in its orientations, it gave priority to arbitration over prosecution. Prior to that, since the 1980s a number of police stations and municipal governments had started to create special offices to receive women's reporting on domestic or other type of violence, and some training for civil servants was provided through PROMUDEH, although this was deemed insufficient by civil society observers (Grupo Impulsor Nacional 2000b, 47).

Another domain of high importance for the feminist movement was the development of employment and revenue-generating projects for women. On this plane, some of the rights that had been erased in the wake of the 1993 constitution, such as maternity leave provisions and protection for breast-feeding women, were reinstated some years later. The State promoted various forms of micro-credit schemes, but the situation of women's role in the labor market was still quite unequal, with higher percentages of women being unemployed or underemployed in comparison to men, as stated in Chapter 2. Moreover, the various forms of women's contribution to the economy continued to be inadequately recognized, especially in the agricultural sector (Grupo Impulsor Nacional 2000b, 63–68).

The other domains of central concern in the feminist movement's agenda for women's citizenship were the reform of discriminatory laws and the promotion of women's political participation and representation in decision-making bodies. These issues form part of the analysis presented in Chapter 5 and will not be addressed here. Important gains were made in these fields, all of which requiring long campaigns led by feminist NGOs together with the SWRS, some Congressmembers and sympathetic media.

Critics point out that PROMUDEH did not contribute to the institutional strengthening of already existing mechanisms for women's empowerment. For example, the advances in the field of women's police stations, which were due to the lobbying efforts and training provided by some feminist NGOs since the late 1980s, were not carried forward by PROMUDEH. While there were twenty-eight women's police stations or special sections for women in police stations throughout the country in 1996 when PROMUDEH started to function, the ministry remained passive and did not make it a priority to strengthen this process. It signed a contract with the NGO *Centro de la Mujer Peruana Flora Tristán* for the training of police forces in the field of domestic violence, but it did not provide financial resources to these programs. The NGO managed to secure the resources from external donor agencies, but neither PROMUDEH nor the Ministry of the Interior got involved in actively promoting the professionalization of police forces on issues related to domestic violence (Loli 2000, 60–61).

The relationship between PROMUDEH and feminist NGOs was shaped along the lines of the above example, in that the Ministry resorted to the NGOs's skills and capacity to attract foreign funding, while limiting NGO input into the policy-making process to a selective consultative process including some NGO professionals. The Ministry appointed an advisory committee including a few feminist leaders. But again, the feminist leaders were consulted only on the initiative of the Ministry and as individual experts rather than as representatives of civil society organizations (Grupo Impulsor Nacional 1997, 30). The end result was an informal and ad-hoc process of consultation by the ministry, rather than the creation of transparent and inclusive mechanisms of coordination and consultation between the Ministry and civil society actors.

Still, the government agreed to form a few inter-institutional coordinating working groups in which, aside from government officials, international donors and some civil society organizations were represented. Two working groups were set up to monitor the implementation of the commitments made by the Peruvian State at the World Conference on Population and Development and at the Fourth World Conference on Women. Maruja Barrig's analysis of the *Mesa tripartita de seguimiento a la Conferencia mundial sobre población y desarrollo* (Tripartite Working Group on the Follow-Up to the World Conference on Population and Development) reveals a pattern of limited negotiating capacity on the part of the feminist NGOs that participated in it, since the latter did not, according to their own description of their role, represent the women's nor the feminist movement (Barrig 2000a, 18). Moreover, this type of mechanism was not conducive to holding the State accountable for its commitments and actions. Instead, it consisted in a technical exchange of information and points of view in which the NGOs could not exercise any significant political pressure (Barrig 2000a, 18).

The conceptual and political framework within which feminist NGOs were brought to work when collaborating with PROMUDEH was quite different from the ideal of women's citizenship described in their own NGO policy and advocacy documents. Women appear in PROMUDEH's terminology as "leading the list of vulnerable groups that need state support under anti-poverty schemes" (Tamayo 1997, 9). When signing agreements with PROMUDEH for the implementation of specific programs, most of them financed by international donors, Olea and Vargas go as far as claiming that, within the politically restrictive context prevailing during Fujimori's rule, feminist NGOs accepted some form of clientelistic relationship with the state. In any case, most of the programs implemented by NGOs under an agreement with PROMUDEH were designed according to the government's poverty eradication objectives rather than corresponding to a gender equality policy framework (Olea and Vargas 2000, 71).

Conclusion: Autonomy as a Choice?

As explained throughout this chapter, two factors are central to explain the choices embedded in the feminist NGOs' strategies in the 1990s. First, the feminist movement moved from seeking an absolute autonomy in the early 1980s to a stance emphasizing dialogical and negotiation-prone autonomy aiming at influencing policy making in the 1990s. Second, and in relation to the former, a central objective of the feminist NGOs in the 1990s was creating spaces within the State for restructuring the public institutional sphere in a gender equal fashion.

While the autonomy of the feminist movement from other social movements and political parties resulted from a decision made inside the movement in the early 1980s, the political context of the early 1990s precipitated and deepened it in a radical way, following on the general trend of fragmentation and weakening of the Peruvian civil society. As described in Chapter 2, the failure and near disappearance of the democratic Left, the fear instilled by years of insurgent and counter-insurgency violence, and the attacks on democratic institutions by the Fujimori regime formed the background within which the feminist movement consolidated its own institutional basis. Key in this process were the resources and legitimacy granted by an empowering international context. The series of UN Conferences and the new international norms on women's rights that derived from them prompted the donor community to devote significant resources to several key policy issues in that field.

In the context of the Fujimori government, the feminist NGOs' strategy of influencing political decision making in order to generate legislative and policy changes meant a reliance on individualist strategies such as targeting powerful individuals and appealing to their political interest in promoting women's rights issues.[23] Congresswomen, Fujimori himself, powerful senior bureaucrats and politicians joined in the call of the feminist NGOs to embark in their efforts at eliminating violence against women, reforming discriminatory laws, making more space for women in the political sphere and recognizing their right to benefit from modern family planning methods.

The gains of the feminist movement in Peru seem to converge with the general trend observed in the Latin American region in the 1990s, whereby the advances in the promotion of women's rights revolved around reforming the law, creating specialized offices responsible for implementing a gender perspective in public policy, ratifying international human rights covenants on women's rights, and some progress in opening up formal political institutions such as the Congress to greater participation by women (Barrig 2000b, 13).

While all of this happened in Peru in a particularly rapid and important fashion, the legal norms, institutions and policies that were adopted in general did not challenge the basic socioeconomic structure of profound class, ethnic and gender discrimination that continue to affect Peruvian society. In the words of Virginia Vargas, herself a leader of the feminist movement,

> Even if, with rights granted from above, women's citizenship expands in a formal sense, especially in its political dimension, this expansion is not connected to greater economic rights nor to improved democratic processes, rather it accompanies reduced democratic spaces. . . . And this is bad for feminisms because it confronts them with an access to equality that does not modify even in a minimal way the authoritarian and exclusionary processes that are at the roots of women's exclusion and inequality. And this makes us discover, in our own experience, that citizenship and democracy do not always go together. (Vargas 2000a, 12–13; my translation)

Acknowledging the formal character of this "access to equality" provided for under Fujimori's rule, Vargas questioned the feminist strategies that dominated the 1990s. What was at stake was the meaning of the struggle for women's citizenship rights within the political context of the 1990s, a struggle that has, more often than not, been waged independently of a concern for the broader political framework and without addressing the structural conditions that impede the exercise of fundamental citizenship rights for the majority of women. This is explained in part by the fact that the agenda of the feminist NGOs in the 1990s was defined and advocated for in great measure without the popular sector women's movement.

Within the neopopulist context of the 1990s, some divisions arose within the feminist movement around the posture to adopt vis-à-vis the Fujimori government on several occasions where it exhibited a clearly unacceptable behavior from the point of view of democratic principles and respect for women's rights. How to deal with the forced sterilization cases constituted one strong line of division, the other being the project Promujer to promote women's political participation in the context of the new gender electoral quotas, as will be discussed in Chapter 5. The relatively isolated feminist movement could only count on the support of a few Congresswomen to face Fujimori who had high stakes in reaping the harvest of key policies framed to be in "women's interests."

Another indication of the degree of contradiction embedded in the relationship between the feminist NGOs and the Fujimori regime is related to the personal behavior of the president himself. Fujimori made his famous speech on women's rights at the Beijing Conference during the same period when his divorce case was brought to court. Violeta Bermúdez, a prominent feminist lawyer from the NGO *Movimiento Manuela Ramos*, was the lawyer representing Fujimori's wife. Thus, when Fujimori made his speech in Beijing, "era un poco incoherente para [nosotras] las feministas" (it was a little incoherent for [us] feminists)[24] because on the one hand they were defending his wife in her divorce case involving accusations of domestic violence, and on the other they were applauding a president who had made the most progressive speech on women's rights ever in Peruvian history.

As evident throughout this chapter, the feminist movement was far from behaving in a monolithic fashion in its relationship with the Fujimori government. The political initiatives taken by the MAM or the MUDE—as opposed to the main feminist NGOs—acted as the moral voice of feminists and women more generally who opposed the authoritarian practices of the regime. While recuperating a capacity for political opposition in the late 1990s, a capacity that was largely left aside by the feminist movement in the late 1980s, the loosely organized movements were significant at crucial junctures of political mobilization against Fujimori. On this issue, it must be noted that this revival of political protest paralleled the trend witnessed in Peruvian civil society in general (Burt 2006).

However, these movements did not compensate for the absence of a broad-based alliance of social forces defending a woman's agenda as a key component of and as inextricably connected to a broader democratization program. The resources and energy of the main feminist NGOs was invested in pursuing research, advocacy, training and legal aid to promote women's civil and political citizenship rights. The opportunities offered by the Fujimori government and the international context for significant gains to be made in the feminist agenda's implementation were used strategically, but at the cost of abandoning a broader vision of citizenship addressing the actual conditions for the exercise of these rights by the majority of low-income women. Just as well, the weakness of the institutional framework and lack of respect for the rule of law, as revealed in the limits of PROMUDEH's performance and in the implementation of the state family planning program described above, did not provide solid foundations for institutionalizing these rights. Fujimori's use of a woman-friendly politics to sustain his neopopulist appeal was consistent with the international opportunities available and coincided with some of the priorities of the feminist movement. Other sectors within the women's movement had to face the paradoxical mix of opportunities and threats presented by Fujimori's neopopulist rule, as will be shown in the next chapter.

Chapter 4

Women Organizing in Shantytowns

State Co-optation and the Exhaustion of Solidarity

Since around half of the population in Peru's capital city is poor or extremely poor, analyzing the social construction of women's citizenship requires looking at the dynamics of Lima's shantytowns.[1] This chapter is about the millions of women who live in the sandy hills that surround the city—in Lima's *conos* as Peruvians call them. More precisely, this chapter is based on a case study of a particular type of women's organization, neighborhood-based collective kitchens. Its leadership relied first on the formation of a National Commission of Collective Kitchens and then on the Federation of Collective Kitchens of Metropolitan Lima. Both played important roles in mobilizing popular sector women in the 1980s and early 1990s.

In great part because of the clear strategy of the Fujimori government to co-opt and destroy the autonomous popular sector women's organizations, the latter have not achieved many of their proposed goals such as a satisfactory improvement of their community's living conditions. They also failed to sustain an organizational model that could survive the radical transformation of Peruvian society in the early 1990s led by Fujimori's neopopulist rule. Finally, this movement was not able to go beyond its original agenda based almost exclusively on the right to food aid and the right to participate in food aid program management. While the National Commission was at its peak in terms of political legitimacy, protagonism, and innovativeness at the time of Fujimori's first electoral victory, a profound crisis of the collective kitchens' organization occurred during Fujimori's ten-year rule. The chaos generated by the spread of political violence in Lima's shantytowns, the magnitude of the economic shock following the application of structural adjustment measures, and the reorganization of food aid programs into a centralized, state-controlled clientelistic strategy, all contributed to its weakening.

To understand this process, this chapter looks at the conditions and possibilities for mobilizing women on the basis of traditional gender roles—in this case, feeding their family and community–and whether this was politically empowering. I will look at the development of the movement's organization, its core political battles and the various postures that Peruvian political authorities have adopted to respond to, exploit, or attack the autonomous forms of organizing around daily needs that popular sector women have put forward. I will show how Fujimori's neopopulist strategies succeeded where other governments had largely failed. In the course of the analysis, I will examine the content of popular sector women's claims, the forms and limits of their political action, and what this reveals about their citizenship. Although we cannot reduce the political experience of all popular sector women to the organization of collective kitchens, the latter has been recognized extensively as an innovative form of political participation deriving from the material and social conditions prevailing in these sectors.[2]

Shantytowns and Popular Organizing in Lima

Shantytowns around Lima have grown in size in a very significant fashion since the mid-twentieth century. Migration of rural population from all parts of Peru accompanied the dual process of modernization and economic crisis. Lima's population grew from 591,000 in 1941 to 3.3 million in 1972 and 6.5 million in 1993 (Dietz 1998, 66). The National Statistics Institute projected that Lima's population was around 8 million in 2005 (INEI Web site). Of course, migration accounted for part of this growth, natural population growth doing the rest. Lima's share of Peru's total population rose from 8.3 percent in 1941 to 23.3 percent in 1972 and 29.4 percent in 1990 (Dietz 1998, 66). The city expanded 120 percent between the early 1970s and the end of the 1990s (Sagasti 2000, 205).

Community life in Lima's shantytowns has gone through various phases following the necessities related to settling in previously empty areas. Shantytowns were built on the basis of land invasions by rural migrants in the sandy hills around Lima in the 1960s and 1970s. The battle for legal titles over land and the recognition of state responsibility to provide basic infrastructure such as roads, water, sewage, and electricity was launched early on and last until today. Many new districts have been created since the 1970s as a result of the formalization of the settlements. At each step, community organizing was key for undertaking collectively the various tasks involved in constructing houses and infrastructure, as well as for negotiating with municipal and other government authorities (Blondet 1991a; 1991b).

In the initial years when shantytowns were being built by the new migrant population, women adopted the role of supporting their husbands in the struggles for settling in and constructing a home and a community, bearing the primary responsibility for taking care of domestic chores and child rearing. With the majority of migrant women coming from indigenous rural communities, their inclusion in the city culture was conditioned by their low level of formal education, which often meant illiteracy and lack of knowledge of the Spanish language. Younger women of course had greater possibilities of mingling with their new social environment, with many working as maids for middle class families (Guzman and Pinzás 1995).

The dominant form of organization in shantytowns was the *organización vecinal* (neighborhood organization), many of which were created under the initiative of the Velasco military government. Named COPRODE (*Comités Pro Desarrollo Comunal*), these Community Development Committees functioned from the 1970s onwards. A number of these at one point joined in the ranks of the new left-wing parties that dominated shantytowns' politics throughout the 1980s. The *organizaciones vecinales* were mostly concerned with infrastructural and community issues for which they had to negotiate with the State and the Church. Men often had to go into the city to work, which left women having to deal with daily problems. Disregarding the importance of women's work in the community, the neighborhood organizations rarely included them in their leadership (Blondet 1991a).

Beginning in the early 1980s, the panorama of organizing in the shantytowns took another configuration with the formation of women's organizations. The *organizaciones de supervivencia* (survival organizations), also called *organizaciones sociales de base* (social grassroots organizations), gradually displaced the *organizaciones vecinales* as leading the process of mobilizing and working for communities. In contrast to the latter, the survival organizations were led by women and their membership was almost exclusively female. Córdova explains this entry of women as part of the return to a democratic regime in 1980 and the holding of elections at the municipal level, which drove the male leaders of the neighborhood organizations into municipal government (Córdova 1996, 30). However, a key factor explaining the predominance of women in these organizations is the nature of their activities, as well as the justification for their initial establishment. All of these organizations had as a common feature the collective endeavor of feeding the families of their communities on a daily basis.

The rise of these organizations can be explained by a series of factors. First and foremost, the various cycles of economic crisis starting in the late 1970s and continuing throughout the 1980s and 1990s affected the entire Peruvian population, but with obviously greater magnitude in the rural areas and Lima's shantytowns. Simply put, hunger was the main causal factor for the emergence of these organizations. High levels of unemployment and underemployment were the other side of the same coin, and the fact that these uneducated and unskilled women were even further handicapped in the labor market explains their availability for working in the survival organizations.

The other key element to consider is the availability of food donations as of 1979, when the United States government signed an agreement with its Peruvian counterpart whereby it would send its agricultural surpluses as food aid channelled through church-based organizations and the state agency *Oficina Nacional de Apoyo Alimentario* (National Office for Food Aid). This new variable modified the options available for survival by introducing a new source of food supplies. Access to the latter, however, was conditioned upon the performance of collective voluntary work or activities for the benefit of the community such as contributing to the construction of community centers, picking up garbage, or even receiving religious education (Blondet 1991, 96). Popular sector women then started to participate in group activities in order to receive food donations.

The role of the Peruvian State is also to be underlined. Indeed, the Peruvian State's approach to social assistance in periods of economic crisis or structural adjustments has relied on food assistance programs of different types since at least the 1950s. These programs linked food assistance to the realization of communal works or the granting of small financial subsidies to accompany food staples. Also constant over the years was the targeting of women as the chief recipients and executors of food assistance programs. In fact, as decried by many, what were deemed to be short-term compensation programs became the norm, mainly because these programs did not address the root causes of poverty, while the various economic models implemented were unsuccessful in promoting sustainable development (Portocarrero et al. 2000, 109). As a result of sustained crisis and increased food aid from abroad, women's organizations revolving around survival activities grew importantly throughout the 1980s and 1990s.

Aside from their fundamental origin based on economic need, these organizations corresponded to a rich and multifaceted experience of mobilization and organization of popular sector women, in which not only the latter were involved, but a plethora of other entities such as Church-based social organizations, feminist or development nongovernmental organizations, left-wing parties, and municipal and state authorities. Each contributed in its way to the character and development of these organizations, contributing resources, training, inspiration, institutional support, and political legitimacy.

Organizations such as collective kitchens were set up as alternatives to state-led work-for-food programs. They were inspired by their predecessors, the *Clubes de madres* (Mothers' Clubs) and *Ollas comunes* (Soup Kitchens), that emerged respectively in the 1950s and late 1970s in Lima's shantytowns and some of Peru's rural areas. *Clubes de madres* and *ollas comunes* were based on the collective work of women who received no wages in both cases. In the case of the *Clubes de madres*, which were promoted by the State in conjunction with the Catholic Church, they were granted food donations and given tools such as sewing machines to produce and sell small items. The dependence of the *Clubes* on the government or party in power that controlled the distribution of food staples and goods often led to political clientelism. In the case of the *Ollas comunes*, women spontaneously set up temporary collective kitchens for the purpose of feeding their neighborhood in moments of strikes, protests or economic crises. They then put together either food donations or more likely some of their own resources to produce meals that they sold at a popular price. In comparison to the collective kitchens created in the 1980s, the *Clubes de madres* were closely tied to the government of the day; the *ollas comunes* lacked a stable organizational structure that could ensure their long-term sustainability (Lora 1996).

THE FORMATION OF COLLECTIVE KITCHENS

The first *comedores populares* (collective kitchens) were born in the late 1970s but became more popular in the 1980s.[3] These reflected a new kind of experience of women joining to carry out activities related to the survival of their communities, based on the same basic idea of collective, free labor organized around shared preparation of meals that was central in the *Clubes de madres* and *ollas comunes*.

However, the *comedores* were unique in that they were associated with the progressive Catholic Church and with popular education centers that claimed, at the end of the 1970s, that women should organize not simply on the basis of clientelistic networks of passive reception of food donations, but rather with the project of developing autonomous and more holistic solutions to the problems of poverty and hunger (Lora 1996, 23–25). Either religious or popular education was included in the routine activities of the *comedores*. Through this training, women developed some skills such as the ability to run a basic organization and understand better the sources of their social condition as poor women.

The collective kitchens movement was always composed of two broad types. On the one hand, there were the autonomous or *autogestionarios* (self-managed), that eventually became affiliated in a federation with various levels of delegative representation and associated with the development work of the progressive sectors of the Catholic Church or nongovernmental organizations. On the other hand, there were other *comedores* that took on different names such as *Clubes de madres* or *Comedores del Pueblo* (People's Soup Kitchens) and were associated with the government or political party that "created" them. This second type continued even as the autonomous movement started and grew.

In fact, when talking about collective kitchens, most authors only refer to the *comedores autogestionarios*, since these are judged to be more autonomous[4] and hence more politically and socially significant. Because they received more attention from the progressive church, nongovernmental organizations and parties of the left, they were the more organized and critical of state policies in relation to popular sectors. Moreover, the history of the construction of this movement is intimately related to the various attempts by the state and political parties to challenge its autonomy and control its membership through the creation of the second type of collective kitchens, in parallel with or competing for food donations. What distinguishes both types is the internal life of the *comedores autogestionarios*' multilevel organization and their willingness to challenge political authorities, claim rights, and entitlements. This chapter addresses principally the dynamics around the construction of the autonomous collective kitchens, since they formed an important component of the popular sector women's movement and, as such, one of the key sites for the construction of women's citizenship.

The number of *comedores* has varied over time, fluctuating according to the strength of the organization of *comedores autogestionarios*, the conditions under which the state or other agencies provided food donations, the general economic situation, and other variables such as the existence of alternative sources of revenues for popular sector women. While it is impossible to give exact figures as to the number of *comedores autogestionarios*, they have approximately increased from 300 in 1986 to 3,000 in 1989 (Córdova 1996, 41). Another source claims that there were 5,329 *comedores* in Lima in 1991, of which 35.5 percent—1,892 *comedores*—were part of the organization of *comedores autogestionarios* (Cuentas 1995, 270).

In 1997, the figures had remained relatively stable for the comedores autogestionarios, which were 1,800 with a total of 45,000 women members; whereas the *Clubes de madres*, most of which hosting some version of a *comedor* (kitchen), were 5,200, with a total of 70,200 women members (Comisión de la mujer de la municipalidad metropolitana de Lima 2000, 93). If these figures were right, then the number of members per organization was almost double in the case of the *autogestionarios*. It is estimated that each *comedor* served approximately between 100 and 300 individuals.[5] Hundreds of thousands of Peruvians used the services of collective kitchens throughout the 1990s, which is why they are so often deemed to have saved the population from starvation in crucial moments such as the drastic economic shock implemented by the first Fujimori government in 1990.

Internal Democracy?

The collective kitchens are based on the principle of shared collective tasks: reception of food donations, buying of additional staples, administering these staples and the revenues coming from the sell of the food rations, or meals, at *menú* prices[6], and the activities related to the preparation and distribution of meals. Each *comedor autogestionario* has a democratically elected executive of a few individuals who oversee these tasks and have the monopoly over the political functions of negotiating and participating in decision-making processes outside of the *comedor*—at the higher levels of the *comedores'* organization and with the municipality, the parish, civil servants, and nongovernmental organizations.

There is a rich debate in the Peruvian literature on whether and to which extent the *comedores* is an organization promoting democratic practices at the grassroots level and throughout its pyramidal structure.[7] Some aspects of this debate are worth mentioning in order to illustrate the contribution and limits of this experience as a means for fostering alternative forms of political participation for popular sector women. A positive evaluation of the collective kitchens sees it as a tool for empowering women. This view is often presented by individuals who were involved in the creation or strengthening of the movement through their role as nongovernmental *asesoras* (advisors) or *promotoras* (trainers). They emphasize first and foremost the importance of creating a space outside of the home and protected from men's control, in which women can express themselves freely and experience new forms of female solidarity.

A former advisor for the collective kitchens' federation, Rocío Palomino described this experience as "a sort of revolution," where "the achievements were lived collectively."[8] Because this type of organizing was based on traditional Peruvian women's primary responsibility for feeding their family, it provided the basic legitimacy required by women to be accepted at least minimally as new social actors in their community. This claim falls in line with the literature on the forms of organizing women develop around daily needs and that generally do not challenge traditional gender roles per se. As some authors have shown, in the process of organizing and initiating collective projects that seek to have some impact on the social, even if at a modest, local level, women gain greater self-awareness of their gender identity, some confidence in their capacity to perform activities outside of their home, and can eventually aspire to other, more politically challenging forms of organizing (Stephen 1997; Molyneux 2001). Of course, this is not to say that survival-based organizations represent an easy organizing experience for women. They often face strong opposition from their husbands, among others, who often refuse at least initially to see their wife involved in such activities.

For the members of the Peruvian collective kitchens, the process of organizing, developing a voice and power base of their own learning skills and participating in rallies has been described by some analysts such as Blondet (1991) and Lora (1996) as giving rise to a new political awareness and sense of identity as poor women. This process was sought as the seed of change in gender relations and class oppression in popular neighborhoods. A number of feminist leftist activists invested their faith in this type of social grassroots organization as a vehicle for expressing the daily reality of shantytown women with the objective of developing their citizenship claims (Sara Lafosse 1984, Blondet 1991, Lora 1996, Córdova 1996).

On the other side of the debate, critics who do not deny this potential still emphasize the often authoritarian character of the relationships within the *comedores*, based on the desire of the leaders to retain the small margin of power they were able to gain within the organization.

As the collective kitchens—or other types of grassroots organizations for that matter—were often the only opportunity women had to have power and exercise it, a tendency to want to retain it was just a natural consequence. As a result, the organization suffered from a frequent lack of turnover in leadership positions. Moreover, the high level of dependency of the *comedores* on outside institutions, either the church, nongovernmental organizations, or state agencies was deemed to compromise the liberating and autonomous features of the *comedores* (Barrig 1986, Delpino 1991).

Organizing Politically

Notwithstanding this ambivalent global portrait, the *comedores* movement became a political protagonist of some importance in the late 1980s. This was made possible by the formation of a higher-level organizational body, or what is referred to in the Peruvian literature as the "centralization process of the *comedores autogestionarios*." The idea of creating a centralized organization, which would develop a set of institutional rules for its membership and represent the interests of the *comedores autogestionarios*, originated in 1986 in the first *Encuentro Nacional de Comedores* (National Meeting of Collective Kitchens), under the auspices of the *Comisión Episcopal de Acción Social* (Bishop's Social Action Commission—CEAS). As clearly expressed in the brief submitted by the newly created *Comisión Nacional de Comedores* (National Commission of Collective Kitchens—CNC) to then president of Peru, Alan García, the decision to put together a centralized organization that could address the interests of the *comedores autogestionarios* was directly connected to the recurrent attacks on their autonomy by both the Belaúnde government elected in 1980 and the APRA government elected in 1985.[9]

The two major political parties had set up their own brand of *comedores* as of the early 1980s, the *cocinas familiares* (family kitchens) under *Acción Popular*'s leader's wife patronage, and the *comedores del Pueblo* (People's Soup Kitchens), linked to the APRA. In both cases, these *comedores* received various kinds of support, either financial or through food staples or kitchen equipment. The other, nonpolitically affiliated *comedores* only had access to the food donations channelled through church-based organizations. This unfair treatment did not prevent the autonomous movement of collective kitchens from growing during the first half of the 1980s. Yet the increasing frustration at not being recognized as legitimate social organizations fulfilling an essential role in the survival of the poorest sectors of Lima got only worst when the García government implemented the *Programa de Asistencia Directa* (Direct Assistance Program—PAD) in 1986.

The PAD established a fund to assist survival organizations, but only those that registered officially with the State and took on the label of *Clubes de madres*. While the latter name resonated with old-style assistencialism, the program was seen by the *comedores autogestionarios* as a clear policy to dismiss their autonomous experience and destabilize their organization. It appeared as a discriminatory and politically motivated program oriented toward the reinforcement of the survival organizations that were loyal to the APRA (Cuentas 1995, Lora 1996).

As of 1986, the autonomous collective kitchens had already created a second level organization, the "*centrales*" (District Head), within each district, mainly for logistical purposes. Advisors from nongovernmental organizations and some popular sector women leaders argued that there was a need to create a strong political organization that could face the problems of decreasing international food aid and unequal state support (Lora 1996, 41). The creation of the CNC, with the election of a *junta directiva* (board) of three women at the top, and a multilevel centralized structure—at the district, regional, and metropolitan levels—responded to these preoccupations. The influence of left-wing parties of the United Left among the ranks of the *comedores* also contributed to the creation of the organization, although it maintained its independence from any political party.

Therefore, from 1986 onwards, the autonomous collective kitchens had an explicitly political character embodied in its leadership and organization that mobilized the hundreds of thousands of women members on various occasions around proposals and demonstrations that sought to advance the claims of the movement. As Martha Cuentas summarizes it, "the basic idea was that 'united we are strong', and they started to see that through creating a central organization they could make the State listen, assert their claims and proposals to obtain concrete benefits" (Cuentas 1995, 280; my translation).

Through their new Lima-wide organization, the autonomous collective kitchens could aspire to move up the scale from being a purely grassroots movement to becoming a social movement, following the distinction put forward by Alain Touraine (Touraine 1989, cited in Tocón 1997, 189). That is, they could move from being a movement that attends the interests of its members without making demands on the political system as such, to a movement with broader political implications that can potentially shift the balance of political power.

This was exactly the objective pursued by the nongovernmental organizations and the church-based organizations that had been advising the *comedores autogestionarios* for a number of years and had been able to convince them of the benefit of creating a *central de centrales* (union of district organizations). The way some of these advisors describe the experience testifies to their ambition of creating a new powerful social movement capable of influencing the State and exercising power from the bottom up. María Mercedes Barnechea, former advisor to the *comedores* for the NGO TACIF (Workshop for Family Training and Research), in describing the birth of this new political actor, emphasizes its "autonomy" while showing that only at that stage did the movement start to experience a clear political identity: "The first confrontation with the State comes after a long process of building the movement . . . At this point, when they have a direct dialogue with the State, they start feeling clearly that they are a social actor endowed with their own rights, seeing the right to food as a social right which they could win" (Barnechea 1991, 96; my translation).

This quote reveals the newly formed notion of a right to food that developed in conjunction with the politicization of the movement. The NGO advisors saw the process of centralization and the role of the CNC as the beginning of a women's social movement that had the potential for becoming a key political actor representing popular sector women and their communities.[10] The collective social struggles based on mass mobilization that the organization of *comedores* engaged in starting in 1986 was an extension of the broader popular organizing process that had built up in the 1970s and early 1980s, exemplified by the formation of a strong union movement, strong community organizations, and political parties on the left.

The Golden Age of the CNC

The CNC's actions did not always attain their stated goals, but were strong demonstrations of popular mobilization and capacity for policy proposal. In 1986, as already mentioned, the CNC sent a brief to President García requesting equal access to the benefits granted to the *Clubes de madres* and proposing a series of measures that the government could adopt such as making water more accessible, setting preferential prices for kerosene, controlling multinationals' prices on basic food staples, and creating sustainable employment generation programs.[11] Although the government did not respond to the brief, the latter marked the first step in the CNC's process of addressing the State with its demands.

The political protagonism of the CNC increased further in 1988 when, in the midst of the economic crisis generated by the first anti-inflation adjustment measures implemented by the government of Alan García, the organization developed a proposal to address both the nutritional needs of Lima's poorer sectors and the lack of support experienced by national agricultural producers. The CNC and their advisors put forward a *"Propuesta de subsidios directos de la Comisión Nacional de Comedores"* (CNC's proposal for direct subsidies) that explicitly referred to people's right to food.

As the document recalled, this right was guaranteed by the Constitution of Peru that acknowledges the State's duty to ensure the welfare of its population, particularly the poorest. The proposal also criticized the adjustment measures that were affecting all Peruvian citizens and more dramatically the sectors that were already barely surviving. On that basis, the document called on the State to subsidize directly 58 percent of the autonomous collective kitchens' food staples. The proposal also included a critique of the country's high level of food dependency on international markets and proposed that the food staples that were to be subsidized be bought from national producers to stimulate domestic production and limit the tendency toward increasing the foreign debt. It also called on the State to generate employment opportunities for the poorest sectors, both men and women, going beyond mere compensation policies. Finally, it asked for the participation of survival organizations in the management of the *Programa de Apoyo Alimentario Nacional* (National Food Aid Program), created by the García government to accompany the drastic anti-inflation measures.[12]

To make sure that this proposal was noticed and debated, the CNC organized a demonstration several days after its submission to the Cabinet. It mobilized thousands of women from their bases as well as from other grassroots women's organizations such as the *Coordinadora del Vaso de Leche* (Glass of Milk Coordinating Committee) and the *Federación de Mujeres Populares de Villa El Salvador* (Federation of Women from the district of Villa El Salvador). These organizations also managed to get the support of various political figures, mostly from the left. While the proposal did not make its way on to the García government's agenda, the mobilization and credibility the CNC achieved through this political strategy gave it a new status as a key player in civil society. Because of its innovativeness as a basis for social policy making, the proposal formed the matrix for subsequent policy proposals presented by the CNC as national welfare and development alternatives.

The CNC continued to make public statements denouncing governmental practices contrary to the interests of its members, and to propose alternatives. In 1989, one year after its major subsidy proposal, it reiterated its demands through a public statement underlining the lack of any response from the government and the continuing intensity of the economic crisis.[13] In this statement, the CNC also added the demand for public provision of social security benefits—pension and health-care—for the women working in the collective kitchens, pointing to the responsibility of the State for the crisis and poverty.

The 1990 electoral campaign was also the opportunity for political mobilization by the CNC against what it perceived as discriminatory policies intended to win votes from popular sector women. The García government decided during the campaign to grant many privileges to the *Clubes de madres*, such as ownership of the kitchens' utensils, stoves, and sewing machines that had been lent to them by the State; tax exemptions on the buying of similar tools; direct subsidies covering half the price of the daily ration prepared by the *Clubes de madres* (which amounted to almost the same subsidy demanded by the *comedores autogestionarios* in 1988), and finally, the donation of food staples sold by public enterprises. Only the *Clubes de madres* received such benefits, which caused indignation among the members of the CNC. The following statement summarizes the spirit of their public statement in May 1990: "We are not against the benefits to the *clubes* PAD, but we do reject the way in which the APRA government promotes programs that divide our organizations and the political use of the needs of our people, favoring some and discriminating against others, inciting confrontations among the poor."[14]

The political protagonism of the CNC reached its peak in 1990 in a period of great political change with the defeat and disintegration of the democratic left and the unexpected victory of Alberto Fujimori. By then, the CNC had followed the idea of some of their NGO advisors and developed a bill providing for the official recognition of grassroots social organizations, mechanisms, and norms regulating State collaboration with social organizations in the implementation of social programs. While the bill started to be written and debated within the ranks of the CNC months before the general elections of 1990, it was submitted to the newly elected Congress in September 1990. The bill was approved in January 1991 and signed into law the following month through a rapid procedure in light of the consensus it generated in Peruvian society (Alternativa 1993, 10).

Law 25307, a major political victory for the CNC,[15] resulted from the preceding years of political lobbying, mass mobilization, and participation at various interinstitutional committees responsible for the implementation of social compensation programs. All of this led to and reflected the capacity of the CNC to become a credible public actor representing popular sectors. Added to their demonstrated expertise in managing food donations in periods of economic crisis, the bill received almost immediate unanimous support from parliamentarians. Moreover, the seriousness with which the technical aspects of the bill had been thought through commanded respect from all. As Rocío Palomino, one of the NGO advisors at the time of the presentation of the bill, recalls, to vote against the law would have amounted to "voting against the Virgin Mary."[16]

This law became a symbol of recognition and legal empowerment that remained present in the discourse and claims of the *comedores* movement throughout the 1990s. It recognized grassroots social organizations and their central representative bodies registered with the municipal authorities as legal entities endowed with rights and duties. Among the most important was their right to participate in social programs administration, particularly in the new food aid program created by the law. Participation was envisaged in a management committee formed by central state and municipal officials. The new *Programa de apoyo a la labor alimentaria de las organizaciones sociales de base* (Food aid program for grassroots social organizations) created by law mandated that the State subsidize 65 percent of the cost of the daily ration, based on a regionally approved integral food basket comprising basic national food staples. It also included the obligation for the State to promote revenue-generating activities for grassroots organizations in order to promote their autonomy, as well as provide various forms of training and education to the members of these organizations.[17] The status and rights granted by the law, a national precedent, explains why it constitutes the principal victory cited by the leaders and observers of the *comedores* movement.[18]

Yet the victory was far from being complete, as witnessed the path followed by the law left in the hands of the Fujimori government. When the general budget for 1992 was discussed in Congress, including a discussion on financial provisions for the implementation of Law 25307, the government sought to impede the approval of the proposed budget by using its veto, arguing that it contradicted its economic policies. Congress, disregarding the executive's hold on the budget law, claimed that this was not one of its prerogatives and adopted the law. A couple of months later, Congress was unconstitutionally dissolved by Fujimori, and some observers concluded that Law 25307 was among the many contentious points between the executive and Congress that prompted the abrupt closure of representative institutions by Fujimori (Alternativa 1993, 10).

Following the self-coup of 1992 and the drastic transformation of the political landscape that accompanied it, the *comedores* movement lost most of its political protagonism and gradually ceased to be the strong popular mobilization force it had been in the late 1980s and early 1990s. Law 25307, its main victory, was never implemented.

"We Have Been Abandoned by All"

The difficulties and decline suffered by the organization of the autonomous *comedores* are, on the one hand, related to the multiple factors that have shaped the political landscape of Peru since the crisis of the early 1990s, most notably the exacerbation of political violence in the shantytowns. On the other hand, the organization itself, particularly its lack of capacity to sustain its development and adapt to the new circumstances brought by Fujimori's neopopulist strategies, provide another source of explanation for the dramatic loss of protagonism experienced by these popular sector women.

Political Violence in the Shantytowns

The complexity of the situation in the early 1990s was increased by the intensification of guerilla activities—mainly by the Shining Path—in popular districts, which prompted a low-intensity war between them and the military and paramilitary groups. The popular sector movement—with women's organizations being its most vibrant element by then—was trapped in the logic of confrontation and violence deriving from the conflict, which polarized and politicized every aspect of community life. Popular organizations' leaders became key targets of the Shining Path. This had a devastating impact on the organizations' lives and activities.

When the Shining Path's new strategy of focusing its attacks on Lima started to be implemented in the late 1980s, life in popular districts was transformed.[19] Shining Path used threats and all kinds of tactics to destabilize and destroy the social organizations that were reluctant to join its ranks. On the other side of the battle, the leftist tendencies of the social grassroots organizations made them perfect suspects in the eyes of state counterinsurgency forces.

Women's organizations, which by the time of the 1990 economic shock had become the most effective social organizations putting forward solutions to the immediate consequences of the crisis in popular neighborhoods, became one of the key targets of the Shining Path. The latter claimed that survival organizations, by reducing the magnitude of the impact of the government's structural adjustment policies on the poorest sectors, impeded the "natural" growth of despair and eventually also popular adherence to revolutionary uprising (Blondet 1996; Burt 2006). These organizations were labeled by the Shining Path as the "*colchón del gobierno*" (the government's mattress), to describe the consequence of their choosing to organize to counter hunger on a daily basis rather than through more radical transformative "solutions." Various kinds of tactics were used by the Shining Path to discredit and disorganize, intimidate and destroy the popular sector women's organizations on the basis of this rationale.

Yet it took a certain amount of time for women to realize that they were facing a very dangerous enemy. Since the Shining Path gathered some popular support and gradually gained members among their children, their husbands, or even among women's organizations' ranks, organized women initially perceived the Shining Path as part of the popular struggle for social change. Even if they generally disagreed with the violence or even the ideology of *Sendero*, many popular sector women initially thought that it was defending their cause. Only when the direct targeting of popular sector women leaders started in 1991 did they start to think that this was not the case, that what *Sendero* was seeking was state power and authoritarian rule, rather than to defend people's interests (Guzman and Pinzás 1995, 108–10).

In August 1991, *Sendero* killed Juana López, a leader of the Glass of Milk organization. The shock was immediate among the ranks of survival organizations, and they reacted by organizing a "March against Hunger and Terror" that succeeded in bringing thousands of women to the streets. But the strength of these organizations, which was still manifest in events such as this demonstration, was undermined by the continuing strategy of *Sendero Luminoso* of targeting popular leaders. One of the three leaders of the CNC, Emma Hilario, was attacked at her home twice, first by two women *senderistas* who insulted her and beat her, and then by five *senderistas* who shot her in the head. She miraculously survived through protecting her head with her arm and blankets, but then decided to flee to Ecuador with her family. In February 1992, *Sendero* killed María Elena Moyano, a famous leader from

Villa El Salvador district who had worked for years in women's grassroots organizations and had by then been elected as deputy-mayor of her municipality. She was shot dead and her assassins put dynamite in her body, which exploded in front of her children and friends who were accompanying her at a public neighborhood celebration.

The cruelty and horror of María Elena Moyano's killing made her an immediate martyr within popular sectors and the women's movement, nationally and even internationally. As a distinguished social leader, she had contributed to the construction of strong women's organizations and had been central in the development of Villa El Salvador in the 1980s. Her strong character was acknowledged by all as a quality for her social endeavors, yet this probably caused her death, as she constantly refused to abandon her social protagonism in the face of increasing threats directed at her by the Shining Path (Blondet 1996).

The impact of this violence against women leaders was devastating. The organizations, especially at the highest levels, ceased to function. It became too dangerous to attend meetings, organize public events, or make public statements. Faced with the disintegration of the social and political fabric that had sustained their action and given meaning to it, and with the growing risks involved in maintaining a public profile in the midst of political violence, the women members of the *comedores* movement retreated (Blondet 1996). The three leaders of the CNC flew into exile, and the leadership of the newly formed *Federación de comedores autogestionarios de Lima y Callao* (Federation of Autonomous Collective Kitchens of Lima and Callao) only kept a minimal level of presence while the self-coup in 1992 opened the space for more massive repression on the part of security forces. The situation was further complicated by the fact that within the organization of *comedores* itself there was a debate among pro-*Sendero*, pro-government, and neutral sectors.[20]

Institutional Crisis within the *Comedores* Movement

This period of violence, intimidation, and high fragmentation hit the *comedores* movement at a crucial time in the evolution of its organization. In October 1991, a few months after beginning to be targeted by *Sendero*, the first Congress of *comedores autogestionarios* was held in Lima on the basis of a proposal to create a formal structure to replace the CNC, which had always been conceived of as a temporary body.[21] The battle between the proponents of a new organization and the defenders of the old leadership of the CNC who had constructed the movement was a difficult one, but the Congress concluded with the creation of a Federation for the Lima and Callao region, the *Federación de centrales de comedores populares autogestionarios de Lima y Callao*. The more than 2,000 *comedores* represented at the meeting elected a first *Junta directiva*, or executive, for the Federation, and transferred the control of district *centrales* from the CNC to the Federation. The CNC was then given a specific mandate of organizing the autonomous *comedores* movement at the national level outside Lima (Lora 1996). Since the vast majority of the autonomous collective kitchens were in the Lima and Callao region, the task given to the CNC amounted to having to build a national constituency out of scratch and with little resources. Moreover, the leaders of the CNC were the historic leaders of the movement concentrated in Lima. When cut off from their base, they became politically impotent and irrelevant.

Within the group of former leaders of the *comedores* movement, the interpretation of this change in the form and structure of the movement vary according to their respective position. Rosa Espinal, the president of the second *Junta directiva* of the Federation (1994–97), argues that the decision to create this new body was motivated by the desire to strengthen the organization at the level of metropolitan Lima. The problem emerged when the CNC, "for lack of clarity within the organization as to how to redefine its role," showed it was not capable of maintaining its leadership when expanding to the national level.[22] Relinda Sosa, president of the third *Junta directiva*, also claims that the CNC was a limited-term body created for the specific purpose of building the movement and organizing it politically, developing its proposals, and lobbying the State. In 1991, the goal behind the transformation was to give the movement a formal structure. Relinda Sosa also admits that there was a problem of competition between older and younger leaders. This was not resolved through the dual existence of the CNC and the *Federación*, which rather exacerbated the division and conflict.[23]

Rosa Landavery, one of the three former heads of the CNC, understands the change in a very different light. She argues that the main reason explaining the replacement of her organization with the Federation was related to the power that the CNC had accumulated. Its capacity to gather huge crowds in public demonstrations, to lead social protest and develop alternative proposals, made the CNC compete on the terrain of the left-wing political parties.[24] Landavery believes that the power of the CNC had become threatening for a number of left-wing actors who then promoted the creation of a new representative body.

According to the women from the NGOs who were advising the movement at the time, there was a high level of disagreement among the bases about the way the leadership of the CNC sought to retain its power, not allowing a new generation to come to power. The compromise of creating a new structure with a new leadership while maintaining, formally at least, the old CNC with the same leaders, amounted to this mix of respect for the work the old leaders had done and the desire to rejuvenate the organization.[25]

But the clash between both tendencies had strong repercussions on the capacity of the new Federation to function at full speed. As mentioned by Benedicta Serrano, first president of the Federation's *junta*, the CNC did not facilitate the transition for the Federation to organize its work. The latter had to start from scratch. The political context of violence and killings in popular sector districts also contributed to the dispersion of resources and energy. The CNC leadership all fled abroad for a time and the new *Junta directiva* of the Federation had to go through the trauma of being the official representatives of the *comedores* movement in a period when it was the most dangerous and impossible to develop an effective work strategy.

Another line of division inside the movement revolved around the issue of which stand to take vis-à-vis the government of Alberto Fujimori. While popular sectors had been fooled by the new president for whom they voted in great numbers on the basis of his promise not to impose a structural adjustment program—a promise he did not respect for more than few months after starting his mandate—Fujimori's popularity remained relatively high in popular districts including after the *auto-golpe* of 1992. If the older leadership of the movement was closer to left-wing parties and more prone to criticize Fujimori's government, most of the younger leadership tended to adopt a more cautious, pragmatic stance in line with the majority of the grassroots membership.

Transforming the Bonds with the NGOs

This troubled period (1991–92) also saw the beginning of the transformation of the relationship between the *comedores* movement and their closest allies, the NGO advisors. The group of nongovernmental organizations (Alternativa, CESIP, TACIF, *Servicio de Educación de El Agustino*—SEA, Calandria, FOVIDA, Flora Tristan, among others) that had been advising and promoting the development of the movement, its organization and proposals throughout the second half of the 1980s, retreated in the face of increasing threats and attacks in popular neighborhoods. They also became targets themselves, and ceased to go in popular districts. This meant that they stopped having regular contact with the bases of the movement, and distanced themselves even from the leadership of the movement with whom they had maintained a close relationship mixing friendship, political ideals, and professional advice.

This distancing affected the level of trust existing between NGO professionals and the leaders of the *comedores*, breaking the sense of sharing a common cause. As revealed in a study of the social networks around the CNC leader Emma Hilario, in this period of crisis, "middle class professionals were increasingly perceived as being privileged, as having access to financial resources because they work with popular sectors" (Guzman and Pinzás 1995, 78; my translation). Since it can easily be argued that most of the key events shaping the political and organizational life of the movement would have been unthinkable without the support of the NGO advisors, this distancing had direct consequences for the capacity of the organization to maintain its political protagonism. As Miyaray Benavente, one of the NGO advisors, put it, "hasta las cartas se los hacía" (we were even writing letters for them).[26] The work around the creation of the CNC, its statutes and mandate, the conceptual, legal, and political aspects of the proposal that led to Law 25307, are only the most obvious instances where the inspiration, orientations, and direct input of the NGO advisors were fundamental. As a result of this transformed relationship, advising became more technical and exceptional, rather than the daily exchange of information and joint strategy building that had prevailed before.[27]

Another factor explaining the reconfiguration of interactions between the *comedores* movement and the NGOs is the development of new expectations on both sides. As told by NGO professionals who compare the initial period of construction of the *comedores* organization with the reality of the 1990s, not only were there more popular sector women leaders who were trained and informed by the 1990s, which justified a different approach on the part of the NGOs, but also the latter had new incentives to restructure their links with the *comedores* movement based on new donor-imposed requirements including carrying out specific projects with measurable goals (Guzman and Pinzás 1995, 78; 146–47).

Indeed, the requirements and modes of functioning of donor agencies became much more complex and demanding in the 1990s as a general trend. Funding was reoriented toward results-based projects, rather than supporting a general advisory role for the NGOs involved with the *comedores*. Since NGOs function in large part according to the rules accompanying the funds they receive from foreign donors, they gradually had to move their human resources into executing projects.[28] In addition, the NGOs also disagreed increasingly with the *Federación* on many issues of strategy and political behavior, especially when some of the leaders were approached by political parties to run as candidates or when they did not react in the face of increasing state cooptation and clientelistic maneuvers, as will be described further.[29]

On the side of the *Federación*, this distancing was due to an explicit willingness to assert greater autonomy vis-à-vis the NGOs, especially as of the election of the second *Junta directiva* in 1994. The *Federación* claimed its capacity to make decisions on its own and its wish to transform itself into a nongovernmental organization capable of receiving funding and executing projects. According to Elena Caro, advisor from the NGO FOVIDA, the *Federación* wanted to develop an identity on more equal terms with the NGOs. This new orientation led it gradually to focus its energy on projects rather than sustaining or reformulating its political role, its capacity to mobilize and participate in the public sphere.[30] Thus the NGOs and the Federation started to "compete" on the same terrain of project implementation funded by foreign donors.

The Federation's perception of having been abandoned by the NGOs started around the period of intense violence in the shantytowns, but got even stronger throughout the 1990s, as the latter moved away from working primarily with survival organizations toward a focus on local government.[31] The Federation had to face its contradictions of wanting to behave autonomously from the NGOs without having the training and background necessary to sustain itself as a quasi-NGO, while seeking to maintain its political protagonism. Unclear as to its primary identity—that of a mass movement or that of a technical body—the *Federación* had to face the even greatest challenge presented by Fujimori's strategy to dominate the space occupied by survival organizations.

The Battle Against Neopopulist-Style Clientelism

As of the late 1970s with the end of the Velasco regime, the Peruvian State retreated substantially from the sphere of popular sector politics, with the partial exception of APRA's attempts to control women's organizations in the late 1980s. This left the space open for the left-wing parties, the Church, international cooperation, and nongovernmental organizations to further their work with popular organizations in the 1980s. The reverse shift took place in the early 1990s with the regime of Alberto Fujimori. His government focused its neopopulist discourse on Fujimori's willingness to work for the poor. The president encouraged popular adherence to his regime through a number of social programs grounded in the notion of targeted social compensation benefits for the poorest sectors. As described in Chapter 2, the Fujimori government marked a whole new era in Peruvian politics. Neoliberal economic policy accompanied renewed social spending focused exclusively on short-term assistance to the poor and extremely poor. The reinsertion of Peru into the international financial system was made through this combination of structural adjustment, liberalization of the economy, and privatization of most public services, to which a number of programs were added to "give a human face to adjustment."

Similar social compensation programs had been attempted under the García government, but without the financial and administrative capacity to be implemented, given the rising fiscal crisis. In contrast, the international support granted to the Fujimori government provided the needed funds and some expertise for the creation of such programs as the FONCODES (*Fondo de Compensación y Desarrollo Social*, Social Development and Compensation Fund), the PRONAA (*Programa Nacional de Ayuda Alimentaria*, National Food Aid Program) and other initiatives. These programs were initially centralized under the Ministry of the Presidency that became one of the most powerful and endowed ministries, especially as it channeled the international cooperation funds.[32]

The development of the social programs apparatus under Fujimori is connected to his need to consolidate a political support base within the popular sectors who suffered most from the drastic economic shock therapy implemented as of 1990. Even if the regime maintained a relatively high level of popular legitimacy, especially among the popular sectors, while it shut down democratic institutions and increased the power of security forces, there was a need to respond to the critics and the immediate needs of the population, as well as to build a credible international image. The redrafting of the constitution, holding new elections, and developing a set of social programs gave the Fujimori regime the capacity to proclaim it was implementing a whole new political project designed to attend to the interests of the poor.

The PRONAA, created in 1992, was later brought under the authority of the Ministry of the Presidency. As the official state agency for food aid, PRONAA was the product of the merging of the PAD (*Programa de Asistencia Directa*, created under García) and the ONAA (*Oficina nacional de ayuda alimentaria*, created under Belaúnde but which had almost stopped functioning in practice). The PRONAA was the main entity with which the women of the *comedores* had to deal throughout the 1990s. Its creation was facilitated by the important changes occurring in the panorama of food aid in the early 1990s. First, USAID stopped donating food surpluses as development assistance and replaced them by financial aid for developing countries to buy their own national food products. This contrasted with the earlier situation leading to the establishment of collective kitchens, whereby USAID-donated food staples were channelled to them through church-based NGOs. The PRONAA used the new foreign aid to concentrate within one agency various state programs revolving around food aid for children, pregnant and breast-feeding women, collective kitchens and Mothers' Clubs, as well as for people displaced by political violence (Portocarrero et al. 2000, 76).

PRONAA and FONCODES managed large budgets throughout the 1990s, even though they were originally conceived as temporary programs. PRONAA was to become the main tool through which the State penetrated the life of popular neighborhoods and rural areas, as it replaced and centralized the various sources of food aid previously available through church-based charity or nongovernmental organizations. Created a few months before the promulgation of Law 25307, it led to a confusing situation for the *comedores* movement that had won its legal battle but was seeing a new, powerful state agency being created without explicit reference being made to the law or what it mandated the State to do. Moreover, control over international aid was now exercised by the Ministry of the Presidency and all forms of food aid were centralized under PRONAA's authority, leaving few options but to go to the State.

In fact, Benedicta Serrano, then president of the *Junta directiva* of the *Federación* that reinitiated its activities in 1993, recalls that the initial reaction of the *Federación* was to seek to establish a collaborative relation with the PRONAA. The fact that PRONAA controlled all the food donations distribution channels was certainly key in explaining this move, but it also corresponded to the willingness on the part of the *Federación* to exercise its rights and prerogatives as defined by Law 25307. While the *Federación* launched a campaign to train the grassroots *comedores* on the content and goals of the Law, it also encouraged women to claim their identity as autonomous *comedores* with respect to the PRONAA. It eventually decided to draw listings and maps of its affiliates to submit them to the PRONAA in order that they be recognized as autonomous social grassroots organizations, as provided for in the Law, and granted food supplies like the *Clubes de madres*.[33]

PRONAA's refusal to recognize them led the *Federación* to organize a demonstration in 1994 that ended in the occupation of PRONAA's Chief Director's office. The *comedores*' leaders insisted that an agreement be signed between the state agency and the *Federación* respecting the latter's autonomy and stipulating that they coordinate food distribution jointly. The agreement was signed, which constituted a great victory from the point of view of previous experiences between the autonomous *comedores* movement and the State's various food aid programs. Finally, the *comedores* were entitled to receive state-provided food supplies. But as underlined by Leonor Espinoza, an advisor from the NGO Incafam, the organization was so politically weak by then that it did not even claim this recognition as a victory nor use it to boost its political profile[34]. This low profile attitude reflected the power imbalance between the *Federación* and the PRONAA. The latter's strategy, far from wanting to acknowledge the Federation as a partner, was to absorb the autonomous *comedores* through a gradual process of cooptation, discrediting, and threatening.

The agreement was respected only until the second round of the 1995 elections, when the PRONAA revealed its "true" nature, that of a government party tool for the promotion of Fujimori and the elimination of autonomous or opposition political voices in the poorest sectors.[35] The PRONAA then stopped respecting the structure and functioning of the *comedores* organization, proceeding to destabilize and compete with it over control of its grassroots bases. The resources at its disposal were plentiful. Its central leverage was its monopoly over food donations. As it gradually displaced the pyramidal organizational structure of the *Federación*, going as far as creating its own local distribution centers as of 1997 to establish direct links with the grassroot *comedores*, it rendered the autonomous organization irrelevant.

The competition between the PRONAA and the various levels of the *Federación* slowly but surely eroded the membership of the latter, even if, formally, a lot of *comedores* remained affiliated to the *Federación* while also dealing directly with the PRONAA. Financial and other material gifts were offered to the *comedores* to increase their support for the PRONAA. For the recalcitrant women leaders, threats and blackmail prevailed until they eventually ceded under the pressure either of the PRONAA or their own bases. As the leaders and former leaders of the *comedores* organization echoed when interviewed, what the bases told them in arguing for a close collaboration with the PRONAA was, "What does the *Federación* give me?" Since the PRONAA managed food supplies, the *Federación* had a hard time defending its role as an autonomous organization worth defending.

Social programs, among them PRONAA as one of the key ones, became increasingly central in the political strategy of the Fujimori government to remain in power. In the first months of the regime, the president received the CNC at the Presidential Palace. Law 25307 was approved not long after, and the PRONAA initially played on the confusion generated by the contradiction between the content of the law and the neoliberal project implemented by the Fujimori government. It claimed to be the response to the State's commitment towards poverty-alleviation programs and direct support to the population most affected by the structural adjustment process. This allowed it to invade the field left by the preceding government who only offered assistance to the *Clubes de madres* and, eventually, to absorb a large part of the autonomous *comedores* movement.

From the mid-1990s onwards, the PRONAA developed a sophisticated system of distribution and control, going into all districts and even sending staff to meetings at the various levels of the *comedores* organization or holding its own meetings at the same time so that the women who wanted to benefit from the food distribution had to choose between the two.[36] The reception of food donations was also conditioned upon performing a series of activities in support of the State and the president. Women were "asked" to participate in demonstrations in support of the regime, parades, to attend the president's birthday celebrations, to make flower tapestries for religious holidays, and others (Portocarrero et al. 2000, 234). During electoral campaigns, these requirements increased significantly and took on a different tone, embedded as they were in the high stakes of losing or keeping control over the State. In the electoral campaigns of 1995, 1998, and 2000, the PRONAA literally became an agency working for the government party, distributing posters and all kinds of items with political propaganda in favor of the president and his candidates.[37] Women had to attend political rallies called by the government party and often suffered the additional humiliation of being offered a free bus ride to go to the rally, but having to walk back home because they could not afford the cost of a bus fare. They were threatened by PRONAA staff and misled into thinking that the State would "know" whether they voted or not for the president and his party.[38] It was clear that if they wanted to maintain their access to food staples, the only rational choice to make in the short run was to support Fujimori.

At the level of the grassroots *comedor*, it is understandable that the PRONAA would be able to slowly but surely win over women's "allegiance" with such pressure tactics at its disposal, even if in practice this often amounted to silent submission filled with humiliation and rage, or else indifference. The dynamics at the level of the pyramidal structure of the *Federación* is somewhat more complex. Because of the lack of control over the main power resource, food staples, the *Federación* had to deal with the new political posture of being a "client" of the State for the provision of food staples to its network of *comedores*. In contrast to the era of the CNC, when the *comedores* movement coalesced around claims for state recognition and the setting up of standards on the right to food security, the *Federación* faced a situation of clear yet very unequal competition with the State, disguised under a supposedly more inclusionary food aid program. This led to the destruction of its organization. The Federation had a hard time convincing its bases that they had to oppose those who were feeding them, even if the quality and quantity of food staples was often highly questionable and PRONAA staff's way of treating women often humiliating and paternalistic (Portocarrero et al. 2000; Alternativa 1998, 1999, 2000).

This contradictory situation, combined with the less vocal political profile of the higher leadership of the *Federación*, led to the organization's paralysis and its incapacity to react to its membership's erosion. As explained by Relinda Sosa, former president of the third *Junta directiva*, within the *Federación* itself women were divided as to how to perceive the PRONAA and its encroachments. She explains the dilemma as she saw it: "Those women who are far away from political power had to solve their problems, they had to eat. . . . I think that we the leaders, what we have to do is to interpret how the women we represent feel . . . I would have liked to be in the newspapers' headlines to denounce, but the question was whether this would really change the life of people."[39]

The fate of the *Federación* was further endangered by the fact that its higher leadership was approached by political parties at the time of the 1998 municipal elections to run as candidates. In the context of a new gender quota provision in the municipal elections law that mandated each party list should include at a minimum 25 percent of male and female candidates, the women leaders of survival organizations appeared as very interesting candidates who could potentially carry their bases' votes. Both *Vamos Vecino*, the political movement created by the Fujimori regime, and *Somos Perú*, the main opposition movement, sought to have women from the *comedores* organization in their lists. Their recruitment process differed, though. *Somos Perú* asked for each candidate's financial contribution but organized local primary elections for the selection of candidates. *Vamos Vecino*, on the other hand, gave greater resources to the women from popular sector organizations whom it sought to nominate directly.

Two former presidents of the *Junta directiva* of the *Federación*, Benedicta Serrano and Rosa Espinal, ran as candidates for *Vamos Vecino* and were elected. The candidacy of Rosa Espinal was particularly important since she ran at the level of Metropolitan Lima, whereas Benedicta Serrano ran in the popular district of Santa-Anita. As explained by Felicita Gallegos, president of the fourth *Junta directiva*, both former *junta* presidents entered in the political race "independently" rather than in representation of the *Federación*, but received the informal support of the latter. This situation generated a controversy within the ranks of the organization, especially as some women from lower levels of the organization ran for *Somos Perú*.[40] Yolanda Mariluz, who ran in the district of Independencia, was one of them. She managed to get the support of the *comedores* organization in her district and eventually won a seat, but was denied her victory in favor of the candidate of *Vamos Vecino* in one of the many cases of suspected fraud occurring during the troubled elections of 1998.[41]

This confusion over the political posture to be adopted by the *Federación* and the divisions that ensued following the decision of some women to run for opposing parties only precipitated the crisis of the organization. The level of fragmentation and frustration reached an unmanageable level by the end of the 1990s, when the Fujimori regime itself entered into crisis and proceeded to increase the pressure, manipulation, and cooptation in order to retain state power. The divisions within the *Federación* ran not only between the higher leadership, the district level and the grassroots. They also existed between districts, as some had a much stronger history of popular mobilization and organization, such as in Villa El Salvador, San Juan de Lurigancho and El Agustino, whereas others were open fields for the State to enter and set up its parallel food aid organization relatively more easily[42]. In general, though, the movement was paralyzed by a dynamic whereby it was reacting to the PRONAA's tactics to destroy its organizational structure and legitimacy.

Citizenship Construction through the *Comedores* Experience

Because of the variety of factors described above, including divisions in the movement, the impact of political violence and changing donor policies, the collective kitchens' movement was far more vulnerable to the Fujimori regime's neopopulist project combining neoliberal economic policies with an authoritarian, clientelistic approach to social assistance. An individualistic, market-based model gradually settled in to dominate Peru in the 1990s, facilitated by the failure of the democratic left, the drastic weakening of the union movement and the damage and trauma caused by the war between *Sendero luminoso* and security forces. This new model meant the erosion of the *comedores*' ideal of autonomous organizing based on solidarity.

Panfichi (1997) makes an argument to explain the exhaustion of grassroots popular mobilization in the 1990s based on the rise of individualism in Peru as a result of neoliberal economic policy and the disappearance of traditional political actors. According to his view, shared by some of the women I interviewed, the younger women leaders and members of the collective kitchens in the 1990s were not inspired by the collectivist values based on solidarity that had been so present in the formation of the movement. They were rather more prone to pragmatic and rational calculations oriented toward the satisfaction of individual or family needs.[43] This would explain grassroots' abandonment of the *Federación* in the face of PRONAA's pressures. Within the higher leadership of the *Federación*, this would account for the willingness to collaborate with the state agency in exchange for the granting of opportunities for greater personal political power within municipal government or the State.

The analysis presented in this chapter indicates that more was at stake in the case of the *comedores*. If it is undeniable that the changing political and social framework generated an individualistic current throughout Peruvian society, the apathy of the grassroots membership and the active collaboration of some of the leadership with the PRONAA also point to the limits of the collective kitchens movement itself. I would argue, building on the critiques of Maruja Barrig, Jeanine Anderson, and Irma Chávez, that the particular notion of citizenship embodied in the movement's discourse and claims explains better both its successes and shortcomings in the face of Fujimori's neopopulism (Anderson 1996b; Barrig 1996; Chávez 1997).

The *comedores* movement put forward a definition of citizenship centered primarily on social rather than civil or political rights (Chávez 1997, 130). The right to food and to adequate state support for grassroots survival organizations formed the core of its project and claims. In that regard, collective kitchens followed on the dominant model of citizenship based on social entitlements developed in Peru in the 1960s and 1970s and most expressly represented by the military regime of General Juan Velasco. But they also and most problematically conformed to the limits of social citizenship as reproduced by the Peruvian State throughout the 1980s and 1990s: a social assistance model targeted at specific sectors of the population rather than a universal definition of citizenship rights (Barrig 1996). In the words of Barrig, the *comedores* were projecting a "restricted identity revolving around consumption" rather than citizenship rights as such (Barrig 1996, 70). This identity left them vulnerable to fall within the logic of paternalistic and clientelistic intervention from governmental or nongovernmental origins. This intervention was institutionalized with the creation of the PRONAA.

Yet, as I show in this chapter, as part of the steps they followed in their political strategies, the leaders of the *comedores* introduced a broader dimension through claiming state recognition of their autonomy and expertise, as well as the state's obligation to contribute national resources to their work. As such, this entry into the domain of national public policy, with the emphasis put on the legal guarantees encompassed in Law 25307, introduced a new profile for popular sector women's political participation. They thus became actors in the public sphere, not only outside their homes, but in the more formal political realm, claiming and winning access to the State and the Legislature. Even though the object of their political participation revolved around an exclusive focus on basic needs, the means taken and the role developed by the leadership of the movement brought a political and even a civil rights component to their project. They claimed their right to be political actors, to see their basic claims transformed into normative obligations for the State, and for political and state institutions to abide by these obligations.

Yet, as Chávez has shown, there is a gap between this broader notion of citizenship as exercised mainly by the higher leadership of the collective kitchens' organization, and the daily reality of grassroots *comedores* members. The latter delegated political authority to the former on the basis of their need for a regular supply of food staples. This "instrumental delegation logic" (Chávez 1997, 124) embodied in the relationship between the bases and the leadership does not allow the formation of citizenship practices that would go beyond the subject matter for which the organization is created, that is, the collective provision of prepared food to the membership and community. This would explain why, from the perspective of the majority of popular sector women members of collective kitchens, when the control over food staples delivery was taken over by the State through PRONAA, there seemed to be little value in continuing to support the political struggle led by the *Federación*. The same difference in political practice and awareness between the bases and the higher leadership would explain why the former generally endorsed President Fujimori's self-coup in 1992, while the older leadership condemned it, generating a further process of distancing and conflict.

Similarly, the movement's insistence on its autonomy may have caused its gradual weakening and long-term political irrelevance. Autonomy, a fundamental principle on which the organization was built, was seen as necessary both for the formation of a strong women's organization based on gender identity—be it that of mothers' or women community leaders'—and for the capacity to negotiate with various political entities as freely as possible. This choice certainly contributed to the development of greater self-confidence among women in their capacity to act as autonomous individuals in the public sphere, a condition essential to the development of citizenship. Yet as Jeanine Anderson emphasizes, this political posture impeded the formation of political alliances.[44] The latter could have been crucial at two levels: first, in the realm of political resources it could have given greater profile to the *comedores* movement, especially at crucial political junctures; second, it could have contributed to the development of a broader discourse of citizenship based on the experience, interests and needs of the popular sector as a whole, rather than perpetuating the traditional dichotomy between women's affairs located in the sphere of social reproduction and men's affairs associated with the broader public sphere and the economy.

Yet this latter view forgets the context dominated by Fujimori's neopopulism where political alliances outside of the government party were not attractive at all, to say the least. To be sure, the autonomy of the *comedores* movement was always only relative. Its close links to the Church and development of women's nongovernmental organizations showed the practical limits of such a discourse. Again, Jeanine Anderson underlines the confusion that may have arisen through time in mixing social programs with political aspirations, especially in a context whereby the dependency on food donations made women particularly vulnerable to the whims of larger political interests, be it of well-intentioned women's NGOs, their own organizations' leaders, state officials or even the President of Peru.[45]

Furthermore, the *comedores* model, as other kinds of survival organizations based on women's voluntary work, was problematic for the long-term development of the popular sector women's movement and for the development of women's citizenship. By not providing solutions to the issue of women's lack of access to paid employment, which go along with many related citizenship issues such as access to education, childcare, and equality in the domestic sphere, the strategy of empowerment based on the *comedores* model was bound to exhaust itself[46]. Those women who became leaders of the movement eventually developed aspirations for greater leadership and responsibilities that could not be satisfied within the organization; those who remained at the grassroots level had a greater stake in income-generating activities, or easily abandoned the struggle for the autonomy of the movement when the PRONAA told them to do so.

Yet the very condition of their protagonism resided on their legitimacy as popular sector women seeking to satisfy the basic needs of their families. As put forward by Arturo Granados: "The image of poor women who struggled against poverty and exemplified mothers' self-sacrifice gave them significant social prestige. This is the common idea underlying the organization: poor mothers struggling for their children" (Granados 1996; my translation). This was exactly the identity Fujimori emphasized in his appeal to this sector. Portraying the PRONAA as the State's responsible response to Peruvian poor mothers' needs, Fujimori had an easy terrain on which to build emotional and material linkages with them to sustain his rule. It thus could be argued that the basis for articulating women's presence and claims in the public sphere also constituted, paradoxically, strong limits to their developing more-encompassing citizenship claims. They could hardly get rid of their fundamental movement identity without risking losing their legitimacy. Fujimori's neopopulism reinforced this vicious circle by undermining the perceived need for autonomous organizations and replacing them with state agencies.

Conclusion: The Limits of Daily Needs Politics

If the struggle for recognition by the State has led to important victories such as Law 25307 and the participation of the collective kitchens' organization in food aid programs, this chapter has also showed the incomplete character of such victories in relation to the initial goals of the movement. Moreover, Fujimori used the issue of food aid as a central element of his neopopulist strategy for building a political clientele among women and for controlling popular sectors' organizations. Through the PRONAA's increasing presence in popular districts and the power it exercized over grassroots collective kitchens, Fujimori managed to exacerbate fears, submission or unconditional support among popular sector women who were left traumatized by the crisis of the early 1990s. Fujimori's tactics were in many ways a continuation of the preceding governments' treatment of economically vulnerable popular sector women who could easily be transformed into a captive political clientele. However, the PRONAA represented a major improvement in the capacity of the State to control these sectors, at a time when the autonomous organization of *comedores* was facing important challenges. The institutionalization of a clientelistic relationship between popular sector women and the State was one of the main achievements of the Fujimori regime based on its neopopulist character.

On a more positive note, the collective kitchens can be credited for having created a space for popular sector women to take on a new role in the public sphere, contributing to the development of women's political participation and the emergence of a discourse, even if circumscribed, on their citizenship as popular sector women. The movement also produced a number of women leaders willing to take on new public and political responsibilities. In that regard, the experience of some of these leaders who have run as candidates in municipal and even national legislative elections is to be highlighted. In less than twenty years, popular sector women have managed to cross the boundaries of the home and community to access the national public sphere and the formal political sphere. Yet the existing space for these women leaders remained reduced, as will be discussed in the following chapter, and the losses associated with the declining membership and political relevance of the autonomous collective kitchens organization were not compensated by the rise of new forms of mobilization during Fujimori's rule.

CHAPTER 5

ENTERING THE MAINSTREAM
POLITICAL SPHERE

WOMEN AS ELECTED REPRESENTATIVES

If traditional political science equated the low number of women in partisan politics with their being absent from the political sphere (Duverger 1955), feminist critiques have now well shown that this equation was based on a limited view of what is to be considered political (Jones and Jonasdottir 1988; Barrett and Phillips 1992; Vickers 1997). However, it remains true that a low level of participation in political institutions potentially implies a severe deficit in women's capacity to influence a central decision-making space. Running as candidate and being elected as representative is an important facet of citizenship, yet it is also one of the greatest challenges facing women in their efforts to penetrate the public sphere in democratic regimes.

The particular obstacles or factors facilitating women's entry in electoral and party politics are not related to a democratic regime's consolidation process. For instance, long-established democracies such as France or the United States still have low proportions of women being elected at the national level, a reality testifying to the ambivalent relationship between representative democracy and women's inclusion in the political sphere. The situation of Peruvian women is no exception in that regard. In that sense, a striking feature of Fujimori's rule is the rapid increase in the number of women participating in elections and being elected during the 1990s. While there is a region-wide trend in Latin America where women have entered the electoral scene in greater numbers since the 1990s, due in part to affirmative action measures, in Peru, Fujimori was a central figure in the politics of promoting women to high political positions (Htun and Jones 2002; Franceschet 2005; Rousseau 2010). The deterioration of political democracy because of his neopopulist concentration of power did not impede women from entering the electoral sphere. Some feminist organizations' agenda included the goal of promoting women's political participation. Did feminists find an ally in the president over this key women's citizenship issue?

This chapter will explore the factors that, taken together, account for the increased number of women taking an important role in the political institutions of Fujimori's regime. In addition to his neopopulist agenda of building a constituency among women, this major transformation in Peruvian politics can also be assessed from the point of view of its impact on women's citizenship rights. In this spirit, I will analyze to what extent elected women at the Congress have been able to elaborate and defend laws and policies addressing key women's issues. This is important to show that, even if Fujimori used the promotion of women's participation to enhance his democratic legitimacy, this had some positive effects on the legislative process from a gendered perspective. However, I will also show that the arguments used by many key actors to defend efforts at including more women in electoral politics reinforced traditional gender representations based on essentialism. Finally, within civil society and some sectors of the feminist movement, investing efforts to increase women's presence in representative institutions at a time when Fujimori's neopopulist concentration of power was manifest turned out to look like a dangerous divorce between women's political rights and democracy, a rather paradoxical situation.

The chapter is divided as follows: first, I present an overview of Peruvian women's historical and contemporary challenges in their attempts to penetrate the electoral political sphere. I then proceed to analyze the role of women in the 1995–2000 Congress and at the municipal level at the end of the 1990s. The subsequent sections consider the collaboration between elected Congresswomen and feminist organizations in civil society to highlight positive outcomes for women's citizenship rights. Finally, I show how Fujimori's neopopulism has contributed in significant ways to allowing for such progress to be made, but that this situation was filled with contradictions and difficulties for opposition Congresswomen and some feminist organizations in particular.

Women in Peruvian Electoral Politics

In Peru, women were granted political rights at the national level only in 1955, the same year as Nicaragua and Honduras, and followed in 1961 only by Paraguay. By way of comparison, in Ecuador, women were granted the right to vote in 1929, in Brasil in 1932, and in Argentina in 1947. Peruvian President General Manuel Odria decided to give women the right to vote in 1955 in a paternalistic gesture motivated by the belief that they would vote for him. This historic move did not emerge out of a sustained struggle led by women, but rather from an opportunistic political calculation on the part of a dictator who wanted to legitimize and perpetuate his power.

This is not to say that Peruvian women had never claimed political rights before. The first feminist group formed in Lima in 1914 by María Jesús Alvarado, *Evolución Femenina* (Female Progress), centered its discourse on the need to redress women's unequal status in the Civil Code, as well as to give women suffrage (Villar 1994, 31). Another prominent feminist journalist, Zoila A. Cáceres, founded a group called *Feminismo Peruano* (Peruvian Feminism) in 1924 and became the key advocate for women's suffrage rights. However, the debate around women's right to vote soon became dominated by the struggle between conservative parties supporting the oligarchic regime and anti-oligarchic parties with working class and middle class bases led by the populist *Alianza Popular Revolucionaria Americana* (American Popular Revolutionary Alliance—APRA) founded in 1930). As Eliana Villar explains it, women's political rights as such were not the focus of the debate, but rather used as another terrain for class-based male-dominated party politics (Villar 1994, 32–33).

From the 1930s onwards, conservative forces were generally in favor of extending the right to vote to literate women only, whereas the APRA was in favor of granting the vote to working women only, as well as to illiterate men. As only literate adults over twenty-one had the right to vote, the "real" issue at stake for parties was how best to enlarge the electorate strategically in order to win more votes. The APRA's argument was that women were prone to vote in a conservative fashion because of the influence that the Catholic Church supposedly had on them and because the majority of literate women belonged to the oligarchy. The APRA advocated granting working women the right to vote mostly because it was thought they would vote similarly to their husbands and, to a lesser extent, because they believed that working class women were more politically progressive. Conservative sectors refused to include illiterates, but argued that there were no difference to be made between women and men in terms of their political aptitudes.

This debate was part of a larger constitutional reform process that ended in 1933, providing for women's right to vote at the municipal level only (Villar 1994, 33). This debate took place mostly within a Constituent Assembly where there were no female representatives. The following period was marked by recurrent attempts by conservative politicians to bring back the issue of women's right to vote, until General Manuel Odria's authoritarian government approved a law modifying the constitution to grant women full citizenship, but retaining the restriction of suffrage to literate Peruvians (Villar 1994).

Peru's two traditionally strong parties, the APRA and the AP (*Acción Popular*—Popular Action, established in 1956), never inserted women on equal terms into their rank and file. Women were integrated early on in the very well organized APRA, but always within specialized commissions or committees and with secondary functions through the 1970s. This was also the period when a number of new left-wing parties emerged in Peru, many of which provided women with the opportunity to get political experience. Only as of 1980, when a democratic regime with universal suffrage was first established, did women start to participate in greater numbers in electoral politics, although still facing strong limitations. The 1979 Constitution significantly increased the legitimacy of women's participation in electoral politics, since the previous exclusion of illiterates from full political citizenship particularly affected women.

The first pioneer women parliamentarians were elected in 1956, one at the Senate and eight at the House of Representatives. In 1963, only two women were elected. In the 1979 Constituent Assembly elections, again only two women were elected (Villar 1994, 51–52). Then in every election from 1980 through 1995, women managed to win a total of around 11 percent of the parliamentary seats, except for the 1992 Constituent Congress election, where women held 8.8 percent of the seats (Promujer 1998, 30; Movimiento Manuela Ramos 1996, 26; Foro-Mujer 1995, 18). At the time of the self-coup in 1992, four out of sixty senators and twelve out of 180 deputies were female representatives. The bicameral parliament was eliminated by the 1993 Constitution. However, this constitutional change did not affect the percentage of women holding seats, which remained stable with 10.8 percent of the 120 Congress seats in the period 1995–2000.

In terms of women's participation in the candidate lists, their numbers actually decreased slightly between 1980 and the first half of the 1990s. For the Senate, almost 15 percent of candidates were female in the 1980 and 1985 elections, whereas in 1990 this number fell to 12 percent. For the House of Representatives, in 1980 15.7 percent of the candidates for the Lima department were female, and in 1990 they were 16.9 percent, which compensates a little for the decrease in the Senate. In 1995, only 13 percent of the candidates for the unicameral

Congress were female (Foro-Mujer 1995, 19–20), yet this does not appear to have led to a significant decrease in their electoral success rate.

The end of the 1990s saw a new breakthrough in women's participation in institutional and electoral politics. Women more than doubled their numerical presence at the Congress in 2000. The main explanatory factor for this notable and rapid increase in women's parliamentary representation seems to be the "quota law" (*"Ley de cuotas"*), an amendment to the Electoral Code approved by Congress in 1997.[1] The amendment only provided for a minimum number of candidates of each sex. But figures speak to the impressive progress made by women in electoral performance. In 1995, 12.4 percent of the candidates to the Congressional elections were female, with 10.8 percent of the seats won by women. In the municipal elections of 1998, when the quota was first implemented, 25 percent of candidates were female, and women won about 25 percent of the seats. In the 2000 Congress elections, 26 percent of women candidates led to 21.6 percent of the seats being held by women.[2] At the 2001 congressional elections, 36 percent of candidates were women, a figure that went even beyond the mandatory quota. But the number of elected women declined to 18 percent of the seats in the Congress elected in 2001, for reasons that I will explore later. Overall, however, women had significantly increased their numerical presence at the Peruvian Congress and in municipal governments at the end of the 1990s after the adoption of the electoral gender quotas.

These advances, even if still far from the ideal of equal gender representation, can surely be attributed in great measure to the affirmative action legislation embodied in the gender quota. This not only allowed more women to run, but it was part of a process of increasing popular support for women candidates. The legislated quota is one among other factors such as women's increasing visibility in the public sphere, as well as the positive image they have been able to generate as public actors. Indeed, women's performance as administrators, political representatives or community leaders was increasingly valued by Peruvians throughout the 1990s. Surveys in that period have shown that, especially within the capital Lima where a third of all Peruvians live, women were seen as having as much to offer or even more than men in terms of public leadership and responsibilities (Blondet 1999a; Alfaro 1998; Calandria 2000).

The nongovernmental organization Calandria undertook regular surveys since 1996 and noted a constant increase in the percentage of Peruvians supporting women's active role in politics and measures designed to promote gender equality (Calandria 2000, 20). When asked to compare male and female politicians, public polls revealed a clearly more positive opinion about women at the close of the 1990s. One such survey revealed that 64 percent of Peruvians living in Lima thought that women politicians were more honest, whereas three percent thought men were more honest and 21 percent thought that both were as honest; 49 percent thought women were better administrators compared to 15 percent for men and 30 percent for both sexes. On the other hand, 62 percent thought that men were more authoritarian, with 16 percent opting for women and 19 percent saying that both sexes were equally authoritarian (Blondet 1999a, 11).[3] Women politicians' positive image may explain why the gender quota received 75.6 percent of popular endorsement in 1998 and 80.9 percent in 2000 according to these surveys[4] (Calandria 2000, 20).

A striking example of such support is that when asked if they would vote for a woman candidate for the presidency, 67.6 percent of Peruvians living in Lima answered positively in 1996, whereas 79.7 percent of Peruvians living in five major cities including Lima answered positively in 1998 (Alfaro 1996,10; Calandria 1998, 3). This favorable public opinion later became strong enough that, for the first time in Peruvian history, a woman running as presidential candidate in the 2001 and 2006 elections got very close to winning.[5] Lourdes Flores Nano, a distinguished career politician, got one less than the second most favored candidate, former President Alan García, in the first electoral round in 2001. Many later argued that had she passed on to the run-off elections, she would have won over Alejandro Toledo and would have been the first Latin American woman to win presidential elections based on her own merits and not on some family links to famous male politicians. Again, at the 2006 presidential elections, Flores Nano lacked a little over 60,000 votes to pass on to the second round, which was finally won by Alan García.

An interesting observation emerging from the Peruvian case is that some of the traditional gender characteristics attributed to women have in fact become one of the bases of popular support to their political leadership. In the context of the 1990s where politicians in general were perceived to be corrupt, authoritarian, lazy, and self-centered, electing women came out as an alternative worth experimenting in the eyes of many Peruvians. When asked to compare male and female mayors, for example, respondents in a 1998 survey indicated that while men work more and are more efficient, women are more honest, loyal, just, and sensitive to social and human issues (Alfaro 1998b: 24–25).

The mothering and caring characteristics that the average Peruvian values in women politicians were seen as necessary to "clean up" the electoral-institutional sphere and provide more trustworthy political leadership. Seeing women and men as having different attributes and political skills did, in this case, lead to favorable public opinion toward women's involvement in political affairs, even if some prominent women played a key role within the corrupt web of the Fujimori regime as will be described later (Blondet 2002). On the other hand, commenting on these public polls carried out in Lima, social communicator Rosa Alfaro claimed that there is a general "spirit of equality and respect for gender equity . . . which reflects a process of modernization of our citizenship" (Alfaro 1997, 29; my translation). However, gender roles and responsibilities in the household remained traditional and unequal, even if this is also changing with the youngest generation (Alfaro 1998b, 27).

These findings would seem to nuance the arguments put forward by Pippa Norris and Ronald Inglehart according to which "there are substantial differences in attitudes toward women's leadership in postindustrial, postcommunist, and developing societies"; "traditional attitudes are a major barrier to the election of women in parliament"; and "as a result of the process of modernization and value change, these cultural barriers have been fading most rapidly among younger generations in postindustrial societies" (Norris and Inglehart 2001, 132). What these authors claim is that traditional culture would be the main explanatory factor for the low level of women's representation in elected legislatures. Yet in light of the above, it is obvious that traditional gender representations are not necessarily adverse to women's equal access to the political sphere, even if this means reifying distinct and somewhat essentialized gender characteristics. Moreover, cultural change may be more rapid than predicted by the indicators of economic development and democratization, considering that younger generations in Peru are more favorable to gender equality in the household and in public life, thus revealing similar patterns of generational attitudinal change in developing countries—at least some of them—and postindustrial societies.

THE POLITICAL SYSTEM AND WOMEN'S POLITICAL PARTICIPATION

Peru has a presidential system with an open-list proportional representation system, like most Latin American States. The electoral system suffered from several deficiencies because of how the party system evolved in the 1990s. First, the lack of internal democratic procedures within most political parties was compounded by the fact that no specific legislation regulated political parties in this period. As a result, since the late 1980s as explained in Chapter 2, parties were often created for an election and disappeared or merged when the next election came.[6] The selection of candidates was a process guided by informal criteria rather than established, democratic mechanisms. Not surprisingly, parties were not particularly representative of the Peruvian social diversity, and were rather strongly personalistic. In that context, women had a hard time competing and only a minority were really making a career within parties as of the mid-1990s.[7]

In terms of the electoral system, the double preferential vote in place since 1985 had an ambiguous impact on women's electoral performance.[8] In Peru, a high proportion of voters does not use the preferential vote option, limiting their choice to the party in general, or use it incorrectly.[9] Moreover, the 2000 and 2001 elections showed that parties were still not very inclined to give good positions to women, a fact that may influence voters negatively in their propensity to choose women candidates. In 2000 for example, the first 10 positions of all parties' lists had only 17 percent of women, and the first 20 positions had only 18.5 percent of women. The majority of women, that is 59 percent, were positioned in the last half of the lists.[10] Without assessing the full impact of this double-preferential vote system, it should be underlined that in the 2000 elections, 16 women were elected in a position higher than the one they were assigned in their party list, and 10 women were elected in positions lower than the one they were given.[11]

Another important aspect to consider in the Peruvian electoral system in the 1990s is the single national electoral district that accompanied the turn to a unicameral parliament in 1993. Prior to this, the Senate was elected according to a single national district, whereas the House of Representatives was elected according to departmental districts, thus providing for regional representation. The impact of this change on women's electoral opportunities seems to have been null in the context where there were no quota measures. At the 1995 elections, the number of elected women remained low but constant in comparison with prior elections. However, comparing the 2000 and 2001 elections provides another perspective. The electoral reform in 2001 abolished the single national district to introduce a departmental district system. The effect of this change is noticeable since the number of women elected went down from twenty-six in 2000 to twenty-two in 2001, with the total number of Congressmembers remaining the same. When remembering that 11 percent more women ran as candidates in 2001 compared to 2000 (36 percent versus 25 percent), this difference in the results cannot totally be disconnected from the change in the district system. Some expert explanations point to the lower level of women's leadership and greater prevalence of traditional gender roles outside Lima, where women had a harder time as candidates.[12]

WOMEN AT THE CONGRESS AND MUNICIPAL LEVEL

As noted above, the second half of the 1990s corresponds to a significant leap in the presence and visibility of women at the Congress. Within the factors that explain it, the international context around the Beijing World Conference on Women certainly played an important part. A few active Congresswomen used the new opportunities offered by the favorable international scene. Few months after the installation of the Congress elected in 1995, several Peruvian Congresswomen participated either with the official Peruvian delegation to the Beijing Conference or at the parallel NGO meeting. Congresswomen's international exposure to new ideas and proposals to increase women's political participation led to the creation of a Permanent Commission on Women at the Peruvian Congress. The proposal to set up this Commission was introduced in Congress by Beatriz Merino, a prominent opposition member.[13] The initiative was supported by most Congresswomen, but when the time came to formally install it, Martha Chávez, President of Congress and member of Fujimori's party, delayed it for a year. Once created, the commission also suffered from not having the ordinary status granted to all the other congressional commissions, including the power to submit bills. Only in 1997 did it become a commission with full powers, reinforcing further its importance as a vehicle for Congresswomen's collaboration and legislative innovation. Competition between Martha Chávez and other prominent Congresswomen from the opposition or the government parties played a part in the delay. Underlying this competition was also deeper ideological opposition from Chávez to any affirmative action measure to promote women.

The Permanent Commission on Women rapidly became a very powerful focus of attention for politicians and the media. "*Había una inmensa expectativa política*" (There were huge political expectations), recalled Beatriz Merino, who also mentioned that the Commission was always very well portrayed in the media, including in some of the comic shows where the character of Beatriz Merino, the commission's first chair, was dressed up in a Superman costume.[14] It should not come as a surprise that Congresswomen from Fujimori's party wanted to lead the commission as soon as its impact was received so positively, and in fact only during its first year of existence was its president an opposition Congresswoman. Coinciding with it being granted full powers and after building a very good reputation from its first year of activism, its leadership was transferred to and maintained under the control of Congresswomen from Fujimori's party.

The Commission on Women contributed to enhancing the collaboration between most Congresswomen on bills of direct interest to women. Beatriz Merino claims that Congresswomen proceeded along the logic of consensus rather than interparty fighting, acting *"como si fueramos del mismo partido"* (as if we were from the same party). Contrary to most of the rest of congressional practices at that time, Congresswomen from Fujimori's party collaborated with opposition Congresswomen in promoting bills, with the exception of the otherwise influential Martha Chávez and another of Fujimori's pawns, Carmen Lozada. *"Yo creo que es el único tema que funcionó en el Congreso* (I think that this [women's issues] is the only topic that worked out well in the Congress)," said Beatriz Merino in interview, connecting voters' increased support for women candidates in the 2000 elections to the fact that Congresswomen in the 1995–2000 Congress had been seen as acting responsibly and capable of consensus building.

The collaboration between women from different parties came with a price: very few bills were accepted as such if they were presented by an opposition member. Most of the time, opposition Congresswomen would present a bill that would then be "stolen" by a Congresswomen from Fujimori's party and presented anew in a slightly modified version to be approved with less difficulty by the Plenary controlled by Fujimori.[15] In many instances, this rewriting of bills was done with the approval of opposition Congresswomen, who knew that this was the only way to proceed under the circumstances of tight control by the governing party over the legislative process. This constraint, if frustrating and time-consuming because of the duplication of work, did not impede women from wanting to continue collaborating, since it was the only way to make progress on women's issues. "This is what allowed us to survive as happy and creative human beings, in this context. We had clear agendas, this is what we wanted, we were doing it, and we achieved it" explained Beatriz Merino when she recalled the experience of this small group of active Congresswomen in the period 1995–2000.[16]

A side effect of this dynamic was the opportunities it gave to the governing party to further boost its popularity based on the significant advances made on several issues belonging to the women's movement's agenda. Some of these issues had gained wide popular support, as was mentioned in Chapter 3. This unusual degree of interparty cooperation resulted from a compromise on the part of opposition Congresswomen who deemed it more important to ensure that these bills be adopted rather than act cohesively as opposition members. Klatzer (2000, 226) notes that Congresswomen were allowed by their parties to collaborate on issues concerning women's rights. It may be that Congressmen did not consider these issues to be worthy of attention and therefore left the terrain open for interparty cooperation. Yet the intensity of the debates in plenary sessions on some of the bills submitted by the Commission on Women does not lend a lot of credibility to this argument. The remaining possibilities are that, first, Congresswomen personally took greater interest in and therefore devoted more energy to these issues and were willing to fight harder and use various strategies. Alternatively, it might be argued that under a Congress controlled to a great extent by the Executive, there were clear interests on the part of the latter to see advances in some issues relating to women's rights, thereby clearing the way for collaborative behavior on the part of concerned Congresswomen.

At the municipal level, the *Ley de Elecciones Municipales* (Municipal Elections Law) was approved in October 1997, providing for a minimum of 25 percent of each sex in the lists of candidates for *regidores* (municipal councillors). At that time, the number of elected women at the municipal level was even lower than at the Congress. In 1996, women represented 7.9 percent of the elected municipal authorities, the majority of them being elected as councillors (Promujer 1998, 69). In contrast, at the 1998 elections after the new quota had been applied for the first time, 25 percent of the elected district councillors were women (CESIP 1999, 18).

The inclusion of quota provisions in the municipal electoral law resulted from a proposal made by Luz Salgado, then president of the Commission on Women at the Congress and member of Fujimori's party elite. Following a meeting of the *Asociación de Municipalidades del Perú* (Association of Peruvian Municipalities) wherein some women mayors asked for a municipal electoral quota system, a bill was well received by Congress without the difficulties that Congresswomen had encountered when proposing the first electoral quotas for the legislature in 1995 (Promujer 1998, 26). Salgado, when justifying her bill, explicitly stated that "it's not that we are feminists, but we women make up 50 percent of the population; logically we should increase our participation in municipal lists like we already have for parliamentary lists" (Promujer 1998, 26; my translation).

Salgado's statement on the "nonfeminist" character of the bill can mean several things. First it may be a strategic move in light of the fact that feminism is not particularly well appreciated among the majority of Congressmembers. Alternatively, for this Congresswoman and possibly others, this kind of affirmative action measure does not have anything to do with feminism. The rest of her statement indicates that bringing more women to participate in elections is a desirable goal in itself. One may conclude that Salgado's perspective went along the descriptive representation model highlighted by Pitkin (1967), emphasizing a discrepancy between the proportion of women in society and the proportion of women elected as representatives.

In any case, the first municipal elections following the adoption of quotas were characterized by an intense search for female candidates by political parties and movements, which meant that many women were approached before even thinking about the idea of running as candidate. Once involved in the process, the majority of recruited women had difficulties negotiating a good position in the lists and was not given a lot of opportunities by parties to speak at public events. This contradicted the general public perception that women had a lot to offer to municipal politics, as revealed by public opinion surveys discussed above. Because of women candidates' scarce economic resources and generally limited political experience, many of them reported experiencing frustration and marginalization during the electoral campaign.[17]

Compulsory quotas explain the greater level of participation of women in the 1998 municipal elections, which led to increasing women's numerical presence in municipal bodies. However, as reported by the women's nongovernmental organization CESIP, the majority of women running as candidates remained insecure and shy. Those who had been members of parties for a while were in a better position than those running as independent candidates recruited by parties at the last minute (CESIP 1999, 57–58). Nonetheless, 25 percent of municipal councillors elected in 1998 were female, a proportion equivalent to the space they occupied in the lists.

Instilling a Feminist Content to Women's Presence at the Congress

To understand the progress made by women in the mainstream political sphere, it is necessary to go back to the evolution of the feminist movement, which has moved from a very autonomistic discourse toward a clear strategy of influencing the State and political institutions, as explained in Chapter 3. Although women have entered the formal political sphere "naturally" following the changes in the social structure generated by women's access to education and their entry into the workforce in the 1970s and 1980s, the space and strength they developed in that sphere is connected in a significant fashion to the work of women's organizations in civil society.

In the 1980s, feminist groups made up of young professionals and intellectuals invested their energy and time in defining their own identity and language, establishing the basis of their citizenship claims. They then chose to work primarily in popular neighborhoods, organizing poor women and "teaching" feminist values and ideals. Their close links with the emerging and increasingly strong networks of grassroots women's organizations based on survival needs provided for a strategy based on autonomous organizing, outside of the realm of party politics. But at the same time, the links that feminist organizations maintained with the democratic Left and the continuing presence of the women's agenda in the debates of the various leftist parties led to some incursions of prominent feminists in the formal political sphere. In the 1985 elections, two women from key feminist organizations were included in the lists of candidates running under the banner of *Izquierda Unida* (United Left).[18]

This electoral episode was both a contradiction and a necessary experiment for the feminist movement. It was a contradiction because of the feminist movement's insistence on the theme of autonomy and the ambivalence it had shown toward associating itself with the United Left, the latter being in practical terms the natural ally of the feminists, but without genuinely including the feminist agenda in its platform. Yet it was seen by some feminists as a necessary experiment because of their need to enlarge their support base. The idea of running as candidates came both from outside the feminist movement—in the media, in parties—as well as from internal discussions about the need to break the tendency of the feminist movement to isolate itself from other social or political movements (Vargas 1989, 53–70).

As Maruja Barrig, Peruvian analyst of the women's movement, puts it, two central errors were made in that experiment. First, the rapid insertion into formal politics led to a premature and confusing abandonment of the feminist movement's option for autonomy. This move was further contradicted by the choice not to compromise this autonomy by remaining independent from the United Left throughout the electoral campaign.[19] The candidates were therefore left in a political vacuum vis-a-vis their own base and within their new political role. Second, the political slogan chosen by the candidates—"*Vota por tí, mujer*" (Vote for you, woman)—implied that these feminist candidates were to represent all women, whereas they were very far from representing the experience and claims of most Peruvian women, especially from popular classes. Emphasizing issues like abortion, sexuality, domestic violence, and the sexual division of labor within the family, the candidates' strategy did not succeed in attracting popular classes' support. The latter's priority were rather hunger and unemployment. Moreover, the feminist candidates' desire to represent all women also generated some tensions between feminist organizations and nonfeminist women candidates running either for the United Left or other parties (Barrig 1986, 31; Vargas 1989, 53–70).

Neither of the two feminist candidates got elected. In fact, only two women from the United Left list were elected in 1985. The latter had not made particular statements concerning women's status, but had benefited from the clear support won by their political organization in their districts to succeed in the preferential vote (Vargas 1989, 69). Nonetheless, this electoral politics experience provided a number of lessons for the feminist movement, such as the need to bridge the gap with the majority of poor women and find more successful ways to penetrate the formal political sphere. Indeed, the closing campaign discourse by United Left presidential candidate Alfonso Barrantes demonstrated in a very telling way that feminists had a long way to go before they could trust political parties. On that occasion, Barrantes stated that he had the certainty that a woman's problems were not due to her sex, but rather to her class, dismissing the contribution made over the last years by the feminist movement in articulating a gender-based analysis of discrimination and oppression (Vargas 1989, 67).

As detailed in Chapter 3, during the end of the 1980s and the 1990s women's organizations consolidated, transforming the first feminist groups of the 1970s into sophisticated professional nongovernmental organizations (NGOs) with wide national and international networks. This consolidation went together with a shift in feminist practice and discourse. Organized women focused increasingly on formulating policy proposals, using legal strategies and calling on state institutions to address women's needs and rights. In this new framework, women's organizations decided to invest in the traditional political sphere, developing lobbying and advocacy tools. This strategic choice materialized in a very visible fashion in 1990 when *Foro-Mujer* (Woman's Forum) was created. A forum made up of six feminist nongovernmental organizations, *Foro-Mujer* was born to address explicitly the issue of women's political participation.[20] It became a focal point for the development of strategies for increasing women's access to power and politics. The efforts of *Foro-Mujer* led to the creation of the first parliamentary group of Congresswomen in 1991, but the political turmoil in which the country was enmeshed at that time did not facilitate any type of sustained coordination. The self-coup of 1992 destroyed this initial impetus within Congress, yet *Foro-Mujer* continued to function until 1995.

The Forum organized a "Women's Campaign for a Vote of Conscience" for the referendum on the constitution designed by Fujimori in 1993, highlighting the fact that this new constitution, contrary to the previous one, did not specifically provide for affirmative action measures to enhance gender equality. Prior to that, it had also successfully struggled against the proposal to include an article in the new constitution stating that abortion is a homicide.[21] *Foro-Mujer* was also the first to propose a quota system to be included in a law on political parties that would make mandatory a minimum of 30 percent of female candidates in the lists for parties' internal elections as well as for general elections at the municipal and national levels. The initiative was presented to the Constituent Congress in March 1994 but did not receive enough support to be enacted into law. Interestingly, a survey done by the Peruvian polling firm IMASEN revealed that at the time this project was presented, 82.3 percent of Peruvians supported it (cited in Foro-Mujer 1994, 25).

The strategy behind the creation of *Foro-Mujer* included two goals: to increase women's presence in formal political institutions, and to influence the content of the agenda of these institutions, mainly the legislature. At that time, it was assumed that by bringing more women into the legislature, the capacity to bring forward legislative initiatives favoring women would increase. The question of the institutional and political environment surrounding the inclusion of more women was not seen as a problem in the way it would later be following Fujimori's self-coup.

Foro-Mujer disappeared after the 1995 elections because of divergent views among the member organizations. *Movimiento Manuela Ramos*, one of the pioneer and largest women's organizations, continued the *Foro*'s work by publishing a monthly newsletter for Congressmembers at the time of the installation of Congress in 1995.[22] This newsletter sought to circulate information on women's issues, promote bills, and educate Congressmembers so that they would be willing to take on new bills that addressed women's claims. The newsletter generated sustained interest on specific bills directly connected to the agenda of the feminist movement, especially among a group of women Congressmembers. *Movimiento Manuela Ramos*, as well as other women's organizations, maintained regular contacts and collaboration with this group and together managed to pass a number of important laws.

Some of the legislative advances favorable to women's rights coming out of the initiatives of Congresswomen with the input of women from civil society are cited by feminist activists as proofs of the positive contribution made by women's participation in Congress.[23] However, it is important to note that the increase in the number of elected women in 2000 has not had an equivalent impact in the legislative advances for women because of the political turmoil generated by the flight of Fujimori and Montesinos and the installation of a transitional government at the end of 2000. The Congress elected in 2000 was abrogated and lasted only one year. It was totally absorbed by the tasks involved in investigating and sanctioning the corrupt authorities of the Fujimori regime. Therefore, it was not possible to effectively gauge the difference made by the significant numerical increase in the presence of elected women at the 2000 Congress.

This limit notwithstanding, it is interesting to analyze the main legislative advances made in the 1990s in order to trace Congresswomen's involvement and strategies. Chronologically speaking, the first that comes to attention is the "Law on the Policy of the State and Society on Domestic Violence" (Law no. 26260) approved in December 1993, as a result of the collaboration between *Foro Mujer* and the Senate. Early in 1990, *Foro Mujer* initiated the debate around the lack of a legal framework defining domestic violence and the absence of state responsibility to protect victims and sanction the perpetrators. Two prominent Congresswomen took up the issue and developed the bill until Congress was closed down in 1992. Because of the important profile gained by the issue in public debate, the bill was revived in the Constituent Congress and approved. Subsequent modifications to the law were made during the 1990s, some leading to its improvement while others such as the obligation to go through conciliation procedures between victims and perpetrators of violence were much more problematic from a feminist point of view (Boesten 2006).

The creation of the *Comisión de la Mujer* (Permanent Commission on Women) at the Congress in October 1995, through a motion of the thirteen Congresswomen elected that year, represents another clear case of progress in the institutionalization of women's citizenship. As mentioned above, the commission rapidly became a focal point of women's legal activism, as well as a forum for Congresswomen to unite around shared goals. Of course, not all Congresswomen were equally active within the commission—in fact not all of them could be appointed to it at the same time because of the limited number of seats—and a few of them became strong critics, like *fujimorista* Martha Chávez. The collaboration between women from civil society and Congresswomen was guaranteed by the fact that the advisors to the commission, who were part of its staff, were feminists coming out of women's organizations. As such, these advisors provided a high level of coherence to the work of the commission, as well as direct channels of communication with civil society.[24]

The "Quota Law" was proposed by *Foro-Mujer* in March 1994 at the Constituent Congress. This proposal came back at the Congress elected in 1995 among the many projects to reform the electoral code presented by various Congressmembers in 1995 and 1996. Of the thirty-nine projects discussed by the Constitutional Commission of the Congress, four included some clauses establishing quotas for parliamentary lists. Two of these latter were presented by female Congressmembers, while the other two were introduced by male Congressmembers from the opposition. The first project, submitted by opposition member Lourdes Flores Nano in 1995, had been received "with loud laughs" and archived almost immediately. Then Martha Hildebrant and Luz Salgado, two prominent Congresswomen from Fujimori's party, were sent to an international conference on women's political participation organized by the Interparliamentary Union. They came back convinced of the importance of providing the Peruvian political system with a legal tool to favor more participation by women. According to Beatriz Merino, they then agreed with Lourdes Flores Nano and herself that the most astute thing to do would be for them to present a new project, which would have a better chance of being approved compared to the one presented by Flores Nano, an opposition Congressmember.[25] A new project was presented by Hildebrant and Salgado.

However, the battle was not won so easily. When the Constitutional Commission rendered its opinion on reforming the electoral code, it recommended adopting one of the projects that did not include quotas—a project presented by Congresswoman Martha Chávez. During the discussion in the plenary in 1997, Chávez tried to sustain her project by going as far as discrediting the opinion of the Commission on Women. As revealed in the polarization around this issue, the electoral gender quotas were never identified either to the opposition's initiative or to the government's. Yet as was pointed out by Peruvian and foreign analysts, at that point Fujimori came out publicly in favor of gender quotas and the article providing for this quota was rapidly adopted by Congress (Schmidt 2003, 3; Yañez and Guillén 1998 cited in Schmidt 2006, 167). In a surprising outcome, the article included a clause from the project initially presented by Lourdes Flores Nano. This clause had the advantage of introducing a gender-blind quota by setting a minimum of candidates from both sexes, thus bypassing the critics saying that this kind of measure was discriminatory (Promujer 1998, 26). The new electoral law however established the quota at 25 percent, which was the floor advocated by the government party, and not 30 percent as stated in the bills presented by opposition Congressmembers.

Another area of the women's agenda that has benefited from the work of Congresswomen concerns the modification of the Penal Code. The feminist movement set for itself the task of reforming the penal code early in the late 1980s, as it identified serious problems related to the definition of the crime of rape, the status of women as victims of rape and sexual violence, and the responsibility of the State in protecting victims and punishing perpetrators. An early reform in 1991 provided some corrections, yet important areas were left untouched. One such area was the existence of a norm that absolved from penal sanction a perpetrator of rape if this person subsequently married the victim. Bill no.1147/95-CR, presented by Beatriz Merino in March 1996, sought to eradicate such a norm. It generated a long battle within Congress that finally led to its adoption in April 1997.

The second significant modification of the penal code in the 1990s introduced the obligation for public prosecution in cases of sexual violence. Prior to this, the prosecution of alleged rapists was left to the initiative and resources of the victims themselves. Two law projects were presented by opposition Congresswomen Ana-Elena Townsend and Beatriz Merino in 1998. Law no.27115, passed in May 1999, was the result of an extensive campaign jointly run by feminist NGOs, women in key positions in the State and the media, and the Congresswomen who put the project forward, together with Congressmembers who were sitting on the *Comisión de la Mujer*, headed during that period by a woman from Fujimori's party. One significant aspect to mention is that the vote on this law was left to the free conscience of each Congressmember, leaving aside partisanship because it was seen as a matter "pertaining to the private or intimate domain, which potentially can affect a family's honor and/or relationships of subordination between men and women" (Dador 2000).

What comes out of this brief review of legal advances in women's citizenship is the varied pattern in political battles surrounding the adoption of different laws. Some attracted the support by Fujimori himself when he could use them to show the modernist character of his regime, such as in the case of domestic violence or electoral gender quotas. Others did not attract such high political support and were left in the hands of determined Congresswomen who had to devise alliances and strategies to provide for the adoption of these bills.

THE FUJIMORI REGIME'S INTEREST IN PROMOTING WOMEN

As was made clear in previous chapters of this book, an avalanche of policies and institutions favoring women's advancement were put forward by Fujimori from the start of his second term. Right after the 1995 elections, Fujimori attracted the attention of the women's movement by being the only president to make a speech during the closing session of the Beijing World Conference on Women, positioning himself as a defender of women's autonomy and family planning. His speech was applauded by most Peruvian women's rights defenders and many saw in this opening an opportunity not to be discarded.

Yet the neopopulist nature of his regime and its authoritarian features greatly compromised the extent to which the women's movement could establish a collaborative and transparent alliance with the government on women's rights. For example, Fujimori's speech at Beijing came just a few days after his new national policy on family planning had been approved in the absence of many Congresswomen who were attending the Beijing Conference. Former opposition Congressmember Beatriz Merino recalls that she and other Congresswomen sent faxes to Congress asking for a delay in the debate over the bill creating the new family planning services. They argued that there was no voice in Congress or in civil society as many key women's rights activists were also in Beijing, to represent Peruvian women during the debate around the adoption of the new state policy.[26]

The contentious element of Fujimori's family planning policy was the inclusion of voluntary sterilization surgery among the range of free contraceptive methods offered by public health clinics, as explained in Chapter 3. With this audacious move, the Fujimori government positioned itself in radical opposition to the Catholic Church and related conservative sectors that voiced clear opposition to this policy development. At the World Conference on Women at Beijing, Fujimori made open remarks against the Catholic Church: "Peruvian women are not going to remain confined or constrained by the intransigence of ultraconservative mentalities that pretend to turn into a dogma their incapacity to accept social change" (Fujimori 1995). Women's organizations were ambivalent since they feared that the Fujimori government was seeking first and foremost to create one more policy instrument in its "antipoverty" strategy, rather than promoting reproductive choice. Yet, overall, when the policy was set in place, women's organizations were willing to give credit to the government for this unprecedented move in favor of women's reproductive rights that responded in great part to their demands (Rousseau 2007).

What is interesting from the point of view of the dynamics within Congress is that women from all parties joined ranks to save the family planning program when major scandals regarding its implementation unfolded in 1997.[27] Opposition Congresswomen decided not to use this issue politically to denounce the Fujimori government for fear that the whole policy would be attacked and eventually disappear.[28] An analysis of the steps taken by the Commission on Women on this case reveals that a pragmatic rather than a politically critical approach was taken to deal with the problems emerging from the implementation of the national policy. The Deputy Minister of Health was called to testify in an extraordinary joint session of the Commission on Women and the Commission on Health in December 1997, the Minister of Health was called in to testify before both Commissions in January 1998 and March 1998, and the Deputy Minister of the Promotion of Women and Human Development and President of the COORDIPLAN (National Coordinating Commission on Family Planning and Reproductive Health Policies) also submitted a report to a joint session of both Commissions in January 1998.

At each session, the members of the commission recommended changes and verified whether the proposed improvements had been adopted.[29] According to several interviewees, this approach had beneficial consequences at least in the short term, as shown by the changes made in the Ministry of Health's procedures manual on reproductive health for public health care professionals. However, in the longer run, the abuses committed under this program were associated with the evils of the Fujimori regime to such an extent that the family planning program was seriously undermined in the immediate years following the end of Fujimori's regime in 2001 (Rousseau 2007).

From the point of view of the dynamics within Congress and the state apparatus, another notable component of Fujimori's politics is the nomination of numerous women in high level positions in his government or in the various parties that he successively created. Right from the beginning in 1990, Fujimori's list for the Senate included 25 percent of female candidates, compared to only 7 percent in other parties' lists. For the 1992 Constituent Congress elections, Fujimori's list included 11.3 percent female candidates compared to 10.3 percent for other parties' list. However, in 1995 Fujimori's list lost this lead (9.2 percent female candidates compared to 10.7 percent in other parties' list), but at the 2000 elections when quotas were first applied at the legislative level, Fujimori's gender politics was revealed through the election of 28.8 percent of his party's female candidates, compared to 16.2 percent female candidates of other party lists winning seats, with a little over 25 percent of the candidates being female for all parties running in 2000 (Schmidt 2006, 154).

In the state bureaucracy, Fujimori's appointments also revealed an unprecedented tendency to nominate many women. Schmidt reports that at the end of his first term, 20 percent of Peru's vice-ministers were women, while in 1999 almost half of the vice-ministers were women (Schmidt 2006, 153 and 159). Many high executive jobs in state agencies or in the Judiciary were also filled by women, and Fujimori nominated three women ministers during his second term (Schmidt 2006, 159).

Beyond quantitative data, what struck observers was that Fujimori's neopopulism relied on several women to play key roles as spokespersons defending the regime from its initial days onward. This is particularly true of a small group of Congresswomen who became central to the Fujimori regime's image and discourse (Blondet 1999b; Schmidt 2006). The main messages conveyed by these politicians consisted in the following: they repeatedly reaffirmed the Fujimori government's unique capacity to protect the nation against terrorism, which most often involved pointing to *Sendero luminoso*'s threat but also indiscriminate accusations against the left in general; they also fed popular distrust and discredit of traditional political parties that was common within some of the media and central to Fujimori's rhetoric; and they generally portrayed Fujimori as a paternalist figure, provider of food aid and security to the majority of poor women.

One of these women, Luisa María Cuculizza, Minister of PROMUDEH (Ministry for the Promotion of Women and Human Development), joined Fujimori's elite group in 1999 when he appointed her as minister, after a long career first as mayor of Huánuco and later of one of Lima's middle class district, San Borja. Her inclusion in the cabinet led her to make several statements in favor of Fujimori's intention to declare Peru out of the InterAmerican Human Rights Court's jurisdiction, at a time when the Court was hearing cases concerning Peru's controversial antiterrorist laws. Cuculizza emphasized how she had "lived the drama of terrorism in her own flesh," arguing that her husband's assassination in 1984 was connected to his refusal to pay bribes to the Shining Path. However, the daily *La República* revealed that official police documents from back then contradicted her version. The murder was committed by a mentally retarded son of a woman who was claiming compensation to Cuculizza's husband for the loss of merchandise in a car accident involving his company's truck. According to police reports, Cuculizza herself had declared to the police back then that she did not feel threatened by the Shining Path.[30]

Martha Chávez was another strong spokesperson leading the Fujimori government's fear campaign and constant emphasis on terrorist threats. At the World Conference on Women at Beijing for example, she stated that "Amidst this difficult and painful context, our women, especially those living in poor areas of Peru, in a decided and courageous attitude turned themselves into the most fearsome opponents of the criminal actions of terrorist groups . . . defying them every day" (Chavez 1995). Cuculizza, Chávez, and other women politicians' willingness to participate in a very personal and emotional way to cover up some of Fujimori's most controversial decisions affecting the rule of law and respect for civil rights constituted some of the backbone of Fujimori's media strategy. The group of highly visible Congresswomen and female Ministers had a particularly important role in Fujimori's political success. As stated by Cecilia Blondet, "many women, independently of their ideological position, 'act as face-saving' to justify the President's behaviour every morning. By so doing, they add those values that the people demand and that are dramatically lacking in the government: honesty, through trivializing the accusations of corruption that it faces; social concern, by underlying the clientelist and populist actions of the President; generally they justify and defend the arbitrary and authoritarian measures that we are accustomed to as Peruvians" (Blondet 1999b, 9; my translation).

This group of women politicians actually marked the imagination of the Peruvian people as a central feature characterizing Fujimori's rule. According to Blondet (2002), their willingness to justify the policies and behavior of their leader in a very outspoken way was due in part to their sense of owing their access to power to Fujimori himself. They perceived the interests of the regime to be directly theirs. Blondet, a key analyst of Peruvian gender politics, went as far as claiming that "they defend him [Fujimori] more than they defend themselves, they protect him in a ridiculous fashion, and their sectarism reveals similarities with the fanatical women who surrounded Abimael Guzman [The Shining Path guerilla organization's leader], or the nuns dedicated to preserve religious rituals, rather than emancipated women who enter politics with freedom" (Blondet 2002, 54; my translation).

The character of the most outspoken Congresswomen or Ministers was a particular combination of very assertive personality combined with a blind loyalty to the president justified on the basis of the latter's strong identification with the Peruvian people's interests against terrorists or corrupt elites. These politicians projected a modern image of the professional woman, autonomous in the sense of pursuing a career, but ultimately dependent upon the good will of a male leader who was seen as the final authority, just like a father is in a traditional family. From this point of view, Fujimori's reliance on women politicians as main spokespersons of the regime signaled a relatively conservative view of women's political contribution, even if it definitely positioned women at the central stage of the country's politics.[31]

Fujimori's strategy of granting women greater presence in political institutions decidedly gave his government a particularly women-friendly outlook in line with public opinion's favorable perception of women's role in politics. This also probably had some role to play in Fujimori's greater electoral success among the female electorate. Post-election polls reported a systematically greater proportion of women among pro-Fujimori voters from 1995 onwards. The pro-Fujimori female vote was four percent higher than the pro-Fujimori male vote at the 1995 elections, then 7 percent and 12 percent higher at the 2000 election's first and second round (Schmidt 2006, 163).

But this women-friendly strategy only partially achieved its goal, for at the same time some of his most noticeable policies unleashed strong popular opposition, including in some sectors of the women's movement. Amidst the steps and policies adopted purportedly to favor women's rights a number of scandals revealed the true nature of Fujimori's instrumental use of women. The most brutal was, as explained, the alleged abuses in public health provision of female sterilization. Another case arose around the electoral campaign of 2000, when the *Defensoria del Pueblo* and some independent media showed that the national food aid program, PRONAA, was in fact a propaganda machine for the reelection of Fujimori through conditioning food delivery to poor women on their electoral support, as described in Chapter 4 (Portocarrero et al. 2000; Blondet 2002).

These contradictory developments led to a renewed mobilization of some middle class women who, for the majority of them, had remained within the NGO sphere of activities for most of the 1990s. To protest against the Fujimori government's abuses committed in the name of women's rights, newly formed movements such as *Mujeres por la Democracia* (Women for Democracy) and the *Movimiento Amplio de Mujeres* (literally, Women's Broad Movement) became one of the highlights of civil society opposition beginning in the mid-1990s. One of the key slogans of *Mujeres por la Democracia* was "lo que no es bueno para la democracia no es bueno para las mujeres" (what is not good for democracy is not good for women), mirroring and complementing the earlier slogan used by Latin American feminists for years: "lo que no es bueno para las mujeres no es bueno para la democracia" (what is not good for women is not good for democracy) (Vargas 2001, 106; Rousseau 2006). The central message voiced by these movements was that democracy cannot be a secondary objective of the women's movement. What may have seemed like progress for Peruvian women, within what was considered by them to be an authoritarian framework, was unlikely to last or correspond to genuine progress, as discussed in Chapter 3.

A notable fact about this mobilization is that opposition Congresswomen—even if some were sympathetic to the protest—remained outside of it possibly to protect its nonpartisan status. One could argue that this was a lost opportunity for opposition politicians to join in with civil society's opposition to the Fujimori regime. This was part of the contradictory situation experienced by opposition Congressmembers who remained within political institutions that were deeply questioned and increasingly described as undemocratic.

Part of the women's NGOs' efforts to promote women's political participation in the formal electoral sphere, in this context, became a very divisive issue. Under the leadership of *Movimiento Manuela Ramos* and four other NGOs, the Project *Promujer* (Pro-Woman) started in 1998 during the municipal electoral campaign.[32] *Promujer* sought to promote women's political participation by disseminating information around the electoral quotas, monitoring its implementation by electoral bodies and political parties, providing assistance and training to women candidates, lobbying for a women's agenda at the Congress, and educating the population about the importance of gender equality in public affairs.

Again and very much like *Foro-Mujer*, *Promujer* assumed a protagonist role by launching public campaigns in favor of voting for women candidates and raising public support in favor of the quotas. It also became a resource center for political parties who looked desperately for women candidates when making up their lists and for women who looked for parties with which to run for election. Yet *Promujer* and its activities were soon accused—by members of *Mujeres por la Democracia* among others—of contributing to legitimize Fujimori's rule. The latter came under serious attack especially from 1997 onward when his intention to run for a third term at all costs became evident. This generated increasing tensions within the women's movement, as some organizations—not part of the *Promujer* project—opposed promoting women's electoral participation in a context where the conditions for holding free and fair democratic elections did not prevail. The 2000 electoral campaign was particularly troubling for the women's movement, just like for other sectors of civil society that split over the question of supporting or opposing the elections. The contradictions embedded in not opposing Fujimori's blatant disrespect for the rule of law were made more evident when the media revealed the extent of the political use of food aid to pressure and manipulate poor women into voting for Fujimori and the former head of the state-run food aid program, himself running as candidate to the Congress.

Conclusion: The Uses and Abuses of Women's Electoral Appeal

In the 1990s, women's greater presence in electoral processes and representative institutions, as well as in high level bureaucracy and the cabinet can be explained by a particular confluence of factors. Organized women in civil society sought to use the traditional political sphere in unprecedented ways to advance their women's rights agenda, ambitious professional women sought access to political power, and Alberto Fujimori used this opportunity to fulfill his need to build political support among these sectors. This coincidence of interests had positive repercussions on women's capacity to enter the political sphere in greater numbers and with greater impact, but it also gave Fujimori further legitimacy through his capacity to claim unprecedented openness to women's "empowerment," at a time when his rule was increasingly being contested.

Fujimori's neopopulist appeal to women promoted their entry into representative institutions and even favored some key legislative advances for women's rights, thereby playing with some values such as gender equality commonly associated with democracy and modernity. At the same time, some traditional feminine values characterized the discourse of the main female politicians defending Fujimori's policies when they claimed security and protection from the "father" of the nation. Their daily appearance in the media to defend the president amounted to a ritualized, highly emotional endorsement of some of his most abusive decisions and policies. These politicians claimed to speak in the name of the Peruvian people and its alleged need to oppose corrupt and self-serving elites and eliminate threats coming from potential or real insurgents.

This being said, this chapter also showed that the participation of a relatively small number of women in parliament can have positive repercussions on the advancement of women's rights, but only in such a context where there is a balance of political forces in civil society and within the state that allows such progress to be made. The notions of political opportunities and political agency are central to understanding the progress made by Peruvian women in the electoral sphere and the legislative agenda of the 1990s. Without the strong and active presence of organized women in civil society who prepared bills and lobbied Congress, Congresswomen would not have had the same capacity to create space for women's issues in the legislative process. Feminist NGOs' active involvement points to some of the conditions required for women's presence in the elected assembly to have some impact on legal progress. On the other hand, within political institutions, the strong hand of Fujimori was used to moderate if not eliminate the typical interparty male alliances against the inclusion of many gender equality legal claims. The neopopulist concentration of power in the hands of the president had unpredictable outcomes in favoring some key legal reforms on women's rights.

However, the Fujimori regime was not devoid of dangers for women participating in formal politics. To mention only a few of the dilemmas and difficulties involved, the critical distance that some sectors of the women's movement have had increasingly to take to oppose the arbitrary, corrupt, and authoritarian features of the regime contradicted their initial goals of promoting women's participation in electoral politics. The project *Promujer* came to be seen by some as an irresponsible or at least highly questionable move by a sector of the women's NGOs, who were unwilling, in that context, to publicly oppose or criticize Fujimori's dubious democratic politics. The problem lied in assuming net benefits from promoting a greater participation of women in political institutions irrespective of whether the latter were in fact discredited and condemned as undemocratic and corrupt, while the party system was also weak.

The legitimacy of promoting greater political participation of women in parliamentary institutions within such a controversial context was at the core of the debate within the women's movement. This dilemma reveals the complex relationship between political democracy and the promotion of women's citizenship. Intuitively, but also very explicitly in the discourse of most women rights' activists, the promotion of women's citizenship is part of a larger goal of democratizing society, which is achieved in part through reforming political institutions. Demanding women's inclusion in these institutions is a fundamental step in this process. Problems may arise when this same discourse is reproduced by political leaders who play on the value associated with promoting gender equality to enhance their legitimacy and even their democratic credentials, while at the same time their politics goes in the opposite direction. What was at stake was whether it was meaningful to promote the participation of all women from all parties when some were clearly the advocates and supporters of authoritarian practices, and more generally whether it was even worth supporting political participation in an electoral process that was increasingly seen as not providing the conditions for fair democratic elections.

This debate was partly influenced by another contentious issue, the claim that women supposedly had a different, morally superior behavior as political actors. In a political system that was notably corrupt, it was argued that women were more prone to act in favor of public interest. As noted, Peruvian public opinion became very favorable to women's participation in electoral politics, a fact that was used by Fujimori in a strategic fashion to increase his popularity. Interestingly, Congress' *Mesa directiva* elected after the controversial elections of 2000 was led by four women in an unprecedented move by Fujimori to salvage his legitimacy in the face of an otherwise very questionable electoral result.[33] While this move also corresponded to Fujimori's need to satisfy different factions of his party *Perú 21*, these Congresswomen standing to defend the regime while the president was highly questioned both internally and internationally was representative of the role assigned to women politicians by Fujimori throughout his rule. This move to appoint an all-women *Mesa directiva* even inspired one women's rights activist to publicly claim that "it's better to have four authoritarian women than four authoritarian men" (as reported in Vargas 2000, 3). On the other end of the spectrum of feminist activists, the goal of working for the establishment of democratic, transparent political institutions, as a prerequisite to include women on equal terms, was openly stated only by a limited number of civil society movements such as *Movimiento Amplio de Mujeres* or *Mujeres por la Democracia* who condemned the cooptation of women's issues by Fujimori.

The Peruvian political system experienced a greater number of women candidates amidst a deeply divisive debate on the state of democracy. Even if the elections in 2001 brought fewer women to Congress than the 2000 elections, an important fact to underline is that they were more numerous in running as candidates, with six percent of female candidates over and above the mandatory quota figure that had been increased from 25 to 30 percent. The risk of losing it all with the fall of the very regime that had promoted women's greater participation in formal political institutions did not materialize, partly because of the quick reaction of the *Promujer* project leaders who added to their slogan for the 2001 elections that voters should vote for women, but only those who were "honest and democratic," in direct response to the criticisms they had received in 2000.[34] This new slogan also had the advantage of clarifying the fact that not all women are, by virtue of being women, better politicians.

CONCLUSION

THE PARADOXES OF CONSTRUCTING WOMEN'S CITIZENSHIP UNDER NEOPOPULISM

Neopopulist politics is a fundamental element conditioning the impact of political democracy on women's movements' opportunity structures in some Latin American countries such as Peru in the 1990s. As shown in this book, neopopulism has negative effects on the institutional checks and balances and undermines collective action in civil society. This has a specific impact on women's citizenship, mediated by class and ethnic social structures. The case of Peru reveals that neopopulism can produce advances in women's citizenship construction even if these are limited and fragile. Overall, a gendered analysis of neopopulism under Fujimori highlights important paradoxes for the study of democratization and gender politics in Latin America.

Contemporary patterns of political rule and the prevalence of poverty combined to create a daunting challenge for Peruvian women in their efforts at engendering citizenship in the 1990s. The discussion of contemporary Peruvian politics presented in Chapter 2 emphasized the weakness of democratic institutions as inherited from the transition of the late 1970s, as well as the incapacity of the main political actors to consolidate democratic rule throughout the 1980s. The rise of an internal armed conflict and the unprecedented economic crisis of the late 1980s led Peruvians to look for a profound transformation of their society in the early 1990s. The nature of the changes that they obtained through the rise of power of Alberto Fujimori was very ambivalent. Personalistic and clientelistic politics increased significantly under his rule, while severe human rights violations and the implementation of neoliberal reforms meant severe setbacks in Peruvians' citizenship rights. Fujimori's neopopulist framework structured new opportunities but also many obstacles for collective actors pushing for women's citizenship claims.

The crisis that eventually led to the installation of the Fujimori regime was prompted in part by the persistent economic crisis that crystallized under the García government's economic populism. Just as well, the dramatic impact of the violent conflict between insurgent guerrillas and state security forces, which took a heavy toll of casualties not only in the civilian population in general, but particularly among popular sectors and left-wing leaders, paralyzed and ultimately destroyed the social organizations in Lima's shantytowns. The growing spiral of violence seemed hopeless at the end of the 1980s. All these factors caused the radical decline of the political party system inherited from the democratic transition period, as well as the weakening of Peruvian civil society. The state and the economy were on the verge of complete breakdown at the time of the crucial elections of 1990.

Fujimori's political "independence" represented an alternative that Peruvians democratically chose to try in 1990. However, this independence was soon to be replaced by an alliance with some sectors of the military and former military official Vladimiro Montesinos as de facto Head of Intelligence Services. Montesinos created a wide corruption net around the president, amounting to the creation of a state-backed mafia. In the balance of power favoring Fujimori's political survival beyond the coup launched by his group in 1992, international financial institutions played an important role. These institutions saw in the regime the best available guarantee that neoliberal reforms would be implemented according to the "Washington Consensus."

The illegal interruption of constitutional order in 1992 and its replacement by a new constitutional and institutional framework allowed the regime to impose its neopopulist political rule in a more systematic fashion by further centralizing power in the hands of the Executive. This meant the weakening of the Legislature's prerogatives, executive control over the Judiciary, and repeated attacks on civil liberties. His self-coup was legitimized by Fujimori on the basis of the need to build a new political and economic project to salvage the country. The restructuring of the economy along neoliberal precepts erased the social rights granted under the reformist military regime of the 1970s. Land, public services, health and pension schemes were all submitted to various degrees of privatization, and labor laws were amended to reduce social protection. All these changes were institutionalized through a new constitution in 1993, with serious impact on Peruvian citizenship.

Fujimori pursued Peru's traditional populist pattern of state-society relations based on an unmediated appeal to the popular sectors who had voted for him in the first place. Building a neopopulist platform based on a political discourse against the political class and democratic institutions, the Fujimori coalition manipulated a democratic façade and made increasing encroachments on the rules it had itself set for the façade's functioning in an attempt to remain in power indefinitely. Because of the weak capacity of democratic institutions to deliver basic public goods such as economic stability and security up to the arrival of Fujimori, these encroachments were not sanctioned by public opinion who instead valued the strong hand of Fujimori's regime.

Fujimori's populist appeal relied on a set of social programs that addressed minimally some of the most basic needs of the poorest sectors. His neopopulism differed from "classic" populism in the absence of a well-structured party that would support the regime, and in the mobilization of Peruvians based on an individualistic framework rather than as collective actors based on well-defined identities. Recurring to the same old populist technique of opposing popular interests to traditional elites and their control over the political system, Fujimori nonetheless carefully avoided creating new organizations that would allow collective subjects to institutionalize their access to the state. This shift away from corporatism corresponded to the increasing importance of the informal sector in the labor market and the transformation of many social organizations in the early 1990s. The demise of labor unions and leftist parties conditioned a move toward pragmatic popular demands seeking immediate material gains in line with dominant state ideology.

Fujimori's neopopulism also differed from Latin America's classic populism in that it applied a drastic set of neoliberal reforms aiming to reshape the Peruvian economy and the role of the state according to the "Washington Consensus." Parallel to the introduction of a free-market economic framework, Fujimori used a set of targeted social programs to create his own basis of political support among the poorest, unorganized sectors of the population who depended on the basic goods provided by the state for their daily survival. Because of the compatibility of these programs' basic rationale with the international policy prescriptions accompanying neoliberal reforms, Fujimori was able to present himself as a legitimate modernizing leader seemingly preoccupied by the poor's fate.

From the point of view of democratic institutional checks and balances, neopopulism manifested itself through the concentration of powers in the Executive, which was facilitated by Fujimori's majority control over the Legislature and the intervention of the Executive in the Judiciary through the creation of ad hoc bodies that controlled the nomination of judges. This seriously handicapped the full realization of political and civil rights, which were the most important areas of progress associated with the advent of political democracy in 1980. While Fujimori's regime provided better overall security to the majority of the population, this improvement had an important political cost. It meant the strengthening of the military's prerogatives, the setting up of mafia-type intelligence services, and the violations of several fundamental rights such as the right to life and physical integrity, freedom of expression in the media and the right to a fair trial.

Feminists, Popular Sectors, and Women Politicians: Alliances, Winners, and Losers

As explained in the preceding chapters, Peruvian women formed various organizations as of the late 1970s to put forward citizenship claims based on different material conditions and perceptions of gender interests. Taken together, the three case studies presented in this book reveal an unequal pattern of gains and losses according to the social position occupied by these collective actors in Peruvian society and depending on the type of citizenship claims they made.

For the middle-class feminist movement, the 1980s were marked by the rise of feminist nongovernmental organizations (NGOs) that emphasized feminist consciousness-raising activities, some of which were undertaken in Lima's popular neighborhoods. The focus of feminist organizations' work was on developing popular awareness of the problems of domestic violence, sexuality, and health care, among others. Relative distance from the formal political system was maintained in the 1980s except when two feminist leaders ran in the 1985 elections. The low electoral support they were able to gather revealed the limits of feminist strategies that had largely remained outside of state and party politics up to then. The lesson learned by the feminist movement was that it could be dangerous to jump into electoral politics without solid backing in society in general. The theme of autonomy, which had been central in the formation of the feminist movement in Peru and elsewhere in Latin America, became more problematic when the feminist movement made its first—unsuccessful—attempt at bringing its discourse and claims onto the formal political terrain. A new opening to influencing state policy was then seen as necessary to go further, and was aided by the changing orientations of international cooperation agencies seeking to engender the new civilian-led state apparatuses in the region.

The Fujimori regime presented new opportunities for the more institutionalized sectors of the feminist movement. Some of the strategies adopted by the main feminist NGOs at the end of the 1980s found a fertile terrain for their implementation once Fujimori was elected. The concentration of power in the hands of the president coupled with the latter's own interests in developing a women-friendly image led to some concrete possibilities of advancement regarding women's political participation and the creation of state institutions addressing women's status. The feminist NGOs' new focus on engendering the state, broadening women's access to the political system and reforming the most discriminatory laws found more space in the political context of the 1990s characterized by the weakness of political parties and the dominance of neopopulist politics.

The gains made by the feminist movement were circumscribed to a select number of areas related to civil and political rights. As shown in Chapters 3 and 5, the decision of the movement to build alliances with influential Congresswomen, irrespective of their political allegiance, and the additional resources generated by a favorable international context structured the political dynamics wherein Fujimori felt an opportunity to benefit from a few bold steps in enhancing women's citizenship. Public opinion's favorable views on women's leadership and political skills provided a politically rewarding background for Fujimori who included more women in the political sphere. The creation of a set of institutions within the state to address women's issues and rights, and the nomination of more women to key positions within the state bureaucracy and the cabinet, responded to converging interests between the feminist movement and the president's desire to construct the image of a women-friendly regime. This is one of the paradoxical outcomes of Fujimori's neopopulism.

Yet these advances were overshadowed by the basic political objectives of the Fujimori regime to remain in power at the cost of blatant disrespect for the rule of law. Neopopulist politics was inimical to institutional strengthening of the state and to the consolidation of democratic checks and balances. Some institutions created under Fujimori's rule to promote women's issues and rights were good allies of the women's movement, while some were clearly a central part of the strategies of the Fujimori regime to consolidate its clientele among women through the use of questionable policies and tools. The Specialized Women's Rights Section at the Ombudsman's Office maintained its independence within the state and worked closely with the feminist NGOs on a number of legal reforms and monitoring state compliance with recognized women's rights. It benefited from the shield created by the international financial support provided to the Ombudsman's Office, managing to protect its independence on most issues it dealt with. The political skills of the Ombudsman himself also explained the capacity of the institution as a whole to navigate through the troubled waters of the Peruvian State under Fujimori.

In contrast, the creation in 1996 of PROMUDEH, the Ministry for the Promotion of Women's Affairs and Human Development, served to further Fujimori's clientelistic goals through the management of several assistencialistic programs. Paradoxically, the ministry responded to the commitments made by heads of states at the Beijing World Conference on Women to create state agencies devoted to the promotion of women and the integration of a gender perspective in public policy. It also represented a great victory for the feminist movement because it was the first portfolio ministry of this rank in Latin America. But it was not conceived in collaboration with civil society women, nor its main policy orientations debated through formal consultations with the movement. As a result, it was difficult for the feminist movement to hold PROMUDEH accountable, as feminists were confined to an ad hoc, individual advisory role to the ministry. Contrary to other national agencies on women in neighboring countries such as Venezuela or Chile, no formal consultative mechanisms were put in place to guarantee civil society's input into the work of PROMUDEH (Friedman 1999; Franceschet 2003). This corresponded to the neopopulist style of Fujimori whereby intermediary channels of representation such as civil society organizations were not recognized as legitimate political interlocutors.

The gender quotas for legislative and municipal elections promoted first by the feminist movement and then also by most Congresswomen, came to symbolize one of the major steps taken to address unequal gender relations under Fujimori's regime. As was explained in Chapter 5, however, the numerical increase was also the result of sustained efforts by organized women in civil society who sought to play a greater role in the public sphere and the state. Yet the capacity to impose positive discrimination measures, a controversial proposal among parliamentarians, was strongly conditioned upon Fujimori's and some of his party's Congresswomen's roles. Also, the interesting results that it generated, that is, an increased number of women elected in 1998 and 2000, were connected to some aspects of the Peruvian electoral system under Fujimori, such as the single electoral district system for legislative elections, and political parties' respect for the new electoral quotas due to the monitoring role of regime-controlled electoral bodies. These two elements had an unintended positive impact on women's electoral success.

Beyond the numerical increase of women at the Congress that came only in 2000, the work of a few Congresswomen collaborating among themselves independently of their party affiliation and in conjunction with some feminist NGOs was in itself significant in explaining some of the advances in women's citizenship rights. Even with a small number of women elected, some important legal reforms were made that corresponded in great measure to the claims made by the feminist movement in the preceding years. The Permanent Commission on Women at the Congress, set up in 1996, acted as a catalyst to create a small institutional space within the larger male dominated Congress. It became a unique site of collaboration and competition between Congresswomen from both Fujimori's and opposition parties, who shared an interest in advancing some of the women's movement's agenda.

In the political system of the 1990s, with the disappearance of traditional political parties and the domination of a set of unstable coalitions of individual politicians, elected women were freer to make a difference on women's issues. As long as the proposed bills did not have any direct impact on economic policy or national security matters, as when they focused on domestic violence, the criminal code, or gender quotas, they often found an ally in the president who played the progressive leader in front of a Legislature that debated these issues quite intensely. Fujimori's neopopulist hold on Congress facilitated the ease with which an interparty alliance of Congresswomen joined in a progressive agenda of reforms on some women's civil and political rights.

However, this scenario was not devoid of serious dilemmas for women's rights activists. The support provided by some important feminist NGOs to the promotion of women candidates through the *Promujer* project raised the question of political participation as the central dilemma facing all politicians (and citizens, for that matter) in the post-1992 framework: whether or not to lend legitimacy to a regime that clearly manipulated democratic rules and institutions in order to remain in power indefinitely. By detaching the promotion of women's political participation from the evaluation of the broader political context, especially during the 2000 electoral campaign, feminist NGOs that worked within *Promujer* decided to side with the dominant logic of the political parties under the Fujimori regime: a short-term willingness to gain political terrain in the electoral sphere. Electoral participation sent the message that conditions for free and fair elections were satisfactory, even when Fujimori clearly violated the constitution in his attempt to remain in power for a third mandate.

This issue was one of several that strongly divided the feminist movement in the 1990s and underlined the danger of separating a women's rights agenda from the broader goal of democratizing Peruvian politics. The improvements in state-provided family planning services formed another instance of major victory for the women's movement that was nonetheless accompanied by disillusions and outrage when the cases of reported forced sterilization were brought forward by some feminist lawyers. This seriously questioned Fujimori's goals behind the promotion of women's reproductive health and autonomy. What initially consisted of the first serious effort by the Peruvian state to provide universal access to modern family planning techniques to Peruvian citizens turned out to be seen as one of the most brutal components of the regime's poverty eradication policies. By encouraging medical personnel to perform speedy sterilizations at the cost of women's right to freely give their consent and their right to bodily integrity, the family planning program ended up being used apparently to limit the number of children born in the poorest sectors. What was first seen as an advance in women's social rights turned out to be a new form of state control over women's bodies. The opposition it generated within different sectors of Peruvian society, including in the feminist movement, as well as the international attention it received, created sufficient pressure for Fujimori to accept partial corrective measures. Yet the battle was hard-fought and divisive for the feminist movement, which struggled over the best strategies to adopt in order to retain state commitments regarding access to family planning.

The vulnerability of the majority of women in the face of some of the Fujimori regime's programs was connected to the regime's policy orientations. Its focus was not on promoting women's citizenship rights, but rather on using women's central, traditional role as provider of family and community well-being to achieve instrumental goals such as distributing food staples or reducing the birth rate in targeted sectors. Fujimori's neopopulist appeal used the material deprivation and the weakness of poor women's organizations to justify the creation of a number of state agencies and programs, most of which were eventually attached to PROMUDEH. These served to strengthen the regime's clientelism. Through these agencies and programs, Fujimori managed to appear as a leader who cared about the popular sectors' material and security needs, particularly those of women. In fact, these programs became major sources of corruption and political control, as highlighted in Chapter 4.

The creation of a state agency that centralized the distribution of food aid (PRONAA) had the dual effect of seriously undermining the autonomous organizations led by popular sector women leaders and creating a new mechanism to control popular neighborhoods. The popular neighborhoods and rural communities' dependence on food aid made it relatively easy for the state to manipulate these sectors' political support for the benefit of Fujimori. This cooptation process weakened the collective kitchens' leadership, which was already fragile at the beginning of the 1990s. After a decade of relative success in building an alternative to traditional state clientelism in the shantytowns, women's organizations were dramatically undermined by the state's unprecedented level of investment in the institutionalization of public food aid programs under Fujimori.

A number of elements contributed to this development. First, the decision by international donors to transform their food assistance into financial assistance for state-led poverty alleviation programs led to a shift in food aid initiative from the hands of church-based NGOs and popular sector organizations to the state. The virtual monopoly over food aid conceded to the state nullified the main power resource on which the autonomous collective kitchens' organization was based, that is, control over food staples for meal preparation and distribution in the community. Paradoxically, Fujimori's decision to create a state program that would deliver food aid to all grassroots collective kitchens, rather than only to the ones formally created by the state as was the case under previous governments, corresponded to one of the historical claims of the autonomous collective kitchens' movement. Recognition by the state of their equal right to benefit from state subsidies was a major victory for this movement. Yet this recognition was not accompanied by the setting up of participatory mechanisms to protect the role of the autonomous collective kitchens' federation in the management of food aid programs. Hence, this meant the gradual erosion of the federation's membership and its growing political irrelevance.

Ultimately, this Peruvian experience points to some of the limits of popular sector women's organizations based on survival activities, particularly when it comes to the representation of popular class women's interests. The fact that they centered their main identity and claims on the right to food and the right to be recognized as the main channel for community food service delivery certainly constituted a strong impediment to survive as an autonomous collective actor once the state managed to dominate the field of food aid successfully. This is in spite of the fact that, when created, these organizations displayed a new political agency for women and carried new claims on the State as social actors with a specific discourse on women's citizenship.

As popular sector women's organizations they were created around women's traditional identity as mothers and spouses responsible for the welfare of their families and communities, giving priority to what could be termed "practical gender interests" (Molyneux 1985). Yet as argued in Chapter 4, the collective kitchens' movement lost the opportunity to develop a more comprehensive and emancipatory vision of women's citizenship. Moreover, the lack of sustainability of the organization as a political actor, which is quite distinct from its social reproduction function, was revealed in a particularly stark way when the collective kitchens' movement lost the active support of its main allies, feminist and development NGOs. The relationship between the NGOs and the autonomous collective kitchens' organization in the early 1990s suffered from the former's decision to develop a more professionalized and technical approach to the work they were pursuing in popular neighborhoods, as well as the latter's desire for greater autonomy and the capacity to manage project funding. Ultimately, what amounted to a depoliticization of the organization led to its increasing marginalization in the popular sectors.

Problems in renewing the leadership of the collective kitchens' movement amidst the worst period of political violence in popular neighborhoods also explain the weakness of the organization throughout the 1990s. The lack of space for popular sector women leaders who had served in these survival organizations and who now aspired to move to higher levels of responsibility and social achievement was only partially solved by the entry of some of them in municipal politics. In the meantime, the living conditions of the women they sought to represent had not improved substantially, and the little progress seemed to be entirely owed to the Fujimori government through its capacity to eradicate political violence, end hyperinflation, and provide sustained food aid.

Overall, the main advances in women's citizenship rights under the regime of Fujimori belonged to the sphere of political and civil rights, while social and economic rights were generally left aside, with the exception of increased universal access to family planning. The neopopulist and neoliberal nature of Fujimori's rule conditioned his government's differential treatment of women's rights claims according to how they related to his broader policy framework. The latter was instrumental in the strengthening of some feminist NGOs who had a greater stake in pushing forward a set of civil and political rights. The popular sector women's movement, on the other hand, was shattered by the multiple crises of the early 1990s and the cooptation of its members by the state. As a result, the limited platform of rights that it had put forward in the second half of the 1980s dissolved as a result of state intervention and its relative isolation in the 1990s.

In both the gains in civil and political rights and the losses in social and economic rights, the influence of international factors cannot be dismissed. On the positive side, the international mobilization of multilateral organizations, women's NGOs, and donor agencies in the first half of the 1990s around the cycle of UN World Conferences provided resources and political support to the agenda of the feminist movement focused on reproductive rights, political participation, and legal equality. It also gave strong incentives to governments in developing countries to endorse part of this reform agenda. In the case of the Fujimori government, this combined with a decision to use a broad discourse on the importance of women's role in society to create a stronger base of popular support among Peruvian women—and men, arguably.

"Transnationalism reversed," a term used by Elisabeth Friedman to describe the feedback effect of transnational organizing on national social movement dynamics, contributed to deepening some trends already present in the women's movement, such as the professionalization of some of its constituents and the distancing of a certain movement elite from the reality of grassroots women (Friedman 1999). However, the involvement of Peruvian feminist organizations in transnational activities was crucial to counterbalance the role that Fujimori decided to play in international fora dedicated to women's issues. Moreover, it is likely that had women's organizations not been involved so intensely in transnational organizing in the 1990s, the president would have found it less attractive to participate himself and to put forward new policies associated with his international commitments.

The other side of the international influence is less positive. The losses experienced in social and economic rights were strongly connected to the agenda of international financial institutions (IMF, World Bank) that supported Fujimori from the beginning of his rule in 1990. The implementation of structural adjustment and liberalization policies promoted by these institutions was accompanied by the introduction of a social policy paradigm focused on social compensation to the poorest sectors. Targeted social sectors received basic needs subsidies but social policy did not provide the tools for the majority of the population excluded from the formal labor market to develop sustainable employment venues. The political use of the new set of social programs financed in part by international funds kept popular sectors in a dependent, clientelistic relationship to the state. This was one of the central tools through which Fujimori consolidated his neopopulist rule. The autonomous collective kitchens movement became one of the first targets of this new policy and was ill-prepared to mount a counter-offensive when many of its members became *fujimoristas*, actively supporting the president.

What Does Democracy Do to Women's Citizenship?

Several contentious issues concerning women's political mobilization in the context of post-transition democratic frameworks can now be reassessed in light of what has been learned from the Peruvian case. As mentioned in Chapter 1, most of the first wave literature on women and democratization claimed that the turn to democratic rule in the 1980s engendered a retreat of women's organizations from the political sphere in comparison to the periods marked by authoritarian rule and regime transitions (Friedman 2000, Jaquette 1994, Waylen 1994).

While the Peruvian women's movement went through several transformations in its organizing since the late 1970s, the transition to democracy as such did not have a profound influence on the movement, in comparison to other Latin American cases. The feminist movement, a central actor in the political struggle for engendering Peruvian citizenship, emerged from the transition to democratic rule in 1980 as a young movement that had only recently created a set of autonomous organizations. A number of feminist women had been active in left-wing parties in the opposition to the military regime, but women's organizations were not at the forefront of antiauthoritarianism. The nature of the military regime in Peru, relying on a much lower level of repression than was the case in other South American authoritarian regimes, may explain the less predominant role of the women's movement in initiating the opposition to the regime. Moreover, Peru's reformist military regime as of the late 1960s was generally favorable to women's advancement, as described in Chapter 2. Overall, the regime did not massively repress unions and other left-wing organizations. This led to a situation where the women's movement did not occupy a "privileged" place in the configuration of the organized opposition to military rule. The transition was accompanied by a decision by the main feminist groups to work outside the political party system in order to build their own identity and organizational tools. The women's movement as a whole, including its popular sector components, was just starting to take shape in the early 1980s. Therefore, the turn to democratic politics in Peru did not lead to a marginalization of women's organizations, contrary to what was reported in the literature on the transitional dynamics in neighboring countries (Alvarez 1990; Jelin 1990; Jaquette 1994; Jaquette and Wolchik 1998; Waylen 1994, Friedman 2000).

In Peru, the first decade of democratic rule in the 1980s was generally favorable to the strengthening of women's organizations in popular sectors, in the wake of the Left's increased political success at that time (Roberts 1998). However, from the perspective of the institutionalization of their citizenship claims, the limited victories of the collective kitchens' movement arose in connection to the first months of the government of Alberto Fujimori at the very beginning of the 1990s, when it acknowledged their claim to public food aid and their quest for state recognition as social organizations. This situation is paradoxical due to the weakening of democracy's rule of law and institutional checks and balances under Fujimori. Moreover, this victory was accompanied by the decline of the organization, rather than its strengthening. Thus the success of the collective kitchens' movement was short-lived.

Taken as a whole, the twenty years of democratic rule from 1980 to 2000 tend to look more favorable to women's political inclusion in the state and in party politics during the time period when democracy was undergoing severe attacks in the 1990s. The fate of women's civil and political rights was relatively more positive under Fujimori, in contrast to the common wisdom found in the literature on his rule that describes the post-coup regime as "electoral authoritarian."

The second factor that needs to be emphasized in order to nuance the findings of the first wave literature on women and democratization is the degree of development of the women's movement itself at the time of the transition to democracy. Women's movements have dynamics of their own that interact with the broader political framework in complex and particular ways conditioned only partly by political regime type. As described in the case of Peru, the fact that the movement was only emerging in 1980 impeded it to engage the broader political arena. Instead, it concentrated its energies on building its organizations, in the feminist and popular sectors, and only in the 1990s did it put forward new strategies to penetrate the formal political terrain, either by seeking to influence policy making or enter the electoral realm, with the exception of the failed and short-lived attempt by two feminist activists to run as candidates in the 1985 elections.

These findings echo Susan Franceschet's call to refrain from using the period of military dictatorships as the norm against which to measure subsequent patterns of women's mobilization (Franceschet 2003, 12). In many ways, the former may constitute an exceptional period in terms of providing women with "a common enemy," as well as alienating them from the state because of the nature of the military regimes' projects, at least in the cases of Chile, Argentina, and Brazil (Franceschet 2003). The political space and opportunities for the women's movement vary under military dictatorships and democratic regimes. Yet the consequences of regime type on women's mobilization are connected to the degree and type of state repression against various collective actors including women's movements as well as particular patterns of state formation. The state, under democracy or authoritarianism, is conditioned not only by regime type but by development models, gender, racial, and other ideologies, depending on the configuration of political forces and institutions.

These observations should not be taken as an undervaluation of democracy. Political democracy in contemporary Latin America is generally perceived as a highly preferable type of political regime. As the yearly survey carried by *Latinobarómetro* demonstrates, Latin Americans value democracy even as they also generally mistrust some of its key institutions such as the Legislature and political parties. Democracy in its liberal-representative form provides at least formally the institutional and constitutional protection of fundamental freedoms and the principle of nondiscrimination that is central to many women's rights claims. Not surprisingly, women's organizations are often at the forefront of civil society's defense of democracy, as was also revealed in the case of Peruvian women's mobilization in the 1990s.

The second wave literature on Latin American women's mobilization discussed in Chapter 1 highlights the fact that the turn to democratic regimes in the 1980s generated new forms of women's mobilization, more oriented toward the state and less politically radical in their discourse (Alvarez 1998 and 1999; Barrig 2000b; Molyneux 2001). Transitions to democracy, sometimes with universal suffrage for the first time as in Peru, were a breakthrough in the expansion of political and civil rights. The women's movement throughout the region seized the opportunity it was given to extend the new logic of political equality and individual freedom and apply it to their struggle for transforming gender relations and ending discrimination (Molyneux 2001).

Throughout the region, the new democratic framework led the feminist movement to focus on women's access to political institutions, since the new rules of the game had to be improved to allow a greater presence of women, an issue that had not been sufficiently or even minimally considered during the transitional processes, including in Brazil or Chile where women participated actively in transitional politics. This was seen by feminists as an important goal in and of itself, as well as a necessary step to increase the pressure for the adoption of many legal reforms aiming at ending gender discrimination. The political and financial support provided by the international agenda of United Nations' World Conferences in the first half of the 1990s boosted the various feminist organizations involved at the international and national levels in pushing their governments to adopt and implement new commitments.

As a result, by the end of the 1990s, most governments in the region had created a state agency or high-level institution overseeing the impact of public policy on women and making recommendations for state policy to address gender discrimination (Barrig 2000b; Molyneux 2001). Yet the autonomy and power of these agencies has generally been shown to diminish over time according to changes in government, as in the case of Brazil's more conservative governments in the 1990s (Alvarez 1994), or even during the rule of a single government. Argentina's President Menem for example showed a sudden reversal of policy vis-a-vis women's rights in the mid-1990s, after initially promoting several positive reforms (Waylen 2000). Chile's SERNAM (*Servicio Nacional de la Mujer*) was also given less autonomy and power than originally envisaged by the first *Concertación* government because of major disagreements within the *Concertación* coalition about politically sensitive issues such as abortion and divorce (Waylen 2000). SERNAM's mandate remained limited to pilot projects and policy reform initiatives, rather than policy implementation (Franceschet 2003, 20–21).

These different cases show that the role of women's mobilization in civil society in the political process leading to the creation of these specialized state agencies did not guarantee continuing influence on how their mandate would evolve. Whether or not the agencies were formed as a result of the mobilization of women's rights advocates during a political transition, like in the case of Brazil and Chile, or through presidential decree following the transition, like in the case of Argentina and Peru, their strength, resource endowments, and policy priorities are dominated by the political interests of the government of the day. Clearly, institutional strengthening is required in that area.

Democracy can also be key to pursue other dimensions of women's political rights. By the end of the 1990s, many Latin American states had adopted positive discrimination measures to increase women's participation in elections as a result of international, regional, and national lobbying by women (Waylen 2000 and 2007; Molyneux 2001; Htun and Jones 2002). The notable exception in this regard is the case of Chile, where quotas were established only at the level of some political parties of the "renovated Left" who created positive discrimination mechanisms for filling party positions (Waylen 2000, 784). The rapidity with which gender quotas were adopted at the level of national elections in Peru under Fujimori and in Argentina under Menem, both with a neopopulist pattern of political rule, contrasted with the difficulties women encountered in Chile, where the party system is strongly institutionalized and democratic politics has an old history (Mainwaring and Scully 1995). In Brazil, where the party system is less stable than in Chile but where democratic institutions have proven more resilient than in Peru under Fujimori or Argentina under Menem, electoral gender quotas have been adopted gradually first at the municipal level in 1995 and then at the national level in 1997. What the Argentinian and Peruvian cases share on this issue is the importance of presidential support to the quotas, as well as the formation of a multiparty coalition of women parliamentarians supported by civil society groups, who lobbied for their adoption. This suggests that neopopulist concentration of power and low barriers to cross-party alliances seem to be two key political conditions facilitating joint collective action in support of positive discrimination measures to redress gender inequality in electoral politics.

While the number of elected women in Latin America increased overall throughout the 1990s, results are very uneven, ranging from 22 percent increase in Argentina to no difference in some countries or even one percent decrease in Brazil (Htun and Jones 2002, 41). In 1999, women held 5.7 percent and 7.4 percent of the seats in each House in Brazil, and 27.6 percent and 5.6 percent in Argentina's Houses. In Peru, in 2001 17.5 percent of Congress seats were won by women. The impact of the quotas overtime is more significant in some countries, with Argentina having 40 percent of women elected at the national level, and Peru 29 percent at the end of 2008. In other countries such as Brazil, progress is more modest and women occupied 9 percent and 12 percent of the seats in each House at the end of 2008 (Interparliamentary Union Women in National Parliament database).

A more encouraging trend is the collaboration between Congresswomen from different parties around proposals to reform discriminatory laws or adopt laws that favor women, as illustrated in Chapter 5. While women's cross-party collaboration on gender issues is not widespread throughout the region, again a contrast can be found between the more constraining institutional features of Chile's coalition politics and Peruvian politics under Fujimori where the dominance of the Executive and parties' relative weakness facilitated Congresswomen's collaboration. The case of Peru under Fujimori confirms other case studies' finding that a crucial element for legal reform success is that women be organized strategically outside the legislature to pressure for gender equality bills and ally with women parliamentarians (Waylen 2000 and 2007; Friedman 2000; Molyneux 2001).

Overall, then, the institutionalization of women's movements' politics, through new relationships between women's organizations and the state, is strongly associated with the restoration or creation of democratic regimes, even if the pace and degree of gender policy development varies importantly from one case to the other. A more negative outcome of this trend is that it generated new sources of exclusion for some sectors of the women's movement that were not able to compete on a equal footing in the institutional terrain (Alvarez 1999; Friedman 1999; Franceschet 2003). As shown in this book, the case of Peru is another example of women's NGOs professionalization often reinforcing "paternalistic" and instrumental relationships between middle class organizations and popular sector women, due in part to state and international funders' project implementation requirements.

Gendered Neopopulism in Peru

To go back to Fujimori's politics, it is unclear whether democracy was a necessary condition for several of his pro-women achievements such as the creation of a ministry on women's status or the inclusion of more women in high-level state positions. This question illustrates the complexity of Peruvian politics in the 1990s. Fujimori's gender policies and rhetoric were framed as 'democratic gains' in the context of the president's high electoral popularity, while in fact they were adopted when democratic accountability was being severely undermined. Moreover, one could well argue that he would have proceeded similarly in his gender politics had he managed to retain the authoritarian regime his coalition set up right after the coup in 1992, before ceding to international pressure. However, as was argued in several chapters of this book, Fujimori's decision to build political support bases among women was strongly related to his willingness to consolidate his electoral success.

Fujimori's neopopulism had a multifaceted impact on state-society relations. The gendered reading of his regime presented in this book reveals a set of unexpected strategies to legitimize his rule, as well as concrete consequences on the women's movement's different sectors. Peru's neopopulism was informed by a gender discourse, and it was consequential for the dynamics of women's citizenship construction.

In contrast to the corporatist model associated with past forms of Peruvian populist politics under Velasco or García, Fujimori's neopopulism combined democratically sanctioned legitimacy through the voting booth with the absence of a solid party capable of institutionalizing the regime's power. The successive electoral "machines" or movements put together by the president to organize and channel electoral support became the norm even outside his circles during the 1990s and even beyond. The instability of the party system allowed the president to pick and choose his allies in an arbitrary fashion to suit his own goals, even going as far as paying his opponents to join his ranks. In light of the very high concentration of power in the hands of the Executive and Fujimori's capacity to win or buy a majority of seats in all the legislative elections following his self-coup, the Legislature could not reasonably be considered an accountability mechanism or a counterweight to executive power during most of the 1990s.

This had paradoxical consequences on women's citizenship construction. Because of the decision made by Fujimori to endorse a vaguely defined "pro-women agenda," important legislative reforms concerning women's rights were adopted. The marginal relevance of political parties as institutions, caused in part by the "independent politician" model successfully imposed by the president himself, facilitated Congresswomen's push for certain women's rights issues promoted by feminist NGOs. Opposition Congressmembers did not follow a strong party discipline, both internally and in their role as opposition, whereas Fujimori's party was relatively easy to mobilize in favor of these reforms because of the President's own positions on some of these issues. An interesting parallel can be made with Weyland's argument on the affinities between neopopulism and neoliberalism (Weyland 1996). Just as neopopulist politics allows the executive to bypass established political channels such as the legislature to impose harsh neoliberal reforms, it can also facilitate the adoption of important advances in terms of gender equality reforms. The staunch opposition to some of these issues such as publicly funded access to modern contraceptives, even among relatively left-to-center parties such as the APRA, was neutralized by Fujimori's capacity to dictate the terms of the reforms. Even the entrenched elite of the Catholic Church was criticized by Fujimori as being antimodern and dogmatic for refusing to allow women to use contraceptives.

The fact that Fujimori's neopopulism was based on his government's commitment to abiding by the dominant development models promoted by the international financial institutions, rather than on classic populism's anti-imperialism, also contributed to inserting a gender policy reform agenda in Peru's politics. Indeed, beyond the

Washington Consensus, the international community in the 1990s carried a strong set of gender policy reform models. These derived from women's rights activism at international conferences, were transformed by the main international aid agencies, and then "trickled down" to national political settings such as Peru. Fujimori seized this opportunity to present his government as resolutely modern, gender-progressive. His image of a women-friendly leader was produced in great measure by the unprecedented number of women he nominated in high-level positions, as ministers, deputy-ministers, prosecutors or directors of state agencies, contrasting importantly with past Peruvian politics. Compared to Argentinian Carlos Menem, another neopopulist president who initially favored some advances on women's rights, Fujimori strikes out as a much more pro-female politician. Menem appointed only one woman as cabinet minister, and only as of 1996 after seven years of rule (Waylen 2000, 778). Moreover, the inclusion of women from shantytown grassroots organizations in the municipal and national party lists, many of them but not all within Fujimori's lists, meant a significant transformation of the gender, class, and ethnic characteristics of political candidates. Neopopulism *a la* Fujimori meant a democratization of the formal electoral sphere by opening it up to the most marginalized social sectors. This is another paradoxical finding in light of Fujimori's frequent abuse of the rule of law including how he intervened during electoral processes.

While promoting women's leadership and creating high-level institutions purportedly devoted to the improvement of women's status, all very significant moves by Fujimori, he also legitimized his policies on the basis of a traditional discourse emphasizing women's central role as mothers. Shantytown and rural women were the key targets of the regime's clientelistic social programs. These programs relied on women's unpaid work in the sphere of social reproduction to deliver their benefits and channel state resources. The president's neopopulist appeal within popular sectors therefore carried through with a conservative vision of women's contribution to society. The traditional gender division of labor within the poorest sectors was largely maintained during Fujimori's rule if one considers state discourse and policies during that period. This affected predominantly women who were recent migrants from rural areas or among the second and third generations of migrants, as well as rural women, most of them being indigenous or *cholas*.

A central facet of Fujimori's neopopulism is how he avoided referring to class categories in his political appeal to Peruvians, preferring to insist on a conflict between the elite and the masses as in old-style populism. In the context of the 1990s, when Peru's Left had significantly vanished from the main political scene, the internationally dominant neoliberal paradigm was rarely questioned by the majority of elected politicians. Added to the volatile nature of the party system and the near-hegemony of political "independents" relying on noninstitutionalized electoral machines, it was difficult to distinguish political actors on the basis of the traditional Left-Right continuum. On some "moral issues" and on the confidence placed in women in key decision-making positions, Fujimori appeared relatively more progressive compared with past Peruvian presidents and other party leaders including most from the Left. As a consequence, it might be questionable to consider Fujimori's political female entourage as another example of right-wing movements such as the one described by Baldez (2002) or Power (2002) in their analysis of the women's movement's dynamics around the 1973 coup in Chile.

However, the nature of the political discourse displayed by *Fujimoristas*, analyzed in its historical context, points to classic conservative tactics. The strategic use of threats about a potential return to the insecurity and violence prevailing during the conflict with the Shining Path allowed Fujimori to win the allegiance of many women and men who had previously been Left supporters or active militants. Supporting and working with the Fujimori regime was, according to the latter's rhetoric, a matter of preserving order and restoring the foundations for a strengthened state and a more productive economy. These objectives were to be pursued with the central help of women as primary caregivers concerned with the good of their community. Not surprisingly, the *Fujimorista* women in positions of power, either at Congress' Permanent Commission on Women, at the head of PROMUDEH or elsewhere in the state, did not come out of a past involvement with the women's movement. They therefore endorsed Fujimori's attacks on left-wing and other critical social organizations.

Notwithstanding the more massive space occupied by women in Peruvian politics under Fujimori, the weakness of civil society limited significantly the extent to which the entry of more women could combine with an enlargement of women's citizenship at the level of social and economic rights. The neopopulist mode of political representation, legitimized by Fujimori's apparent capacity to "impose order" and his claim to "end traditional elite privileges," systematically undermined the power of autonomous organizations in civil society, particularly those making claims that were contrary to his neoliberal model of state-society relations. This had the greatest impact on the majority of poor women who were the most directly affected by this limited form of citizenship devoid of significant transformation in their socioeconomic status.

Similarly, the human rights abuses committed by the Fujimori government included violations of some women's rights, as experienced painfully by women in the cases of the coerced sterilizations or the political manipulation of food aid programs, to name the most obvious. Only in 2009 was Fujimori convicted by Peru's Supreme Court for torture, kidnapping and forced disappearances committed during the early 1990s. During his rule, the weakness of accountability mechanisms, especially in the judicial sphere, represented a particularly difficult aspect of this "electoral authoritarian" government. Neopopulist rule meant that few institutional guarantees existed for the consolidation of policies and institutions created for the purpose of advancing women's citizenship. This created severe dilemmas for feminist NGOs seeking to pursue an institutionalist reform agenda. Their credibility was at stake when they accepted to play by the rules set by Fujimori, even if this could mean concrete gains in legal and formal terms.

If neopopulist leaders have emerged since the 1990s in different countries of Latin America such as Brazil, Argentina, Venezuela, and even Bolivia, their political projects vary extensively, in contrast with older forms of populism. Some are clearly much more respectful of democratic principles and human rights than Fujimori was. The gendered dimensions of these governments also differ on many counts (see Kampwirth 2010; Rousseau 2010). As shown throughout this book, in the case of Fujimori's neopopulism, his top-down control of the state combined with a strong neoliberal reform program. Some organized women managed to strategically advance their claims within the limited space available and with great risks for the sustainability of their action. Neopopulism does not foster civil society's autonomy nor does it work to build institutional channels mediating between the state and civil society. This had profound consequences for the more socially vulnerable categories of mobilized and nonmobilized women, who were the most dependent on the state and who were rendered even more so under Fujimori. Even if popular sector women were the main target and audience for Fujimori's neopopulist appeal, paradoxically they were the ones who lost the most, with the exception of some grassroots women leaders who managed to gain from the openings in party politics and build a new political career.

The use of women as the objects and subjects of his politics particularly characterized Fujimori's neopopulism, allowing his government to legitimize its rule upon an apparently inclusionary project articulated in part along a gender discourse. Peruvian women have made several inroads during that decade to become more equal citizens. However, social inequalities have risen and women were the first to pay the price. When Fujimori flew in exile in 2000, Peruvian women faced the daunting task of (re)building new cross-class bases of solidarity and autonomous organizations. Neopopulism is likely to remain one of the central patterns of political rule in several Latin American countries including Peru, at least in the near future. The challenge for all organized women is to remain firm and defend their emancipatory claims while not losing sight of the need to find more allies outside the state when it threatens to destroy their organizational capacity.

Appendix

Interviews

Rosa-María Alfaro, Founder and Researcher, NGO *Asociación de comunicadores sociales Calandria* (interviewed on May 22, 2001).
Jeanine Anderson, Professor of Anthropology, *Pontificia Universidad Católica del Perú* (interviewed on February 16, 2001).
María Mercedes Barnechea, Coordinator, Gender Equality Fund, Canadian Embassy in Peru, and former advisor to the *Comisión Nacional de Comedores* while employed by the NGO *TACIF* (interviewed on February 22, 2001).
Maruja Barrig, Consultant and Member of *Mujeres por la Democracia* (interviewed on May 16, 2000).
Miyaray Benavente, Professional staff, Food Support Program, NGO *Alternativa* (interviewed on February 8, 2001).
Violeta Bermúdez, Coordinator, Human Rights and Democratic Institutions Program, *United States Agency for International Development* (Peru Office), and Former Coordinator, NGO *Movimiento Manuela Ramos* (interviewed on May 15, 2001).
Cecilia Blondet, Director, *Instituto de Estudios Peruanos* (interviewed on July 17, 2000).
Elena Caro, Professional staff, NGO *FOVIDA* (interviewed on March 14, 2001).
Patricia Carrillo, Professional staff, Program on Women, Citizenship and Politics, NGO *CESIP* (interviewed on April 27, 2000).
Mirta Correa, Director, Gender and Citizenship Program, NGO *Calandria* (interviewed on July 4, 2000).
Gloria Cubas, Professional staff, NGO *Alternativa* (interviewed on May 9, 2001).
Martha Cuentas, Executive Director, NGO *FOVIDA* (interviewed on February 21, 2001).
Rosa Espinal, Municipal Councillor, Metropolitan Lima, former president of the second *Junta directiva* of the *Federación de mujeres organizadas en*

Professional and other titles are those that applied on the date of the interview, unless otherwise specified. All interviews were carried out in Lima, Peru.

centrales de comedores populares autogestionarios y afines de Lima y Callao (FEMOCCPAALC) (interviewed on February 15, 2001).

Leonor Espinoza, Professional staff, Food Security Program, NGO *INCA-FAM* (interviewed on January 24, 2001).

Jennie Dador, Professional staff, Program on Political Participation, NGO *Movimiento Manuela Ramos* (interviewed on February 14, 2000).

Elizabeth Dasso, Civil Society and Social Development Specialist, *World Bank* (Peru Office) (interviewed on July 13, 2000).

Felicita Gallegos, President, *Federación de mujeres organizadas en centrales de comedores populares autogestionarios y afines de Lima y Callao (FEMOCCPAALC)* (interviewed on March 12, 2001).

Aída García, Board Member, NGO *CEDAL* (interviewed on January 19, 2001).

Narda Henríquez, Professor, Social Sciences and Gender Studies Program, *Pontificia Universidad Católica del Perú* (interviewed on May 3, 2000).

Rosa Landavery, *Central nacional de mujeres de sectores populares del Perú « Micaela Bastidas »*, Former leader of the *Comisión nacional de comedores* (interviewed on February 15, 2001).

Yolanda Mariluz, Advisor to the central district office of the collective kitchens in Independencia, former interim President of the first *Junta directiva* of the *Federación de mujeres organizadas en centrales de comedores populares autogestionarios y afines de Lima y Callao* (interviewed on April 19, 2001).

Beatriz Merino, former Congressmember (1990–1992 with *Frente Democrático*; 1995–2000 with *Frente Independiente Moralizador*) (interviewed on May 18, 2001).

Diana Miloslavich, Professional staff, Municipal Government Advisory Program, NGO *Centro de la Mujer Peruana Flora Tristan* and Member of *Movimiento Amplio de Mujeres* (interviewed on May 30, 2001).

Cecilia Olea, President of the Board of Directors, *Centro de la Mujer Peruana Flora Tristan* (interviewed on July 5, 2000 and April 25, 2001).

Rocío Palomino, Consultant, and former advisor to the *Comisión Nacional de Comedores* while employed by the non-governmental organization CESIP (interviewed on February 13, 2001).

Patricia Sanabria, Professional staff, Human Rights Program, NGO *Movimiento Manuela Ramos* (interviewed on February 14, 2000).

Benedicta Serrano, Municipal Councillor, Santa-Anita district, and former president of the first *Junta directiva* of the *Federación de mujeres organizadas en centrales de comedores populares autogestionarios y afines de Lima y Callao* (interviewed on February 16, 2001).

Relinda Sosa, former president of the third *Junta directiva* of the *Federación de mujeres organizadas en centrales de comedores populares autogestionarios y afines de Lima y Callao* (interviewed on March 8, 2001).

Ana Tallada, President, *Red nacional de promoción de la mujer* (interviewed on July 18, 2000 and May 8, 2000).

Ysabel Valverde, former Secretary General of the central district office of the collective kitchens in the district of San Juan de Lurigancho (interviewed on March 9, 2001).
Roxana Vásquez, Director, NGO DEMUS (interviewed on May 8, 2000).
Rocío Villanueva, Head of the Specialized Section on Women's Rights at the *Ombudsman's Office (Defensoría del Pueblo)* (interviewed on April 23, 2001).
Victoria Villanueva, Coordinator, NGO *Movimiento Manuela Ramos* (interviewed on May 15, 2001).
Susana Villarán, Professional staff, *Instituto de Defensa Legal* and Member of *Mujeres por la Democracia* (interviewed on July 13, 2000).
Ana María Yañez, Coordinator, Program on Political Participation and Leadership (*Promujer*), NGO *Movimiento Manuela Ramos* (interviewed on April 20, 2001).
Gina Yañez, Coordinator, Human Rights Program, NGO *Movimiento Manuela Ramos* (interviewed on February 27, 2001).

NOTES

INTRODUCTION

1. Douglas Chalmers defines the politicization of the State in Latin America as when "political institutions are considered tentative and are viewed instrumentally, not as permanent fixtures. Many problems that might be resolved by reference to a fixed set of procedures or laws are likely to be dealt with purely politically, subject to resolution only through a clash of forces. Policy-making institutions are themselves subject to active political questioning and conflict, and their reconstruction is viewed not as much as a violation of basic principles but as the outcome of a particularly important confrontation" (Chalmers 1977, 24).
2. This new literature includes, among others, Schild 1998; Friedman 2000; Waylen 2000; Craske and Molyneux 2002; Gonzalez and Kampwirth 2001; Molyneux and Razavi 2002; Lind 2004; Franceschet 2005; Waylen 2007.
3. For a good critique of gender essentialism, see among others Fuss 1989, 140.
4. Stetson and Mazur define "State feminism" as the contribution of the State to "the formation of feminist policy and increas[ing] the access of women's movement activists to the political process" (Stetson and Mazur 1995, 272). State feminism is typically but not necessarily the product of the activities of state structures specifically created for such purposes. See also Rai and Lievesley 1996; Randall and Waylen 1998; and Lovenduski 2005.
5. In Latin America, political rights like the right to vote were sometimes granted to women under nondemocratic regimes such as in Peru in 1955. Many social rights were granted by Cuba's socialist regime. The most in-depth work on State feminism in democratic states has focused on Europe, North America, and Australia. See for example Lovenduski 2005.
6. These movements had varying importance at the local or regional level. For a discussion of peasant women's movements, see among others Radcliffe 1993 and Francke 1990. Absent from my study is also the case of women in the left-wing guerillas such as the *Sendero Luminoso* (Shining Path) or the *Movimiento Revolucionario Tupac Amaru* (Tupac Amaru Revolutionary Movement-MRTA). For an interesting analysis of their role and motivations see among others Coral 1998.

Chapter 1

1. Victor Raúl Haya de la Torre devoted his life to APRA activism and signed the new Peruvian Constitution on his death bed in 1979.
2. Alan García, also a gifted orator, won the presidency in 1985. In 2006, he garnered 52.6% of the second round vote and was reelected as president.
3. The new APRA government elected in 2006 is generally pursuing neoliberal reform.
4. A "radial" conceptual definition draws upon different sociological dimensions (e.g., economic, political) to define a concept while recognizing that a single manifestation of the concept will likely not equally or adequately cover these different dimensions. See Weyland 2001.
5. Works that do address these issues: Wolfe 1994, Macpherson 2003, and on Eva Perón in Argentina's populism and her legacy, see Taylor 1979; Fraser and Navarro 1982; and Auyero 2000. A forthcoming volume edited by Kampwirth presents for the first time a set of comparative case studies of gender and populism in Latin America (Kampwirth 2010).
6. The conditions leading to the consolidation of new democratic regimes are the subject of much theoretical and empirical research. Democratic consolidation is generally said to exist when there is: 1.) consensus on the part of all political actors to abide by the rules defining a political democracy; 2.) an actual belief among these actors in the value of democracy as the most appropriate form of governance; and 3.) genuine respect among these actors for, and promotion of, the rule of law as enshrined in a constitution (Linz and Stepan 1996). For a critical discussion of the notion of democratic consolidation, see Brachet-Marquez 1997. For a discussion of the proliferation of different democratic regime sub-types see O'Donnell 1994; Collier and Levitsky 1997; O'Donnell 1999b and Levitsky and Way 2002.
7. For another interesting piece on this subject, see Blofield 2006.

Chapter 2

1. Lynch reminds us that neither the *Alianza Popular Revolucionaria Americana* (APRA) Party, nor the *Acción Popular* (AP) Party, the two most important populist parties, called for the granting of political rights for the illiterate, which formed the majority of the population up to the late 1970s. It was only in 1978 that both parties joined the call of left-wing parties for universal suffrage. In Lynch 1999, 103.
2. This label was adopted by some Peruvian scholars and analysts to describe the Fujimori regime, acknowledging the uniqueness of its characteristics combining democratic and authoritarian elements. See among others Cotler and Grompone 2000, Rospigliosi 1995.
3. The Left won a third of the 100 seats of the Constituent Assembly. However, the APRA and the PPC agreed to cooperate, which allowed them

to control the Assembly. See Lynch 1999 and Mauceri 1997, among others.

4. The number of registered politically motivated violent actions at the national level went from 219 in 1980 to as high as 3,149 in 1989, whereas in Lima, it went from 38 in 1980 to as high as 1,374 in 1992. In Lynch 1999, 145.
5. Annual inflation rate was close to 100 percent in the last years of the Belaúnde government. In Contreras and Cueto 1999, 285.
6. García decided that Peru would allocate only the equivalent of ten percent of export revenues as debt repayment, whereas the debt was worth about 362 percent of Peru's exports at that time. In Cotler 1995b, 126.
7. According to surveys reported in Cotler 1995b, García's rate of popular support went as high as 94 percent in the first months of his rule. In Cotler 1995b, 127.
8. The proportion of the economically active population working in the informal sector grew steadily from 32.8 percent in 1981 to 45.7 percent in 1990 (Roberts 1998, 240). Moreover, between 1985 and 1990, workers' average salary in the formal sector lost 50 percent of its value (Guerra 1995, 443).
9. The political independent model also implies the formation of a "movement" as a flexible group of supporters willing to promote the leader (Cotler 1995b).
10. At the Senate, FREDEMO held 32 percent of the seats, the APRA 25 percent, *Cambio 90* 22 percent, *Izquierda Unida* ten percent, *Izquierda Socialista* five percent; at the House of Representatives, FREDEMO held 30 percent, the APRA 25 percent, *Cambio 90* 17 percent, IU ten percent, *Izquierda Socialista* five percent, and seven percent of the seats were filled with Independents (Tuesta Soldevilla 2001).
11. It is a matter of debate whether Fujimori and the Military had agreed on the coup much longer before it was carried out, and therefore the use of the term "delay" is not meant to be understood as necessarily intentional. Indeed, Kenney argues that Fujimori had to convince the military not to carry the coup before his assuming power in July 1990 (Kenney 2004, 248). In any case, the explanations given for the "delay" are useful to understand the context within which the decision to carry the coup was made.
12. The label "political movements," in contrast to political "parties," was increasingly used to describe the rise of numerous political groupings that formed for specific elections, headed by and composed by political outsiders. These movements were made up of individuals more interested in a political career than sharing an ideological stance or political platform. Fujimori's *Cambio 90* is paradigmatic of this trend dominating the 1990s, displacing traditional political parties from the electoral scene. See, among others, Tanaka 1998; Conaghan 2000; Levitsky and Cameron 2001, and Tanaka 2002.

13. One member of the *Jurado Nacional de Elecciones* (Electoral Tribunal) even wrote a discordant opinion on the results of the process, calling for its annulment because of the proven existence of fraud. In Rospigliosi 1995, 327.
14. The single electoral district provided for parties to each present a unique list of candidates corresponding to a nation-wide "district," among which all the Congress members are to be elected by the whole electorate.
15. Fujimori won with 64.4 percent of the vote in the first round. Yet 40.8 percent of the ballots for the legislative elections were declared null. This and other problems related to vote count generated a lot of confusion and a lack of trust in the electoral process. See, among others, Schmidt 1999.
16. For a detailed account of the 2000 elections, see among others Transparencia 2000b.
17. The OAS General Assembly meeting held in Windsor, Canada, in June 2000 adopted a resolution creating a high-level mission to Peru led by Canada's Foreign Affairs Minister, which made a series of requirements on the Fujimori regime to be complied with in the following months under the authority of a "Mesa de diálogo" (Dialogue Group) where opposition and civil society representatives had a strong voice.
18. Cotler and Grompone recall that the support of the CIA to Montesinos and Fujimori's government ended when these made the mistake of lying to public opinion about a supposed arms traffic between Jordanian and Colombian guerrillas that the Peruvian army allegedly unmasked. Following this announcement at a press conference, the Jordanian government denied and claimed that in fact the arms had been sold to the Peruvian army with the agreement of the U.S. government. The end of U.S. support probably prompted greater divisions within the regime. In Cotler and Grompone 2000, 69–70. See also Cameron 2006.
19. The more critical stance found some echo in the more recent North American literature as well. Levitsky and Way proposed the notion of "competitive authoritarianism" to describe the hybrid regimes like Fujimori's (Levitsky and Way 2002). This contrasts with previous efforts at characterizing it as a limited or partial form of democratic regime. Competitive authoritarian regimes differ from authoritarian regimes because of the continued functioning of formal democratic institutions. They differ from limited forms of democratic rule where violations of the minimum criteria defining democracy nonetheless do not reach a level of seriousness which would "alter the level playing field between government and opposition." Competitive authoritarian regimes are therefore characterized by frequent and serious violations of the minimum democratic standards that alter the level playing field in favor of the regime incumbents, yet the latter are incapable or unwilling to eliminate four significant arenas of democratic contestation: the electoral arena, the legislature, the judiciary, and the media. The possibility for the opposition to use these arenas in a creative fashion to challenge or weaken authoritarian rulers is seen as

the distinctive feature of competitive authoritarian regimes. See also the volume edited by Julio F. Carrión (2006) that defines Fujimori's regime as a form of "electoral authoritarianism."
20. Levitsky mentions that the parties that dominated electoral politics in the 1980s with around 90 percent of the vote (APRA, IU, AP, and the PPC) were reduced to around ten percent of the popular vote in the mid- to late-1990s. In Levitsky 1999, 86.
21. The numerous cases of bribery filmed by Vladimiro Montesinos, Head of Secret Services who was controlling the regime's wide patronage networks, were later shown on public television when the regime collapsed. The videotapes included several Congress members from both opposition and government. See Degregori 2001.
22. These polls were carried out by Peruvian firms DATUM and APOYO. Only the Lima population is included in their sample. See Kenney 2004 for details.
23. The military as an institution did not have any direct interest in the implementation of this neoliberal economic program, yet as explained earlier, it was seen by some sectors as a necessary means by which to restructure the economy and reform the state. Both objectives were connected to perceived and real challenges faced by Peruvian society, of which the primary effect on the military was the intense pressure to maintain internal order in light of insurgent war and economic chaos.
24. The so-called "Fujishock" implemented in August 1990 generated price hikes, the elimination of subsidies, and major cuts in public spending. This led to an immediate increase of about 5 million of the population living under the poverty line. In Béjar 1996, 55.
25. As will be explained in Chapter 4, one of the most important women's organizations in Lima's popular sector neighborhoods, the collective kitchens' movement, certainly voted en masse for Fujimori in 1990, due to women's disillusion with the Left and the APRA (Lora 1996, 144).
26. The main such program, the *Programa de Emergencia Social* (Social Emergency Program), was later transformed and renamed *Fondo Nacional de Compensación y Desarrollo Social* (National Fund for Compensation and Social Development—FONCODES). Even if it was designed as a compensatory scheme, it remained in place until the end of Fujimori's rule and followed through afterwards.
27. My argument characterizing Fujimori's regime as neopopulist differs from the views of Peruvian political sociologists Lynch (1995; 1999), who emphasized an irreversible crisis of populism affecting the Peruvian political system when it emerged out of the Velasco military regime, and Cotler and Grompone (2000) who describe *Fujimorismo* as an authoritarian regime that is wrongly seen, according to them, as neopopulist because of its popularity among popular classes. In the North American literature, Burt (2004 and 2006) also disagrees with a broader notion of populism encompassing regimes of the likes of Fujimori's. These dissenting views

rely on a more traditional concept of populism associating a set of redistributive economic policies with a particular mode of interest mediation through mass-based parties dominated by a charismatic leader.

CHAPTER 3

1. Nongovernmental organizations are legal entities recognized formally by the State and that usually sign agreements with funders to carry-out specific projects. Groups are associations of individuals who share similar objectives and/or interests. The difference in status does not, per se, indicate anything about the political or even financial power of both types of collective action.
2. Classifying women's organizations as feminist or nonfeminist is a matter of debate and interpretation, although a few organizations can resolutely be termed feminist. Some of them use the label more explicitly than others and show greater radicalism in their discourse and agenda. The criteria used for categorizing them as feminists is whether they emphasize explicitly the goal of transforming gender relations on more equal terms in their mandate and discourse. For the purpose of this chapter, when I refer to the feminist movement, this will include organizations such as Movimiento Manuela Ramos, Centro de la Mujer Peruana Flora Tristán, DEMUS, Centro de Estudios Sociales y Publicaciones (CESIP), Incafam, Mujer y Sociedad, Aurora Vivar, CENDOC-Mujer. The feminist movement also consists of smaller organizations or associations, individual activists and thinkers, and various networks such as the Red Nacional de Promoción de la Mujer, Consorcio-Mujer, Foro-Mujer.
3. See Chapter 5 for more details.
4. See Chapter 5 for more details.
5. As explained in Chapter 4, the distancing occurred as a result of various processes.
6. Diana Miloslavich, Founding member of MAM, interview with the author, May 2001.
7. Susana Villarán, Founding Member of MUDE, interview with the author, July 2000.
8. The most important was the Women's March during the *Marcha de los Cuatro Suyos* organized by the opposition to rally with Presidential candidate Alejandro Toledo in July 2000.
9. This issue was raised by several NGO representatives interviewed by the author.
10. The integration of the language of human rights in feminist discourse was a global phenomenon in the early 1990s. It was reflected in the gains made at the International Conference on Human Rights held in Vienna in 1993, where the global women's movement successfully lobbied for the official recognition of "women's rights as human rights." See Weldon 2006.

11. This was a Latin American regional trend as described in Olea 1998 and Acosta et al. 2000.
12. This cycle included, aside from the conferences already mentioned, the World Conference on Social Development and the Habitat Conference.
13. Rocío Villanueva, interview with the author, April 2001. Many women's rights activists pointed to the SWRS as a crucial ally.
14. Rocío Palomino, interview with the author, February 2001; also mentioned in Schmidt 2003 and 2006.
15. Roxana Vásquez, interview with the author, May 2000.
16. See Chapter 5 for more details on Luisa Maria Cuculiza's role in Fujimori's second mandate.
17. Roxana Vásquez, interview with the author, May 2000.
18. See more details in Chapter 5.
19. The numerous interviews with feminist NGOs's representatives (see list of interviews in appendix) all indicated a very high level of trust toward and appreciation of the Ombudsman's SWRS. The priorities pursued by Rocío Villanueva's office corresponded in great measure to the ones pursued by the feminist movement in the 1990s. Issues of domestic violence and violence against women in general, reproductive rights, women's political participation, and a gender-sensitive analysis of the law and jurisprudence, were the four areas where most efforts were concentrated at the SWRS. See Defensoría del Pueblo 2000.
20. Rocío Villanueva, interview with the author, April 2001 (my translation).
21. Jennie Dador, interview with the author, February 2000.
22. One of the dangers for women's rights advocates consisted also in not wanting to side with the fierce critics of the state family planning program such as the Catholic Church and other conservative actors.
23. While the political interest of these individuals was at stake in promoting some women's issues, this does not imply that these individuals were not convinced of the importance and validity of promoting women's rights as such.
24. Violeta Bermúdez, interview with the author, May 2001.

CHAPTER 4

1. In 1997, 25.4 percent of Metropolitan Lima's population was extremely poor and 23.1 percent were poor. In 2004, 36.6 percent were extremely poor and 33.2 percent were poor (*Instituto Nacional de Estadistica e Informatica*—INEI Peru, available at: *http://www.inei.gob.pe/Sisd/index.asp*).
2. The organization of the *Vaso de leche* (Glass of Milk) is also an interesting case to study. Committees run by women prepare the milk from milk powder received from the Lima municipality and distribute it on a daily basis to the children and expecting or breastfeeding women of their neighborhoods. For a good overview of the movement, see García 1994.

3. The first *comedores* were set up in the district of El Agustino, between the end of 1978 and early 1979. In Lora 1996, 25.
4. The issue of the autonomy of the *comedores autogestionarios* is of course a matter of debate and interpretation, in light of the fact that, fundamentally speaking, they always depended to some extent on outside food staples providers (nongovernmental organizations, the Church or the State) for their functioning; moreover, the space occupied by the political advising performed by professionals from popular education centers or nongovernmental organizations, as will be described further, also conditioned the autonomy of the *comedores autogestionarios*.
5. Given an average family size of five persons. In Lora 1996, 33.
6. The *menú* is a meal sold at a very low cost for popular consumption.
7. See, among others, Sara Lafosse 1984; Barrig 1986; Blondet 1991; Delpino 1991; Blondet and Montero 1995; Barrig 1996; Córdova 1996; Lora 1996; Tovar 1996; Balbi 1997.
8. Rocío Palomino, interview with the author, February 2001 (my translation).
9. CNC, *Memorial dirigido al Señor Presidente de la República Dr. Alan García Peréz*, August 1986, reproduced in Lora 1996, 221–24.
10. Rocío Palomino, interview with the author, February 2001; Elena Caro, interview with the author, March 2001; Miyaray Benavente, interview with the author, February 2001.
11. CNC, *Memorial dirigido al Señor Presidente de la República Dr. Alan García Peréz*, August 1986, reproduced in Lora 1996, 221–24.
12. *Propuesta de subsidios directos de la Comisión Nacional de Comedores*, September 14, 1988, reproduced in Lora 1996, 225–29.
13. "Protesta con propuesta . . . sin respuesta!" *La República*, September 24, 1989, reproduced in Lora 1996, 234.
14. "Pronunciamiento de la Comisión Nacional de Comedores," *La República*, May 20, 1990, reproduced in Lora 1996, 236 (my translation).
15. Law no.25307 "Declares as priority national interest the work carried out by the Mothers' Clubs, the Glass of Milk Committees, the Autonomous Collective Kitchens, the Family Kitchens, the Family Centers, the Daycare centers and other grassroots social organizations in their activities in the provision of food aid." (my translation)
16. Rocío Palomino, interview with the author, February 2001.
17. Law no.25307, reproduced in García 1995.
18. Interviews with former leaders of the *Comisión nacional de comedores* and the *Federación metropolitana de comedores autogestionarios de Lima y Callao*, Lima, 2001 (see list in appendix).
19. The activities of the Shining Path in Lima's shantytowns intensified as of 1988 and remained a dominant feature of shantytown life until some months after the start of the harsher counterinsurgency strategy implemented by the Fujimori regime after the self-coup of 1992. Popular sector organizations were infiltrated by guerillas or security forces, their members

threatened, coopted or killed; numerous intimidating tactics were used including physical violence, blackmail and looting. See Palmer 1994.
20. Benedicta Serrano, interview with the author, February 2001.
21. As a "commission," the CNC had originally been given the mandate to work for the creation of a more developed and structured organization to represent the autonomous collective kitchens. However, from the beginning of the CNC in 1986 onwards, its leaders focused much more on the consolidation of the collective kitchens movement and on a number of concrete issues.
22. Rosa Espinal, interview with the author, February 2001 (my translation).
23. Relinda Sosa, interview with the author, March 2001.
24. Rosa Landavery, interview with the author, February 2001.
25. María Mercedes Barnechea, interview with the author, February 2001.
26. Miyaray Benavente, interview with the author, February 2001.
27. Ibid.
28. Rocío Palomino, interview with the author, February 2001.
29. Elena Caro, interview with the author, March 2001.
30. Ibid.
31. As explained by Relinda Sosa, interview with the author, March 2001, and by Martha Cuentas, interview with the author, February 2001. This new orientation accompanied the de-politicization of NGO work and the greater technical expertise they were expected to deliver within the projects funded by foreign donors. Training local government leaders and assisting in the building of local capacity for the delivery of health, education, and other services became the focus of many NGOs in the 1990s.
32. Between 1992 and 1999 four ministries (Defense, Economy, Finance, and the Ministry of the Presidency) controlled over 60 percent of the national budget. In Adrianzén 1999, 254.
33. Benedicta Serrano, interview with the author, February 2001.
34. Leonor Espinoza, interview with the author, January 2001.
35. Benedicta Serrano, interview with the author, February 2001.
36. Felicita Gallegos, interview with the author, March 2001.
37. This political manipulation during electoral campaigns was particularly visible during the 2000 elections, documented by many electoral observers and journalists. See, for a good summary, Transparencia 2000.
38. Interview with various leaders of the *Federación de mujeres organizadas en centrales de comedores populares autogestionarios y afines de Lima y Callao*, in the context of the Electoral Observation Mission of the International Federation of Human Rights Leagues, the International Centre for Human Rights and Democratic Development, and the Spanish Federation of Human Rights Associations, Lima, March 2000.
39. Relinda Sosa, interview with the author, March 2001 (my translation).
40. Felicita Gallegos, interview with the author, March 2001.
41. Yolanda Mariluz Quiñone, interview with the author, April 2001.
42. Gloria Cubas, interview with the author, May 2001.

43. Gloria Cubas, interview with the author, May 2001; Rosa Espinal, interview with the author, February 2001.
44. Jeanine Anderson, interview with the author, February 2001.
45. Ibid.
46. Ibid.

CHAPTER 5

1. The *Ley Orgánica de Elecciones* (Organic Law on Elections, Law no.26859) adopted in 1997 provided for a compulsory minimum of 25 percent of male and female candidates in the party lists for legislative elections. The same provision was introduced at the municipal level a few months after (*Ley de Elecciones Municipales*, Municipal Elections Law no. 26864). In 2001 this minimum was increased to 30 percent through a reform of the electoral code voted by Congress (Law no.27387, December 29, 2000). In Promujer, *El Cuarto Femenino* 3 (10), April 2001.
2. Promujer, *El Cuarto Femenino* 2 (8) June 2000: 22.
3. Although no nation-wide survey was available on these issues, the survey performed by the *Instituto de Estudios Peruanos* under the coordination of Cecilia Blondet showed that support for women politicians differed from one region to the other. For example, on the question whether the sex of the candidate had any importance in determining a voter's potential support, 72 percent of the Peruvians living in Lima answered it did not have any importance, with 42 percent of people living in Huancayo (a major city in the Andes) and 58 percent living in Iquitos (a major city in the Amazon) thinking it did not have importance. But on the other hand, in Huancayo 71 percent of respondents felt that the fact of being a woman candidate influenced positively voters' propensity to vote for that candidate, whereas in Lima it was 60 percent of the respondents and in Iquitos 55 percent. In Blondet 1999a, 13–14.
4. Yet only 50 percent of the population knew of the existence of such legislation in March 2000 when asked in the survey by Calandria.
5. The first women running at presidential elections were Mercedes Cabanillas, for the APRA, and Lourdes Flores Nano for the *Partido Popular Cristiano* (Christian Popular Party—PPC) both at the 1995 elections. The APRA got a very low percentage of the vote throughout all of the 1990s, whereas Lourdes Flores Nano dropped out of the race before election day in 1995.
6. For more on the political party system in the 1990s, see Cotler 1995b, 117–41; Grompone and Mejía 1995; Tanaka 1999; and Levitsky and Cameron 2001.
7. These observations also apply to a great extent to the party system prior to 1990. See Enrique Bernales. 1990. *Parlamento y democracia*. Lima: Constitución y Sociedad, as quoted in Klatzer 2000, 224. Matland finds

that internal party democracy is one of the key features enhancing women's participation as candidates (Matland 1998).
8. This component of the Peruvian voting system involves the possibility for voters to select up to two candidates of their liking among the list registered by the party for which they wish to cast their ballot, independently of the position occupied by the candidates on the lists. The number of preferential votes a candidate wins determines if she or he will fill one of the seats won by his or her party.
9. Numerous reports of the civic group Transparencia, which specializes in electoral observation and civic education, have testified to the difficulties voters face in dealing with the double preferential voting system. Some do not understand that the two candidates should come from the same party list; others still do not know that they have the right to choose individual candidates aside from the president. See among others Transparencia 2000a, 1.
10. Promujer, *El Cuarto Femenino* 2 (7) March 2000: 4–5.
11. In *Mujer y Politica. Las mujeres en el nuevo Congreso. Han funcionado las cuotas?* supplement of the daily *El Comercio*, August 26, 2000, 5. This analysis does not report on the women candidates that did not accede to a seat.
12. Ana-Maria Yañez, interview with the author, Lima, April 2001, and International IDEA 2003.
13. The creation of this Commission was first proposed by FORO-MUJER in their "Open Letter of FORO-MUJER to Women Candidates" during the 1995 electoral campaign. In Foro-Mujer 1995. When interviewed, Beatriz Merino mentioned that the idea of forming such a Commission occured to her while in Beijing. Beatriz Merino, interview with the author, Lima, May 2001.
14. Beatriz Merino, interview with the author, Lima, May 2001.
15. This obstruction and lack of respect for the legislative initiatives of opposition members was generalized and did not affect Congresswomen more than Congressmen.
16. Beatriz Merino, interview with the author, Lima, May 2001 (my translation).
17. As stated in a study of women's participation in the 1998 municipal elections, published by the nongovernmental organization CESIP, women candidates often suffered from traditional political practices whereby positions in the lists are "sold" and depend on the party leaders' own preferences. Moreover, women often received very demeaning comments from male candidates and were often relegated to technical tasks in the campaign, having an incredibly hard time in pushing their ideas to be included in the platforms of their respective political organizations. In CESIP 1999, 35–60.
18. Virginia Vargas, from the *Centro de la Mujer Peruana Flora Tristan*, ran for the House of Representatives in the Lima district, and Victoria Villanueva, from the *Movimiento Manuela Ramos*, ran for the Senate. Both

were nominated by their organizations, but through a nonrepresentative and nonconsensual process, and as a result did not represent their organizations officially. However once candidates, they benefited from wide support within the feminist movement. In Vargas 1989, 53–70.

19. Since the United Left was a coalition of parties, it had a flexible structure that included candidates running as independents, such as the two feminist leaders who ran in the 1985 elections.
20. These organizations were: *Aurora Vivar*, *CENDOC-Mujer*, *CESIP*, *Centro de la Mujer Peruana Flora Tristan*, *Mujer y Sociedad*, and the *Movimiento Manuela Ramos*.
21. Diana Miloslavich, former member of *Foro-Mujer*, interview with the author, Lima, May 2001.
22. This newsletter started without any financial support, but the United Nations Population Fund in Lima later decided to fund it. Victoria Villanueva, interview with the author, Lima, May 2001.
23. Ana-María Yañez, Coordinator of the Political Participation and Leadership Program at the NGO Movimiento Manuela Ramos, argued that in the period from 1995 to June 1999, thirty laws were approved that directly or indirectly referred to women's status or rights. She added: "We believe that this is due, in great measure, to the role of Congresswomen who have opened channels of participation for civil society, in particular through the Commission on Women, and insodoing have collected the demands and necessities of women and converted them into binding legal norms" (my translation). In Promujer, *El Cuarto Femenino*1 (4) June 1999: 3.
24. Violeta Bermúdez, interview with the author, Lima, May 2001.
25. Beatriz Merino, interview with the author, May 2001.
26. Beatriz Merino, interview with the author, Lima, May 2001.
27. The contradictions and difficulties this situation generated for women's NGOs are discussed in Chapter 3.
28. Beatriz Merino, interview with the author, Lima, May 2001.
29. Archives of the Commission on Women of the Peruvian Congress, Legislature 1997–1998.
30. As reported in the article "Qué le pasó a la Cuculizza?" published in Lima's weekly *Caretas* available online: *http://www.caretas.com.pe/1999/1590/Cuculiza/cuculiza.htm*
31. For other interesting cases of women's political conservatism in the region, see Kampwirth and Gonzalez 2001 and Power 2002.
32. This project was funded by USAID right after the former coordinator of Movimiento Manuela Ramos, the leading member organization behind *Promujer*, was hired by USAID as key program coordinator (although she claimed not to have been part of the project approval process). Violeta Bermúdez, interview with the author, May 2001.
33. The "*Mesa directiva*" of the Congress is a body made up of four Congressmembers officially elected by Congress to organize the work of the institution and structure its legislative agenda.
34. Violeta Bermúdez, interview with the author, Lima, May 2001.

References

Acosta, Gladys, Maruja Barrig, Sonia Montaño, Cecilia Olea, and Virginia Vargas. 2000. *Las apuestas inconclusas. El movimiento de mujeres y la Cuarta Conferencia Mundial de la Mujer*. Lima, Peru: Ediciones Flora Tristan.

Adrianzén, Alberto.1999. El gasto social, el Estado y la pobreza en el Perú. In *Construyendo una agenda social*, ed. Narda Henríquez. 253–64. Lima, Peru: PUCP Fondo Editorial.

Alfaro, Rosa María. 1996. *Mundos de renovación y trabas para la acción pública de la mujer. Sondeo de opinión*. Lima, Peru: Asociación de Comunicadores Sociales Calandria.

———. 1998. *La política, sí es cosa de mujeres*. Lima, Peru: Asociaciones de comunicadores sociales Calandria.

———. 2000. *Metamorfosis de lo público desde las identidades de género. El caso de la participación de las mujeres en los gobiernos locales*. Paper presented at the Seminar "*Participación política de las mujeres en el Perú: Su impacto en el sistema democrático*," organized by the Grupo Gobernabilidad, March 14, Lima, Peru.

———. 2000. *Liderazgo político de las mujeres en la gestión municipal. Informe de investigación*. Lima, Peru: Asociación de Comunicadores Sociales Calandria.

Alternativa. 1993. *La Ley no.25307. Su viabilidad política y económica*. Lima, Peru: Centro de Investigación Social y Educación Popular Alternativa.

Alvarez, Sonia. 1990. *Engendering democracy in Brazil: Women's movements in transition politics*. Princeton, NJ: Princeton University Press.

———. 1994. The (trans)formation of feminism(s) and gender politics in democratizing Brazil. In *The women's movement in Latin America. participation and democracy*, ed. Jane Jaquette, 13–63. Second edition. Boulder, CO: Westview Press.

———. 1998. Latin American feminisms "go global": Trends of the 1990s and challenges for the new millennium. In *Cultures of politics, politics of culture: Re-visioning Latin American social movements*, ed. S. Alvarez, E. Dagnino, and A. Escobar, 293–324. Boulder, CO: Westview Press.

———. 1999. Advocating feminism: The Latin American Feminist NGO "boom." *International Feminist Journal of Politics* 1(2): 181–209.

Alvarez, Sonia, Evelina Dagnino, and Arturo Escobar, eds. 1998. *Cultures of politics, politics of culture: Re-visioning Latin American social movements.* Boulder, CO: Westview Press.

Anderson, Jeanine. 1985. The UN decade for women in Peru. *Women's Studies International Forum* 8(2): 107–9.

Anderson, Jeanine. 1996a. *El conocimiento, el género, el cambio.* In *El conocimiento como un hecho politico,* ed. Virginia Guzman and Eugenia Hola, 29–52. Santiago, Chile: Centro de Estudios de la Mujer (CEM).

———. 1996b. *Gobiernos inmerecidos: La mujer peruana y el Estado en el Perú.* In *Triángulo de poder,* ed. Geertje Lycklama, Nijeholt, Virginia Vargas and Saskia Wieringa, 271–308. Bogotá, Colombia: Tercer Mundo Editores.

———. 1997. *Pueden los ciudadanos tener familia?* In *La ciudadanía a debate,* ed. Eugenia Hola and Ana María Portugal, 102–17. Santiago, Chile: Isis Internacional.

Arendt, Hannah. 1998. *The human condition.* 2nd ed. Chicago: University of Chicago Press.

Auyero, Javier. 2000. *Poor people's politics: Peronist survival networks & the legacy of Evita.* Durham, NC: Duke University Press.

Balbi, Carmen Rosa, ed. 1997. *Lima. Aspiraciones, reconocimiento y ciudadanía en los noventa.* Lima, Peru: PUCP.

Baldez, Lisa. 2002. *Why women protest: Women's movements in Chile.* Cambridge, England: Cambridge University Press.

Barber, Benjamin. 1984. *Strong democracy: Participatory politics for a new age.* Berkeley, CA: University of California Press.

Bardalez, Elsa, Martin Tanaka, and Antonio Zapata, eds. 1999. *Repensando la política en el Perú.* Lima, Peru: Red para el desarrollo de las ciencias sociales en el Perú.

Barnechea, María Mercedes. 1991. *El proceso de centralización de comedores en San Juan de Lurigancho. Con tu puedo y con mi quiero.* Lima, Peru: TACIF.

Barrett, Michelle, and Anne Phillips, eds.1992. *Destabilizing theory: Contemporary feminist debates.* Stanford, CA: Stanford University Press.

Barrig, Maruja. 1986. *Democracia emergente y movimiento de mujeres.* Lima, Peru: DESCO.

———, ed. 1988. *De vecinas a ciudadanas. La mujer en el desarrollo urbano.* Lima, Peru: SUMBI (Servicios Urbanos y Mujeres de Bajos Ingresos).

———. 1994. The difficult equilibrium between bread and roses: Women's organizations and democracy in Peru. In *The women's movement in latin america. Participation and democracy,* ed. Jane Jaquette, 151–75. Second edition. Boulder, CO: Westview Press.

———. 1996. Women, collective kitchens, and the crisis of the State in Peru. In *Emergences: women's struggles for livelihood in Latin America,* ed. J. Friedman, R. Abers, and L. Autler, 59–77. Los Angeles: UCLA Latin American Center Publications.

———. 1998. Female leadership, violence, and citizenship in Peru. In *Women and democracy: Latin America and Central and Eastern Europe*, ed. Jane Jaquette and Sharon Wolchik, 104–24. Baltimore: Johns Hopkins University Press.

———. 2000a. *La persistencia de la memoria. Feminismo y Estado en el Perú de los 90*. Lima, Peru: Cuadernos de investigación social de la Pontificia Universidad Católica del Perú.

Barrig, Maruja. 2000b. Introducción (o de cómo llegar a un puerto con el mapa equivocado). In *Las apuestas inconclusas. El movimiento de mujeres y la IV Conferencia mundial de la mujer*, ed. Gladys Acosta, Maruja Barrig, Sonia Montaño, Cecilia Olea, and Virginia Vargas, 7–28. Lima, Peru: Ediciones Flora Tristan.

Barrig, Maruja, and Virginia Vargas. 2000. Conclusiones. In *Al rescate de la utopía. Reflexiones para una agenda feminista del nuevo milenio*, ed. Ivonne Macassi and Cecilia Olea, 221–28. Lima, Peru: Ediciones Flora Tristan.

Basu, Amrita, ed. 1995. *The challenge of local feminisms*. Boulder, CO: Westview Press.

Beiner, Ronald, ed. 1995. *Theorizing citizenship*. New York: State University of New York Press.

Béjar, Héctor. 1996. La política social peruana entre 1990 y 1995. *Socialismo y Participación* 70: 53–60.

Bendix, Reinhard. 1964. *Nation-building and citizenship. Studies of our changing social order*. Berkeley, CA: University of California Press.

Bermúdez, Violeta. 1993. Abortion: The debate and strategies in Latin America. The Peruvian Case. In *Women: watched and punished*. CLADEM, 209–21. Lima, Peru: CLADEM.

Bermúdez, Violeta. 1995. Proceso nacional: La sociedad civil. In *Mujer y Desarrollo* (Seminario "Mujer y Desarrollo: Compromisos y Perspectivas de Acción"), 27–32. Lima, Peru: Comisión Permanente de los Derechos de la Mujer del Consejo Nacional de Derechos Humanos—Ministerio de Justicia.

Bernales, Enrique. 1995. La crisis de los partidos políticos. In *Sociedad, partidos y estado en el Perú. Estudios sobre la crisis y el cambio*, ed. Carlos Fernández Fontenoy, 127–90. Lima, Peru: Universidad de Lima.

Blofield, Merike. 2006. *The politics of moral sin. Abortion and divorce in Spain, Chile and Argentina*. New York: Routledge.

Blondet, Cecilia. 1991a. *Las mujeres y el poder. Una historia de Villa El Salvador*. Lima, Peru: Instituto de Estudios Peruanos.

———. 1991b. Las organizaciones femeninas y la política en época de crisis. In *Las mujeres y la vida de las ciudades*, ed. María del Carmen Feijoo and Hilda María Herzer, 141–57. Buenos Aires, Argentina: Grupo Editor Latinoamericano.

———. 1995. Out of the kitchens and onto the streets: Women's activism in Peru. In *The challenge of local feminisms*, ed. Amrita Basu, 251–75. Boulder, CO: Westview Press.

———. 1996. In no-man's land: Poor women's organizations and political violence in Lima's neighborhoods. In *Emergences: Women's struggles for livelihood in Latin America*, ed. J. Friedman, R. Abers, and L. Autler, 79–90. Los Angeles: UCLA Latin American Center Publications.

———. 1998. *La emergencia de las mujeres en el poder. ¿Hay cambios?* Lima, Peru: Instituto de Estudios Peruanos.

———. 1999. *Percepción ciudadana sobre la participación política de la mujer. El poder político en la mira de las mujeres.* Lima, Peru: Instituto de Estudios Peruanos.

———. 1999. *Las mujeres y la política en la década de Fujimori.* Lima, Peru: Instituto de Estudios Peruanos.

———. 2002. *El encanto del dictador. Mujeres y política en la década de Fujimori.* Lima, Peru: Instituto de Estudios Peruanos.

Blondet, Cecilia, and Carmen Montero. 1994. *La situación de la mujer en el Perú 1980–1994.* Lima, Peru: Instituto de Estudios Peruanos.

———. 1995. *Hoy: Menú popular. Comedores en Lima.* Lima, Peru: Instituto de Estudios Peruanos and UNICEF.

Boesten, Jelke. 2006. Pushing back the boundaries: Social policy, domestic violence and women's organisations in Peru. *Journal of Latin American Studies* 38(2): 355–78.

Brachet-Marquez, Viviane. 1997. Democratic transition and consolidation in Latin America: Steps towards a new theory of democratization. *Current Sociology* 45(1): 15–53.

Burt, Jo-Marie. 2004. State making against democracy. In *Politics in the Andes. Identity, conflict, reform*, ed. Jo-Marie Burt and Philip Mauceri, 247–68. Pittsburgh, PA: University of Pittsburgh Press.

———. 2006. "Quien habla es terrorista." The political use of fear in Fujimori's Peru. *Latin American Research Review* 41(3): 32–62.

Calandria and Grupo Impulsor Nacional de Mujeres por la Igualdad Real. 2000. *Buscando la equidad en el Congreso. Encuesta sobre participación política de la mujer.* Lima, Peru: Asociación de comunicadores sociales Calandria.

Caldeira, Teresa. 1998. Justice and individual rights: Challenges for women's movements and democratization in Brazil. In *Women and democracy— Latin America and Central and Eastern Europe*, ed. Jane S. Jaquette and Sharon L. Wolchik, 75–103. Baltimore: The Johns Hopkins University Press.

Cameron, Maxwell. 1997. Political and economic origins of regime change in Peru. The eighteenth Brumaire of Alberto Fujimori. In *The Peruvian labyrinth*, ed. Maxwell Cameron and Philip Mauceri, 37–69. University Park, PA: Pennsylvania State University Press.

———. 2006. Endogenous regime breakdown: The Vladivideo and the fall of Peru's Fujimori. In *The fujimori legacy. The rise of electoral authoritarianism in Peru*, ed. Julio F. Carrión, 268–93. University Park, PA: The Pennsylvania State University Press.

Cameron, Maxwell, and Philip Mauceri, eds. 1997. *The Peruvian labyrinth*. University Park, PA: The Pennsylvania State University Press.

Canovan, Margaret. 1981. *Populism*. New York, NY: Harcourt Brace Jonanovich.

Caro, Elena. 2000. *Algunas reflexiones acerca de la situación política de las organizaciones vecinales*. Lima, Peru: FOVIDA.

Carrión, Julio. 2001. *Understanding electoral authoritarianism: The case of the 1995 election in Peru*. Paper presented at the Meeting of the American Political Science Association, San Francisco, CA, August 30-Sept.2.

———, ed. 2006. *The Fujimori legacy. The rise of electoral authoritarianism in Peru*. University Park, PA: The Pennsylvania State University Press.

Cedano, Maria Isabel. 1999. *Los gobiernos locales y las demandas de las mujeres*. Paper presented at the Seminar "Reflexiones para la agenda feminista del nuevo milenio," Lima, Peru, August 1999.

CESIP. 1999. *Es tiempo de mujeres. Balance de la participacion de las mujeres en las elecciones municipales de 1998 en el marco del Proyecto CESIP-Promujer*. Lima, Peru: CESIP.

Chalmers, Douglas. 1977. The politicized State in Latin America. In *Authoritarianism and corporatism in Latin America*, ed. J. Malloy, 23–45. Pittsburgh, PA: University of Pittsburgh Press.

Chalmers, Douglas, Carlos Vilas, Katherine Hite, Scott Martin, Kerianne Piester, and Monique Segarra, eds. 1997. *The new politics of inequality in Latin America: Rethinking participation and representation*. Oxford: Oxford University Press.

Chaney, Elsa. 1979. *Supermadre: Women in politics in Latin America*. Austin: University of Texas Press.

Chávez, Irma. 1997. *¿Ciudadanía o sobrevivencia? Tensión y posibilidad en las mujeres de sectores populares*. In *Lima. Aspiraciones, reconocimiento y ciudadanía en los noventa*, ed. Carmen Rosa Balbi, 107–34. Lima, Peru: Pontificia Universidad Católica del Perú.

Chávez, Martha. 1995. Speech Given before the IV World Conference on Women, September 6th, 1995, Beijing, China (Unofficial translation). http://www.un.org/esa/gopher-data/conf/fwcw/conf/gov/950907164545.txt (accessed January 21, 2008).

Chuchryk, Patricia. 1994. From dictatorship to democracy: The women's movement in Chile. In *The women's movement in Latin America. Participation and democracy*, ed. Jane Jaquette, 65–108. 2nd ed. Boulder, CO: Westview Press.

Collier, David, and Steven Levitsky. 1997. Democracy with adjectives: Conceptual innovation in comparative research. *World Politics* 49 (April): 430–51.

Comisión de la mujer de la municipalidad metropolitana de Lima. 2000. *Diagnóstico sobre la situación de la mujer en Lima Metropolitana.* Lima, Peru: Comisión de la mujer de la municipalidad metropolitana de Lima.

Conaghan, Catherine. 2000. The irrelevant right. Alberto Fujimori and the new politics of pragmatic Peru." In *Conservative parties, the right, and democracy in Latin America,* ed. K. Middlebrook, 255–85. Baltimore: Johns Hopkins University Press.

Conaghan, Catherine. 2005. *Fujimori's Peru: Deception in the public sphere.* Pittsburgh, PA: University of Pittsburgh Press.

Conniff, Michael, ed. 1982. *Latin American populism in comparative perspective.* Albuquerque: University of New Mexico Press.

Consejo nacional de población. 1993. *Programa nacional de promoción de la mujer (1990–1995).* 4th ed. Lima, Peru: Consejo nacional de población.

Consorcio Mujer. 2000. *Se hace camino al andar . . . Aportes a la construccion de la ciudadania de las mujeres en salud.* Lima, Peru: Consorcio Mujer.

Contreras, Carlos, and Marcos Cueto. 1999. *Historia del Perú contemporáneo.* Lima, Peru: Red para el desarrollo de las ciencias sociales en el Perú.

Coral, Isabel. 1998. Women in war: Impact and responses. In *Shining and other paths: War and society in Peru, 1980–1995,* ed. Steve Stern, 345–74. Durham, NC: Duke University Press.

Córdova, Patricia, ed. 1992. *Mujer y liderazgo: entre la familia y la política.* Lima, Peru: Asociación civil estudios y publicaciones urbanas YUNTA.

———. 1996. *Liderazgo femenino en Lima. Estrategias de supervivencia.* Lima, Peru: Fundación Friedrich Ebert.

Cotler, Julio. 1983. Democracy and national integration. A historical perspective. In *The Peruvian experiment reconsidered,* ed. Cynthia McClintock and Abraham Lowenthal, 3–38. Princeton, NJ: Princeton University Press.

———. 1993. *Descomposición política y autoritarismo en el Perú.* Lima, Peru: Instituto de Estudios Peruanos.

———.1994. *Política y sociedad en el Perú. Cambios y continuidades.* Lima, Peru: Instituto de Estudios Peruanos.

———.1995. Political parties and the problems of democratic consolidation in Peru. In *Building democratic institutions: Party systems in Latin America,* ed. Scott Mainwaring and Timothy Scully, 323–53. Stanford, CA: Stanford University Press.

———. 1995. *Crisis política, outsiders and democradura: El « fujimorismo ».* In *Partidos y clase política en América latina en los 90,* ed. Carina Perelli, Sonia Picado, and Daniel Zovatto, 117–42. San José, Costa Rica: Instituto Interamericano de Derechos Humanos and CAPEL.

Cotler, Julio, and Romeo Grompone. 2000. *El Fujimorismo: ascenso y caída de un régimen autoritario.* Lima, Peru: Instituto de Estudios Peruanos.

Craske, Nikki. 1998. Remasculinisation and the neoliberal state in Latin America. In *Gender, politics and the state,* ed. Vicky Randall and Georgina Waylen, 100–120. London: Routledge.

———. 1999. *Women and politics in Latin America*. New Brunswick, NJ: Rutgers University Press.
Craske, Nikki, and Maxine Molyneux, eds. 2002. *Gender and the politics of rights and democracy in Latin America*. New York: Palgrave.
Cuentas, Martha. 1995. *Perú: Comedores populares, más allá de una estrategia de sobrevivencia*. In *Seminario-Taller Mujer y organización para el consumo en América latina*, ed. Margarita Fernández, 269–86. Santiago, Chile: Programa de economía del trabajo.
Cuentas, Martha, and Ana Zimmermann. 1995. *La ley 25307: entre lo que se manda y lo que se hace. Porcentajes* 3 (April-June):12–16.
Cuentas, Martha. 1996. *Los comedores populares en crisis*? Paper presented at the Seminar "*Situación y perspectivas de los comedores,*" October 1–2. Lima, Peru.
Cueva, Hanny, and Armando Millan. 2000. *Las organizaciones femeninas para la alimentación y su relación con el sector gubernamental*. Lima, Peru: Cuadernos de investigación social, Pontificia Universidad Católica del Perú (PUCP).
Dador, Jenny. 2000. *Alianzas transversales entre las mujeres del Congreso: Una experiencia construida desde la sociedad civil*. Available from http://www.manuela.org.pe (accessed January 14, 2001).
Dahl, Robert. 1982. *Dilemmas of pluralist democracy*. New Haven, CT: Yale University Press.
Deere, Carmen Diana, and Magdalena León. 2001. *Empowering women: Land and property rights in Latin America*. Pittsburgh, PA: University of Pittsburgh Press.
Defensoría del Pueblo. 2000. *Memoria. Defensoría Especializada en los Derechos de la Mujer, abril 1998–abril 2000*. Lima, Peru: Defensoría del Pueblo.
Degregori, Carlos Iván. 2001. *La década de la antipolítica. Auge y huida de Alberto Fujimori y Vladimiro Montesinos*. Second ed. Lima, Peru: Instituto de Estudios Peruanos.
Degregori, Carlos Ivan, and Marvil Francke. 1990. *Tiempos de ira y amor. Nuevos actores para viejos problemas*. Lima, Peru: DESCO.
Delpino, Nena. 1991. *Las organizaciones femeninas por la alimentación: un menú sazonado*. In *La otra cara de la luna. Nuevos actores sociales en el Perú*, ed. Luis Pasará, 29–72. Lima, Peru: CEDYS.
DEMUS. 1997. *Los Derechos de la Mujer* (Volume I). Lima, Peru: DEMUS.
DEMUS. 1998. *Los Derechos de la Mujer* (Volume II). Lima, Peru: DEMUS.
Diamond, Larry. 1996. Is the third wave over? *Journal of Democracy* 7(3): 20–37.
Dietz, Henry. 1998. *Urban poverty, political participation, and the state. Lima 1970–1990*. Pittsburgh, PA: University of Pittsburgh Press.
Dietz, Mary. 1992. Context is all: Feminism and theories of citizenship. In *Dimensions of radical democracy. Pluralism, citizenship, community*, ed. Chantal Mouffe, 63–85. London: Verso.

Durand, Franciso. 1999. *La democracia, los empresarios y Fujimori*. In *El juego político. Fujimori, la oposición y las reglas*, ed. Fernando Tuesta Soldevilla, 165–99. Lima, Peru: Friedrich Ebert Stiftung.
Duverger, Maurice.1955. *The political role of women*. Paris: UNESCO.
Einhorn, Barbara. 1993. *Cinderella goes to market: Citizenship, gender, and women's movements in East Central Europe*. London: Verso.
El Comercio. 2000. *Mujer y política. Las mujeres en el nuevo Congreso. ¿Han funcionado las cuotas?* Supplement inserted in the August 26 edition of *El Comercio* (daily newspaper), Lima, Peru.
El Cuarto Femenino. vol.1, no 1 (September) 1998 to vol.2 no8 (June) 2000. Lima, Peru: Movimiento Manuela Ramos.
Esping-Andersen, Gosta. 1989. *The three worlds of welfare capitalism*. London: Polity Press.
Ewig, Christina. 2006. Hijacking global feminism: Feminists, the Catholic Church, and the family planning debacle in Peru. *Feminist Studies* 32(3): 632–59.
Feijoo, Maria del Carmen. 1994. Women and democracy in Argentina. In *The women's movement in Latin America. Participation and democracy*, ed. Jane Jaquette, 109–29. Boulder, CO: Westview Press.
Feminismo y mujeres de sectores populares. 1986. *Mujer y Sociedad* 10 (May): 4–6.
Fernández, Marisol, Mery Vargas, and Teresa Hernández. 1999. *Innovando rutas legales. Modulo informativo: Mecanismos de proteccion y defensa de los derechos de las mujeres*. Lima, Peru: DEMUS.
Fleury, Sonia. 1997. *Estado sin ciudadanos. Seguridad social en América latina*. Buenos Aires, Argentina: Lugar Editorial.
Flores, Lourdes. 1996. *Violencia contra la mujer: reflexiones desde el derecho*. Lima, Peru: Movimiento Manuela Ramos.
ForoMujer. 1994. *Propuestas políticas desde las mujeres. Conferencia política de mujeres*. Lima, Peru: Ediciones ForoMujer.
———. 1995. *Propuestas desde las mujeres: Políticas públicas*. Lima, Peru: ForoMujer, 1995.
Franceschet, Susan. 2003. "State feminism" and women's movements: The impact of Chile's Servicio Nacional de la Mujer on women's activism. *Latin American Research Review* 38(1): 9–40.
———. 2005. *Women and politics in Chile*. Boulder, CO: Lynne Rienner Publisher.
Francke, Marvil. 1990. *Género, clase y etnia: la trenza de la dominación*. In *Tiempos de ira y amor. Nuevos actores para viejos problemas*, ed. Carlos Ivan Degregori and M. Francke, 79–106. Lima, Peru: DESCO.
Franco, Carlos. 1994. *Ciudadanía plebeya y organizaciones sociales en el Perú (otro camino para "otra" democracia*. In *Democracia emergente en América del Sur*, ed. Gerónimo De Sierra, 95–121. Mexico City: Universidad Nacional Autónoma de México.

Fraser, Nicholas, and Marysa Navarro. 1982. *Eva Perón*. Buenos Aires, Argentina: Editorial Bruguera.
Friedman, Elisabeth. 1999. The effects of 'transnationalism reversed' in Venezuela: Assessing the impact of UN Global Conferences on the women's movement. *International Feminist Journal of Politics* 1(3): 357–81.
Friedman, Elisabeth. 2000. *Unfinished transitions. Women and the gendered development of democracy in Venezuela, 1936–1996*. University Park, PA: The Pennsylvania State University Press.
Friedman, Elisabeth, Kathryn Hochstetler, and Ann Marie Clark. 2001. Sovereign limits and regional opportunities for global civil society in Latin America. *Latin American Research Review* 36(3): 7–35.
Friedmann, John, Rebecca Abers, and Lilian Autler, eds. 1996. *Emergences. Women's struggles for livelihood in Latin America*. Los Angeles: UCLA Latin American Center Publications.
Fujimori, Alberto. 1995. Speech Given before the Fourth World Conference on Women, September 15, 1995, Beijing, China (Unofficial translation). http://www.un.org/esa/gopher-data/conf/fwcw/conf/goc/950915131946.txt (accessed January 21, 2008).
Fuss, Diana. 1989. *Essentially speaking. Feminism, nature and difference*. London/New York: Routledge.
García, Aída. 1994. *Nosotras, las mujeres del Vaso de leche 1984–1994*. Lima, Peru: Centro de Asesoria Laboral del Peru (CEDAL).
———. 1995. *Instrumentos legales para la protección y defensa de las organizaciones sociales de base dedicadas a los programas de alimentación materno infantil*. Lima, Peru: CEDAL.
———. 1999. *Mujeres peruanas: las protagonistas de Junin, Pasco y Huanuco. De la sobrevivencia al desarrollo*. Lima, Peru: Centro de Asesoria Laboral del Peru (CEDAL).
Garretón, Manuel Antonio et al. 2003. *Latin America in the 21st century. Toward a new sociopolitical matrix*. Miami: The North South Center Press.
Gonzales de Olarte, Efraín. 1998. *El neoliberalismo a la peruana. Economía política del ajuste estructural*, 1990–1997. Lima, Peru: Instituto de Estudios Peruanos.
González, Victoria, and Karen Kampwirth, eds. 2001. *Radical women in Latin America. Left and right*. University Park, PA: The Pennsylvania State University Press.
Granados, Arturo. 1996. *Madresantas y maquiavelas bulliciosas. Mujeres y negociación política*. Lima, Peru: Asociación de comunicadores sociales Calandria.
Grompone, Romeo. 1994. *Las mujeres organizadas y la escena pública en Lima*. In *Democracia emergente en América del Súr*, ed. Gerónimo de Sierra, 229–58. Mexico City: Universidad Nacional Autónoma de México.
Grompone, Romeo, and Carlos Mejía. 1995. *Nuevos tiempos, nueva política. El fin de un ciclo partidario*. Lima, Peru: Instituto de Estudios Peruanos.

Grupo Impulsor Nacional Mujeres por la Igualdad Real. 1997. *Del compromiso a la acción. Después de Beijing, qué ha hecho el Estado peruano*. Lima, Peru: Grupo Impulsor Nacional.

———. 2000. *Balance del grado de cumplimiento de la Plataforma de accion mundial en el Peru. Informe*. Lima, Peru: Grupo Impulsor Nacional.

Grupo Impulsor Nacional Mujeres por la Igualdad Real and Asociación de Comunicadores Sociales Calandria. 2000a. *Buscando la equidad en el Congreso. Encuesta sobre la participación política de la mujer*. Lima, Peru: Asociación de Comunicadores Sociales Calandria.

———. 2000b. *Como estámos las mujeres a 5 años de Beijing?* Lima, Peru: Asociación de Comunicadores Sociales Calandria.

Guerra, Francisco. 1995. *La reforma del Estado*. In *Sociedad, partidos y estado en el Perú. Estudios sobre la crisis y el cambio*, ed. Carlos Fernández Fontenoy, 437–62. Lima, Peru: Universidad de Lima.

Guezmes, Ana. 1999. *Los espacios de concertación desde la agenda feminista: Presentación y análisis de la experiencia de la Mesa Tripartita de Seguimiento a la CIPD*. Paper presented at the Seminar "Reflexiones para la agenda feminista del nuevo milenio," August 19–20, Lima, Peru.

Guzman, Virginia. 1990. *Las organizaciones de mujeres populares: tres perspectivas de análisis*. Lima, Peru: Flora Tristan Ediciones.

———. 1995. *El Estado y el movimiento de mujeres, retos y posibilidades*. Lima, Peru: Flora Tristan Ediciones.

Guzman, Virginia, and Alicia Pinzás. 1995. *Biografías compartidas. Redes sociales en Lima*. Lima, Peru: Flora Tristan Ediciones.

Guzman, Virginia, and Patricia Portocarrero. 1992. *Construyendo diferencias*. Lima, Peru: Flora Tristan Ediciones.

Haworth, Lizzi, Cecilia Olea, and Clori Tejada. 1994. *Comisión de asesoría a las organizaciones de mujeres*. Unpublished document produced for Centro de la Mujer Peruana Flora Tristán. Lima, Peru.

Henríquez, Narda. 1989. *Las mujeres en el país de todas las sangres: una aproximación bibliográfica sobre mujer y política*. Lima, Peru: FOMCIENCIAS.

Henríquez, Narda, ed. 1999. *Construyendo una agenda social*. Lima, Peru: Pontificia Universidad Católica del Perú.

Henríquez, Narda, and Josefina Huamán. 1983. *Apuntes sobre la participación de la mujer en las luchas urbano-populares. Perú*. Lima, Peru: Pontificia Universidad Católica del Perú—Programa Académico de Ciencias Sociales.

Htun, Mala. 2003. *Sex and the state. Abortion, divorce, and the family under Latin American dictatorships and democracies*. New York: Cambridge University Press.

Htun, Mala, and Mark Jones. 2002. Engendering the right to participate in decision-making: electoral quotas and women's leadership in Latin America. In *Gender and the politics of rights and democracy in Latin America*, ed. Nikki Craske and Maxine Molyneux, 32–56. New York: Palgrave.

Instituto de la Mujer del Ministerio de Asuntos Sociales de España and *FLACSO*. 1995. *Latin American Women. Compared Figures.* Santiago, Argentina: FLACSO.
International IDEA. 2003. *The implementation of quotas: Latin American experiences.* Available online at: http://www.idea.int/publications/quotas_la/index.cfm (accessed January 2007).
International Labour Organization. *Panorama Laboral* 2001. Available online at http://www.oitandina.org.pe/datoslab/empinf.html (accessed March 11, 2004).
Inter-Parliamentary Union. Women in National Parliaments Database. Available online at http://www.ipu.org/wmn-e/classif-arc.htm (accessed December 11, 2008).
Jaquette, Jane, ed. 1994. *The women's movement in Latin America. Participation and democracy.* Boulder, CO: Westview Press.
Jaquette, Jane and Sharon L. Wolchik, eds. 1998. *Women and democracy: Latin America and Central and Eastern Europe.* Baltimore, MD: Johns Hopkins University Press.
Jelin, Elizabeth, ed. 1990. *Women and social change in Latin America.* London: Zed Books.
Jelin, Elizabeth. 1997. *Los derechos y la cultura de género.* In *La ciudadanía a debate*, ed. Eugenia Hola and Ana María Portugal, 71–85. Santiago, Argentina: Isis Internacional.
Janosky, Thomas. 1998. *Citizenship and civil society: A framework of rights and obligations in liberal, traditional, and social-democratic regimes.* Cambridge: Cambridge University Press.
Jenson, Jane and Papillon, Martin. 2000. "Challenging the citizenship regime: the James Bay Cree and transnational action." *Politics and society*, 28(2): 245–64.
Jones, Kathleen and Anna Jonasdottir, eds.1988. *The political interests of gender.* London: Sage.
Kampwirth, Karen. 2004. *Feminism and the legacy of revolution. Nicaragua, El Salvador, Chiapas.* Athens, OH: Ohio University Press.
———. 2006. Resisting the feminist threat: Antifeminist politics in post-Sandinista Nicaragua. *National Women's Studies Association Journal* 18(2): 73–100.
———, ed. 2010. *Passionate politics: Gender and populism in Latin America.* University Park: Pennsylvania State University Press.
Kampwirth, Karen, and V. Gonzalez, eds. 2001. *Radical women in Latin America: Left and right.* University Park: The Pennsylvania State University Press.
Karl, Terry Lynn. 1997. *The paradox of plenty. Oil booms and petro-states.* Berkeley, CA: University of California Press.
Kenney, Charles. 2004. *Fujimori's coup and the breakdown of democracy in Latin America.* Notre Dame, IN: University of Notre Dame Press.

Klatzer, Elizabeth. 2000. *Un caso de excepción: Las mujeres en la política y la administración pública peruana*. In *El proceso social en el Perú: Investigaciones sobre sociedad, promoción y desarrollo*, 216–32. Lima, Peru: Prom-Perú and Universidad del Pacífico.

Knight, Alan. 1998. Populism and neo-populism in Latin America, especially Mexico. *Journal of Latin American Studies* 30(2): 223–48.

Kogan, Liuba. 1998. *Asociaciones de mujeres de sectores medios-altos de Lima*. Lima, Peru: Instituto de Estudios Peruanos.

Laclau, Ernesto. 1977. *Politics and ideology in Marxist Theory*. London: Verso.

———. 2005. Populism: What's in a name? In *Populism and the mirror of democracy*, ed. Francisco Panizza, 32–49. London: Verso.

León, Magdalena, ed. 1994. *Mujeres y participación política: Avances y desafíos en América Latina*. Bogota, Colombia: Tercer Mundo Editores.

Levitsky, Steven. 1999. Fujimori and post-party politics in Peru. *Journal of Democracy* 10(July): 78–92.

Levitsky, Steven, and Maxwell Cameron. 2001. *Democracy without Parties? Political parties and regime collapse in Fujimori's Peru*. Paper presented at the Congress of the Latin American Studies Association, September 6–8, Washington, D.C.

Levitsky, Steven, and Lucan Way. 2002. The rise of competitive authoritarianism. *Journal of Democracy* 13(2): 51–65.

Levitsky, Steven, and María Victoria Murillo, eds. 2005. *Argentine democracy: The politics of institutional weakness*. University Park, PA: The Pennsylvania State University Press.

Lind, Amy. 2004. Engendering Andean politics. The paradoxes of women's movements in neoliberal Ecuador and Bolivia. In *Politics in the Andes. Identity, conflict, reform*, ed. Jo-Marie Burt and Philip Mauceri, 58—78, PA. Pittsburgh: University of Pittsburgh Press.

———. 2005. *Gendered paradoxes. Women's movements, state restructuring, and global development in Ecuador*. University Park, PA: The Pennsylvania State University Press.

Linz, Juan, and Alfred Stepan. 1996. *Problems of democratic transition and consolidation: Southern Europe, South America and Post-Communist Europe*. Baltimore: The Johns Hopkins University Press.

Lister, Ruth. 1995. Dilemmas in engendering citizenship. *Economy and Society* 24(1): 1–40.

———. 1997. Citizenship: Towards a feminist synthesis. *Feminist Review* 57(1): 28–48.

Loli, Silvia. 1999. *Los derechos de la mujer y los espacios institucionales de politicas*. Paper presented at the Seminar "Reflexiones para la Agenda Feminista del Nuevo Milenio," August 19–20, Lima, Peru.

———. 2000. *La mujer y los espacios institucionales: un balance*. In *Al rescate de la utopía. Reflexiones para una agenda feminista del nuevo milenio*, ed. Macassi, Ivonne, and Cecilia Olea, 55–61. Lima, Peru: Ediciones Flora Tristan.

López, Sinesio. 1997. *Ciudadanos reales e imaginarios. Concepciones, desarrollo y mapas de la ciudadanía en el Perú*. Lima, Peru: Instituto de Dialogo y Propuestas (IDS).
Lora, Carmen.1996. *Creciendo en dignidad. Movimiento de comedores autogestionarios*. Lima, Peru: Instituto Bartolomé de las Casas and CEP.
Los grupos feministas nacionales. 1980. *Mujer y Sociedad* 1 (July): 16–24.
Lowenthal, Abraham. 1983. The Peruvian experiment reconsidered. In *The Peruvian experiment reconsidered*, ed. Cynthia McClintock and Abraham Lowenthal, 415–30. Princeton, NJ: Princeton University Press.
Lovenduski, Joni, ed. 2005. *State feminism and political representation*. New York: Cambridge University Press.
Lovenduski, Joni, and Pippa Norris, eds. 1993. *Gender and Party Politics*. London: Sage.
Lynch, Nicolas.1995. Nuevos ciudadanos y vieja política en el Perú. In *Sociedad, partidos y estado en el Perú. Estudios sobre la crisis y el cambio*, ed. Carlos Fernández Fontenoy, 333–46. Lima, Peru: Universidad de Lima.
Lynch, Nicolas. 1999. *Una tragedia sin héroes. La derrota de los partidos y el orígen de los independientes. Perú 1980–1992*. Lima, Peru: Universidad Nacional Mayor de San Marcos.
Macassi, Ivonne, and Cecilia Olea, eds. 2000. *Al rescate de la utopía. Reflexiones para una agenda feminista del nuevo milenio*. Lima, Peru: Ediciones Flora Tristan.
Machuca, Maritza. 1997. *Las mujeres y el poder en los municipios: Tarma e Independencia*. In *Lima. Aspiraciones, reconocimiento y ciudadanía en los noventa*, ed. Carmen Rosa Balbi, 165–86. Lima, Peru: Pontificia Universidad Católica del Perú.
MacPherson, Anne S. 2003. Citizens v. clients: Working women and colonial reform in Puerto Rico and Belize, 1932–1945. *Journal of Latin American Studies* 35(2): 279–310.
Mainwaring, Scott, and Timothy Scully. 1995. *Building democratic institutions. Party systems in Latin America*. Stanford, CA: Stanford University Press.
Marques-Pereira, Bérengère, and Patricio Nolasco, eds. 2001. *La représentation politique des femmes en Amérique latine*. Paris: L'Harmattan.
Marshall, T. H. 1950. *Citizenship and social class and other essays*. Cambridge: Cambridge University Press.
Matland, Richard E. 1998. Enhancing women's political participation: Legislative recruitment and electoral systems. In *Women in parliament: Beyond numbers*, ed. Azza Karam, chap.3. International IDEA. Online edition available at: http://archive.idea.int/women/parl/ch3a.htm (accessed January 2007).
Mauceri, Philip. 1997. The transition to "democracy" and the failures of institution-building. In *The Peruvian labyrinth*, ed. Maxwell Cameron and Philip Mauceri, 13–36. University Park, PA: The Pennsylvania State University Press.

Mayorga, Fernando. 2002. *Neopopulismo y democracia. Compadres y padrinos en la política boliviana (1988–1999)*. La Paz: Plural Editores and Centro de Estudios Superiores Universitarios de la UMSS.
Mayorga, René Antonio. 1995. *Antipolítica y Neopopulismo*. La Paz, Bolivia: Centro Boliviano de Estudios Multidisciplinarios.
———. 2002. *Outsiders and neopopulism: The road to plebiscitarian authoritarianism*. Paper presented to the Conference "The Crisis of Democratic Representation in the Andes," South Bend, Indiana, May 13–14: Kellogg Institute for International Affairs, University of Notre Dame.
McAdam, Doug, Sydney Tarrow, and Charles Tilly. 1997. Towards an integrated perspective on social movements and revolutions. In *Comparative politics. Rationality, culture, and structure*, ed. M. I. Lichbach and A. S. Zuckerman, 142–73. Cambridge: Cambridge University Press.
McClintock, Cynthia. 1989. Peru's Sendero Luminoso's rebellion: Origins and trajectory. In *Power and popular protest: Latin American social movements*, ed. Susan Eckstein. Berkeley, CA: University of California Press.
———. 1999. ¿Es autoritario el gobierno de Fujimori? In *El juego político. Fujimori, la oposición y las reglas*, ed. Fernando Tuesta Soldevilla, 65–96. Lima, Peru: Friedrich Ebert Stiftung.
McClintock, Cynthia, and Abraham Lowenthal, eds. 1983. *The Peruvian experiment reconsidered*. Princeton, NJ: Princeton University Press.
Melzer, Sara, and Leslie Rabine, eds. 1993. *Rebel Daughters. Women and the French Revolution*. Oxford: Oxford University Press.
Mendez, Juan, Guillermo O'Donnell, and Paulo Sergio Pinheiro, eds. 1999. *The (un)rule of law and the underprivileged in Latin America*. Notre Dame, IN: University of Notre Dame Press.
Merino, Beatriz. 1997. *Matrimonio y violación. El debate del artículo 178 del Código Penal Peruano*. Lima, Peru: Manuela Ramos and UNICEF.
Moghadam, Valentine. 1995. Gender and revolutionary transformation: Iran 1979 and East Central Europe 1989. *Gender & Society* 9(3): 328–58.
Mollmann, Marianna, and Susana Chávez. 2003. *La Regla de la mordaza y la acción política en la lucha por la despenalización del aborto*. Lima, Peru: Flora Tristán.
Molyneux, Maxine. 1985. Mobilization without emancipation? Women's interests, state and revolution in Nicaragua. In *New social movements and the state in Latin America*, ed. David. Slater, 233–59. Amsterdam: CEDLA.
———. 1998. Analysing women's movements. *Development and Change* 29(2): 219–45.
———. 2001. *Women's movements in international perspective. Latin America and beyond*. New York: Palgrave, Institute of Latin American Studies Series.
Molyneux, Maxine, and Shahra Razavi, eds. 2002. *Gender justice, development and rights*. Oxford: Oxford University Press.
Moore, Barrington. 1967. *Social origins of dictatorship and democracy. Lord and peasant in the making of the modern world*. Boston: Beacon Press.

Mosqueira, Edgardo. 1995. *La crisis de la democracia en el Perú: un problema de falta de instituciones.* In *Partidos y clase política en América latina en los 90,* ed.Carina Perelli, Sonia Picado and Daniel Zovatto, 527–54. San José, Costa Rica: Instituto interamericano de derechos humanos and CAPEL.

Movimiento Manuela Ramos. 1996. *El sistema de cuotas.* Lima, Peru: Movimiento Manuela Ramos.

———. *Servicio de información a Congresistas* (newsletter). no.01, July 1995, no.24, April/June 1998.

———. 2000a. *Plataforma de acción por las mujeres. Una propuesta.* Lima, Peru: Movimiento Manuela Ramos.

———. 2000b. *Beijing +5. Qué cambio en la vida de las mujeres peruanas?* Lima, Peru: Movimiento Manuela Ramos and UNIFEM.

———. 2001. *Manuela Ramos en la década de los 90.* Lima, Peru: Movimiento Manuela Ramos.

Mujeres a través de la historia: una aproximación. 1998. Lima, Peru: PROMUDEH.

Navarro, Marysa. 1999. Wonder woman was Argentine and her real name was Evita. *Canadian Journal of Latin American and Caribbean Studies* 24(48): 133–52.

Norris, Pippa, and Ronald Inglehart. 2001. Women and democracy. Cultural obstacles to equal representation. *Journal of Democracy* 12 (July): 126–40.

North, Douglass. 1990. Institutions and their consequences for economic performance. In *The Limits of Rationality,* ed. K. S. Cook and M. Levi, 383–401. Chicago: University of Chicago Press.

Ochoa, Olenka, ed. 2000. *Diagnóstico sobre la situación de la mujer en Lima Metropolitana.* Lima, Peru: Comisión de la Mujer de la Municipalidad Metropolitana de Lima.

O'Donnell, Guillermo. 1979. *Modernization and bureaucratic-authoritarianism: Studies in South American politics.* Berkeley, CA: University of California Press.

———. 1994. Delegative democracy. *Journal of Democracy* 5(1): 55–69.

———. 1999a. Polyarchies and the (un)rule of law in Latin America: A partial conclusion. In *The (un)rule of law and the underprivileged in Latin America,* ed. Juan Méndez, Guillermo. O'Donnell, and Paulo Sérgio Pinheiro, 303–37. Notre Dame, IN: University of Notre Dame Press.

———. 1999b. *Democratic theory and comparative politics.* Paper prepared for presentation at the Annual Meeting of the American Political Science Association, Atlanta.

O'Donnell, G. and Philippe Schmitter. 1986. *Transitions from authoritarian rule. Tentative conclusions about uncertain democracies.* Baltimore: Johns Hopkins University Press.

Olea, Cecilia, ed. 1998. *Encuentros, (des)encuentros y busquedas: el movimiento feminista en América Latina.* Lima, Peru: Ediciones Flora Tristan.

Olea, Cecilia, and Virginia Vargas. 1986. *Qué pasa con las mujeres en la izquierda? Viva* 3 (7) (Sept.-Oct.): 16–18.

Olea, Cecilia, and Virginia Vargas. 1998. *Los nudos de la región*. In *Encuentros, (des)encuentros y busquedas: el movimiento feminista en América Latina*, ed. Cecilia Olea, 139–72. Lima, Peru: Ediciones Flora Tristan.

———. 2000. Los senderos hacia las cumbres. In *Las Apuestas Inconclusas. El Movimiento de Mujeres y la IV Conferencia Mundial de la Mujer*, ed. Gladys Acosta, Maruja Barrig, Sonia Montaño, Cecilia Olea, and Virginia Vargas, 29–80. Lima, Peru: Ediciones Flora Tristan.

Oxhorn, Philip. 1995. From controlled inclusion to reactionary exclusion: Authoritarianism and the international economy in Latin America. In *Civil society: Theory, history and comparison*, ed. John Hall, 250–77. Cambridge: Polity Press.

———. 1998a. *Social inequality, civil society and the limits of citizenship*. Paper presented at the XIV World Congress of Sociology, July 26–August 1 Montreal.

———. 1998b. The social foundations of Latin America's recurrent populism: Problems of popular sector class formation and collective action. *Journal of Historical Sociology* 11(2): 212–46.

———. 1999. *When democracy isn't all that democratic. Social exclusion and the limits of the public sphere in Latin America*. Paper presented at the annual American Political Science Association Conference, September 2–5, Atlanta, Georgia.

Oxhorn, Philip and Graciela Ducatenzeiler, eds. 1998. *What kind of market? What kind of democracy? Latin America in the age of neoliberalism*. University Park, PA: The Pennsylvania State University Press.

Palmer, David Scott, ed. 1994. *The shining path of Peru*. 2nd ed. New York: St. Martin's Press.

Palomino, Rocío. 1987. *El discreto desencanto. Una mirada al feminismo realmente existente. El Zorro de abajo* 6 (January): 21–26.

———. 2000. *Perdidas en el espacio? Las mujeres y los espacios institucionales de políticas*. In *Al rescate de la utopía. Reflexiones para una agenda feminista del nuevo milenio*, ed. Ivonne Macassi and Cecilia Olea, 62–69. Lima, Peru: Ediciones Flora Tristan.

Panfichi, Aldo. 1997. The authoritarian alternative: "Anti-politics" in the popular sectors of Lima. In *The new politics of inequality in Latin America: Rethinking participation and representation*, ed. Douglas Chalmers, Carlos Vilas, Katherine Hite, Scott Martin, Kerianne Piester and Monique Segarra, 217–36. Oxford: Oxford University Press.

Pateman, Carole. 1988. *The sexual contract*. Cambridge: Polity Press.

Patrón, Pepi. 2000. *Presencia social, ausencia política. Espacios públicos y participación femenina*. Lima, Peru: Agenda Perú.

Patroni, Viviana. 1999. A discourse of love and hate: Eva Peron and the labour movement (1940s-1950s). *Canadian Journal of Latin American and Caribbean Studies* 24(48): 153–75.

Perelli, Carina, Sonia Picado, and Daniel Zovatto, eds. 1995. *Partidos y clase política en América Latina en los 90*. San José, Costa Rica: Instituto Interamericano de Derechos Humanos and CAPEL.
Pérez, Andrés, ed. 1997. *Globalizacion, ciudadania y politica social en América Latina: tensiones y contradicciones*. Caracas, Venezuela: Editorial Nueva Sociedad.
Phillips, Anne. 1995. *The politics of presence*. Oxford: Oxford University Press.
Pitanguy, Jacqueline. 1990. Brasil. Políticas públicas y ciudadanía. In *Transiciones. Mujeres en los procesos democráticos*, 13–22. Santiago, Chile: Isis Internacional, 1990.
Pitkin, Hanna. 1967. *The concept of representation*. Berkeley, CA: University of California Press.
Pomar, Nelly. 1997. *Gobierno local, ciudadanía e izquierda en Lima Metropolitana: Independencia y Villa El Salvador*. In *Lima. Aspiraciones, reconocimiento y ciudadanía en los noventa*, ed. Carmen Rosa Balbi, 135–63. Lima, Peru: Pontificia Universidad Católica del Perú.
Ponce del Castillo, Victoria. 1984. *Propuestas políticas y propuestas feministas a las mujeres peruanas*. Lima, Peru: Asociacion peruana para el fomento de las ciencias sociales (FOMCIENCIAS).
Portocarrero, Felipe, A. Beltran, M. E. Romero, and H. Cueva. 2000. *Gestión pública y políticas alimentarias en el Perú*. Lima, Peru: Centro de investigación de la Universidad del Pacífico.
Power, Margaret. 2002. *Right-wing women in chile: Feminine power and the struggle against Allende 1964–1973*. University Park, PA: The Pennsylvania State University Press.
Prokhovnik, Raia. 1998. Public and private citizenship: From gender invisibility to feminist inclusiveness. *Feminist Review* 60 (Autumn): 84–104.
Promujer. 1998. *Poder político con perfume de mujer. Las cuotas en el Perú*. Lima, Peru: Movimiento Manuela Ramos and Instituto de Estudios Peruanos.
Radcliffe, Sarah. 1993. People have to rise up—like the great women fighters. The State and peasant women in Peru. In "Viva." *Women and popular protest in Latin America*, ed. Sarah Radcliffe and S. Westwood, 197–218. London: Routledge.
———. 2002. Indigenous women, rights and the Nation-State in the Andes. In *Gender and the politics of rights and democracy in Latin America*, ed. Nikki Craske and Maxine Molyneux, 149–72. New York: Palgrave.
Rai, Shirin, and Geraldine Lievesley, eds. 1996. *Women and the state: International perspectives*. London: Taylor and Francis.
Randall, Vicky. 1998. Gender and power. Women engage the State. In *Gender, politics and the state*, ed. Vicky Randall and Georgina Waylen, 185–205. London: Routledge.
Randall, Vicky, and Georgina Waylen, eds. 1998. *Gender, politics and the state*. London: Routledge.
Reyna, Carlos. 2000. *La anunciación de Fujimori. Alan García 1985–1990*. Lima, Peru: DESCO.

Roberts, Kenneth. 1995. Neoliberalism and the transformation of populism in Latin America: The Peruvian case. *World Politics* 48 (October): 82–116.

———. 1996. Economic crisis and the demise of the legal left in Peru. *Comparative Politics.* 29 (October): 69–92.

———. 1998. *Deepening democracy? The modern left and social movements in Chile and Peru.* Stanford, CA: Stanford University Press.

———. 2002. Party-society linkages and democratic representation in Latin America. *Canadian Journal of Latin American and Caribbean Studies* 27(53): 9–34.

———. 2006. Populism, political conflict, and grass-roots organization in Latin America, *Comparative Politics* 38(2): 127–48.

Rospigliosi, Fernando. 1995. *La amenaza de la Fujimorización. Gobernabilidad y democracia en condiciones adversas: Perú y los países andinos.* In *Partidos y clase política en América latina en los 90*, ed.Carina Perelli, Sonia Picado, and Daniel Zovatto, 311–34. San José: Instituto Interamericano de Derechos Humanos and CAPEL.

Rousseau, Jean-Jacques. 1972. *Du contrat social.* Oxford: Clarendon Press.

Rousseau, Stéphanie. 2005. Aprismo. In *Encyclopedia of the developing world*, ed. Thomas Leonard, 62–65. New York: Routledge.

———. 2006. Women's Citizenship and neopopulism: Peru under the Fujimori regime. *Latin American Politics and Society* 48(1): 117–41.

———. 2007. The Politics of reproductive health in Peru: Gender and social policy in the global south. *Social politics. International studies in gender, state and society* 14(1): 1–33.

———. 2010. Populism from above, populism from below: Gender politics under Alberto Fujimori and Evo Morales. In *Passionate politics: Gender and populism in Latin America.* Karen Kampwirth, ed., University Park, PA: The Pennsylvania State University Press.

Rueschemeyer, Dietrich, Evelyn Huber Stephens, and John Stephens. 1992. *Capitalist development and democracy.* Chicago: University of Chicago Press.

Ruiz-Bravo, Patricia, ed. 1996. *Detrás de la puerta. Hombres y mujeres en el Perú de hoy.* Lima, Peru: Pontificia Universidad Catolica del Perú.

Rule, Wilma. 1994. Parliaments of, by, and for the people: Except for women? In *Electoral systems in comparative perspective. Their impact on women and minorities*, ed. Wilma Rule and Joseph Zimmerman, 15–30. Westport, CT: Greenwood Press.

Sagasti, Francisco, ed. 2000. *Development strategies for the 21st century: The case of Peru.* Lima, Peru: Agenda Peru.

Sara Lafosse, Violeta. 1984. *Comedores populares. La mujer frente a la crisis.* Lima, Peru: SUMBI, 1984.

Schild, Veronica. 1998. New subjects of rights? Women's movements and the construction of citizenship in the "new democracies." In *Cultures of politics, politics of culture. re-visioning Latin American social movements*, ed. Sonia Alvarez, Evelina Dagnino, and Arturo Escobar, 93–117. Boulder, CO: Westview Press.

Schmidt, Gregory. 1999. *Crónica de una reelección*. In *El juego político. Fujimori, la oposición y las reglas*, ed. Fernando Tuesta Soldevilla, 97–130. Lima, Peru: Friedrich Ebert Stiftung.

Schmidt, Gregory. 2000. Delegative democracy in Peru? Fujimori's 1995 landslide and the prospects for 2000. *Journal of Interamerican Studies and World Affairs* 42 (1): 99–132.

———. 2003. The Implementation of gender quotas in Peru: Legal reform, discourses and impacts. Paper presented at International IDEA Workshop "The Implementation of Quotas: Latin American Experiences," Lima, Peru, 23–24 February 2003. Available online at http://www.quotaproject.org/CS/CS_Schmidt_1_26–11–2003.pdf (accessed June 19, 2005).

———. 2006. All the president's women: Fujimori and gender equity in Peruvian politics. In *The Fujimori legacy. The rise of electoral authoritarianism in Peru*, ed. Julio Carrión, 150–77. University Park, PA: The Pennsylvania State University Press.

Schmitter, Philippe and Terry Lynn Karl. 1993. What democracy is . . . and what it is not. In *The global resurgence of democracy*, ed. Larry Diamond and Marc Plattner, 39–52. Baltimore: The Johns Hopkins University Press.

Siim, Birte. 2000. *Gender and citizenship. Politics and agency in France, Britain and Denmark*. Cambridge: Cambridge University Press.

Somers, Margaret. 1993. Citizenship and the place of the public sphere: Law, community, and political culture in the transition to democracy. *American Sociological Review* 58(5): 587–620.

Staudt, Kathleen. 1998. Women in politics: Mexico in global perspective. In *Women's participation in Mexican political life*, ed. Victoria Rodriguez, 23–40. Boulder, CO: Westview Press.

Stein, Steve. 1999. The paths to populism in Peru. In *Populism in Latin America*, edited by Michael Conniff, 97–116. Tuscaloosa, AL: The University of Alabama Press.

Stepan, Alfred. 1978. *The State and society. Peru in comparative perspective*. Princeton, NJ: Princeton University Press.

Stephen, Lynn. 1997. *Women and social movements in Latin America. Power from below*. Austin: University of Texas Press.

Stetson, Dorothy, and Amy Mazur, eds. 1995. *Comparative state feminism*. Thousand Oaks, CA: Sage Publications.

Stokes, Susan. 1995. *Cultures in conflict. Social movements and the state in Peru*. Berkeley, CA: University of California Press.

———. 1996. Peru: The rupture of democratic rule. In *Constructing democratic governance: South America in the 1990s*, ed. Jorge Dominguez and Abraham Lowenthal, 58–71. Baltimore: Johns Hopkins University Press.

———. 1999. La opinión pública y la lógica política del neoliberalismo. In *El juego político. Fujimori, la oposición y las reglas*, ed. Fernando Tuesta Soldevilla, 201–30. Lima, Peru: Fundación Friedrich Ebert.

Tamayo, Giulia. 1997. Delegaciones policiales de mujeres y secciones especializadas. In *Acceso a la justicia*, ed. Ana Teresa Revilla, 241–62. Lima, Peru: Oficina técnica de proyectos de cooperación internacional del poder judicial.

———. 1997. *La maquinaria estatal: ¿Puede suscitar cambios a favor de las mujeres?* Paper presented at the Conference "Mujer: Espacios estatales y políticas públicas" organized by the Gender Studies Program of the PUCP and CEDEP, June 26, Lima, Peru.

Tamayo, Giulia. 1999. *Nada personal—Reporte de derechos humanos sobre la aplicación de la anticoncepción quirúrgica en el Perú 1996–1998.* Lima, Peru: CLADEM.

Tanaka, Martin. 1998. *Los espejismos de la democracia. El colapso del sistema de partidos en el Perú, 1980–1995, en perspectiva comparada.* Lima, Peru: Instituto de Estudios Peruanos.

———. 1999. *Los partidos políticos en el Perú, 1992–1999: estatalidad, sobrevivencia y política mediática.* Lima, Peru: Instituto de Estudios Peruanos.

———. 2002. *De la crisis al colapso de los sistemas de partidos y los retos de su reconstrucción: los casos de Perú y Venezuela.* Paper presented at the Conference "The crisis of democratic representation in the Andes," Kellogg Institute for International Affairs, May 13–14, University of Notre Dame, Indiana.

Tarrow, Sydney. 1994. *Power in movement.* Cambridge: Cambridge University Press.

Taylor, Julie M. 1979. *Eva Perón. The myths of a woman.* Chicago: The University of Chicago Press.

Tocón, Carmen. 1997. Organizaciones de mujeres para la alimentación en Chimbote (1990–1992). In *Lima. Aspiraciones, reconocimiento y ciudadanía en los noventa,* ed. Carmen Rosa Balbi, 187–217. Lima, Peru: Pontificia Universidad Católica del Perú.

Tokman, Victor, and Guillermo O'Donnell, eds. 1998. *Poverty and inequality in Latin America: Issues and new challenges.* Notre Dame, IN: University of Notre Dame Press.

Torre, Carlos de la. 2000. *Populist seduction in Latin America. The Ecuadorian experience.* Athens, OH: Ohio University Press.

Tovar, Jesús. 1996. *Dinámica de las organizaciones sociales.* Lima, Peru: SEA.

Transparencia. 2000a. *Datos Electorales* (30). Lima, Peru: Asociación Civil Transparencia.

Transparencia. 2000b. *Una historia que no debe repetirse. Perú: Elecciones Generales 2000. Informe de Observación Electoral.* Lima, Peru: Asociación Civil Transparencia.

Tremblay, Manon. 1999. *Des femmes au Parlement: Une stratégie féministe?* Montreal: Remue-ménage.

Tuesta Soldevilla, Fernando, ed. 1999. *El juego político. Fujimori, la oposición y las reglas.* Lima, Peru: Fundación Friedrich Ebert Stiftung.

Tuesta Soldevilla, Fernando. 2001. *Perú Político en Cifras.* Lima, Peru: Friedrich Ebert Stiftung, Third edition.

Turner, Bryan. 1992. Outline of a theory of citizenship. In *Dimensions of radical democracy. Pluralism, citizenship, community,* ed. Chantal Mouffe, 33–62. London: Verso.

Ugarteche, Oscar. 1999. *Globalización y exclusión: La mujer en el Perú de los 90*. In *Construyendo una agenda social*, ed. Narda Henríquez, 141–98. Lima, Peru: Fondo editorial PUCP.
Union interparlementaire. 1997. *Hommes et femmes en politique. La démocratie inachevée. Étude comparative mondiale*. Geneva, Switzerland: Union interparlementaire.
Van Isschot, Luis. 1997. *"Pacificación y Desarrollo"*: Clientelism, community kitchens, and the articulation of social policy in contemporary Peru. Masters Thesis, Simon Fraser University.
Vargas, Virginia. 1988. *Las mujeres en movimiento (o de como somos políticas las mujeres)*. In *Mujeres latinoamericanas. Diez ensayos y una historia colectiva*, Lima, Peru: Ediciones Flora Tristan.
———. 1989. *El aporte de la rebeldía de las mujeres*. Lima, Peru: Ediciones Flora Tristan.
———. 1995. Acuerdos asumidos por las ONGs. In *Mujer y Desarrollo*, 35–41. Lima, Peru: Comisión Permanente de los Derechos de la Mujer del Consejo Nacional de Derechos Humanos and Ministerio de Justicia.
———. 1998. Carta hacia el VII Encuentro feminista latinoamericano y del Caribe. Chile, 1996. In *Encuentros, (des) encuentros y busquedas: El movimiento feminista en America latina*, ed. Cecilia Olea, 13–33. Lima, Peru: Ediciones Flora Tristan.
———. 1998. Nuevos derroteros de los feminismos latinoamericanos en los 90: Estrategias y perspectivas. In *Encuentros, (des) encuentros y busquedas: El movimiento feminista en America latina*, ed. Cecilia Olea, 187–207. Lima, Peru: Ediciones Flora Tristan.
———. 2000. *El Fujimorismo y las mujeres: los riesgos de la democracia en la región*. Socialismo y Participación 88 (September): 11–15.
———. 2000. *Las trampas de la representación de las mujeres en el gobierno de Fujimori*. Texto y Pretexto 1 (December): 1–8.
———. 2001. Mujeres por la Democracia. Los conjuros contra la tentación de la igualdad en clave autoritaria. Una reflexión político personal. *Cuestión de Estado* (27/28): 104–7.
Vargas, Virginia. 2002. The struggle by Latin American feminisms for rights and autonomy. In *Gender and the politics of rights and democracy in Latin America*, ed. Nikki Craske and Maxine Molyneux, 199–221. New York: Palgrave Publishers.
Vargas, Virginia, and Cecilia Olea. 1997. *El movimiento feminista y el Estado: Los avatares de una agenda propia*. Paper presented at the Conference "El movimiento feminista y el Estado: Los avatares de una agenda propia," September 10, organized by CEDEP, Lima, Peru.
Vargas, Virginia, and Victoria Villanueva. 1994. Between confusion and the law: Women and politics in Peru. In *Women and politics worldwide*, ed. Barbara Nelson and Najma Chowdhury, 576–89. New Haven, CT: Yale University Press.

Vickers, Jill. 1997. *Reinventing political science. A feminist approach*. Halifax, Canada: Fernwood Publishing.

Villar, Eliana. 1994. *Por mérito propio. Mujer y política*. Lima, Peru: Ediciones Flora Tristan.

Villavicencio, Maritza. 1987. Articulación del movimiento feminista con los movimientos sociales. Paper presented at the workshop *"Taller de sistematización sobre la problemática de la mujer en el área de organización y participación,"* December 5, Lima, Peru.

Waisbord, Silvio. 2003. Media populism: Neo-populism in Latin America. In *The media and neo-populism: A contemporary comparative analysis*, ed. Gianpietro Mazzoleni, Julianne Stewart, and Bruce Horsefield, 197–216. Westport, CT: Praeger.

Walby, Sylvia. 1994. Is citizenship gendered? *Sociology* 28(May): 379–95.

Waylen, Georgina. 1994. Women and democratization: Conceptualizing gender relations in transition politics. *World Politics* 46(April): 327–54.

———. 2000. Gender and democratic politics: A comparative analysis of consolidation in Argentina and Chile. *Journal of Latin American Studies* 32: 765–93.

———. 2007. *Engendering transitions: Women's mobilization, institutions, and gender outcomes*. Oxford: Oxford University Press.

Weldon. S. Laurel. 2006. Inclusion, solidarity, and social movements: The global movement against gender violence. *Perspectives on Politics* 4(1): 55–74.

Weyland, Kurt. 1996. Neopopulism and neoliberalism in Latin America: Unexpected affinities. *Studies in comparative international development* 31(3): 3–31

———. 1999. Neoliberal populism in Latin America and Eastern Europe. *Comparative Politics* 31(4): 379–401.

———. 2001. Clarifying a contested concept. Populism in the study of Latin American politics. *Comparative Politics* 34(1):1–22.

Wise, Carol. 2003. *Reinventing the state. Economic strategy and institutional change in Peru*. Ann Arbor, MI: University of Michigan Press.

Wolfe, Joel. 1994. "Father of the Poor" or "Mother of the Rich"? Getulio Vargas, industrial workers, and constructions of class, gender, and populism in Sao Paulo, 1930–1954. *Radical History Review* 58(Winter): 80–112.

Yañez, Ana María, and Lisbeth Guillén, eds. 1998. *Poder político con perfume de mujer. Las cuotas en el Perú*. Lima, Peru: Movimiento Manuela Ramos and Instituto de Estudios Peruanos.

Young, Iris Marion. 1989. Polity and group difference: A critique of the ideal of universal citizenship. *Ethics* 99(2): 250–74.

———. 1990. *Justice and the politics of difference*. Princeton, NJ: Princeton University Press.

Yuval-Davis, Nira. 1997. Women, citizenship and difference. *Feminist Review* 57(1): 4–27.

Index

abortion, 71, 81, 87
Alternativa, 115
Alvarado, Juan Velasco, 15, 36–42, 61, 69
Alvarado, Maria Jesús, 67, 131
American Popular Revolutionary Alliance (Alianza Popular Revolucionaria Americana), 14–15, 35–53, 61–65, 105–9, 131–32, 184n1, 184n3
AP. *See* Popular Action Party
APRA. *See* American Popular Revolutionary Alliance
Association of Peruvian Municipalities (Asociación de Municipalidades del Perú), 139

Barrantes, Alfonso, 43, 46, 142
Belaúnde, Fernando, 41, 43, 44, 105, 119
Benavente, Miyaray, 116
Bermúdez, Violeta, 94, 194n32
Bishop's Social Action Commission (Comisión Episcopal de Acción Social), 105

Cáceres, Zoila A., 131
Calandria, 115, 133
Canadian International Development Agency, 83
Caro, Elena, 117
CCD. *See* Democratic Constituent Congress

CEAS. *See* Bishop's Social Action Commission
CESIP, 115, 140, 193n17
Change 90 (Cambio 90), 47, 185n12
Chávez, Hugo, 3, 20
Chávez, Martha, 137, 138, 145, 150
Christian Popular Party (Partido Popular Cristiano), 41, 46, 192n5
citizenship
  and construction, 4–7, 29–32, 37, 68, 123–27, 169–74
  and rights, 28, 39, 86, 93, 124, 166
Civic Unity Solidarity (Unidad Cívica Solidaridad), 21
clientelism, 62–63, 101, 118–23
CNC. *See* National Commission of Collective Kitchens
collective kitchens (*comedores populares*), 97–98, 101–28, 165–69, 187n25, 190n3, 190n4
Commission on the Peruvian Woman (Comisión Nacional de la Mujer Peruana), 40, 69
Communist Party of Peru Shining Path (Partido Comunista del Perú Sendero Luminoso). *See* Shining Path
Community Development Committees (Comités Pro Desarrollo Comunal), 99

CONAMUP. *See* Commission on the Peruvian Woman
CONDEPA. *See* Nation's Conscience
Consumers Protection Institute (Instituto de Defensa del Consumidor), 85
COORDIPLAN. *See* National Coordinating Commission on Family Planning and Reproductive Health Policies
COPRODE. *See* Community Development Committees
Cuculiza, Luisa María, 84, 149, 150

democracy, 19–22, 25–30, 37, 41, 54, 57, 93, 103, 152, 154, 168–71, 184n6, 186n19
Democratic Constituent Congress (Congreso Constituyente Democrático), 52, 53, 57
Democratic Front (Frente Democrático), 36, 46, 47, 51
Direct Assistance Program (Programa de Asistencia Directa), 106, 109, 118
domestic violence. *See* violence

elections, 35, 46, 53–57, 109, 122, 132–36, 139, 141, 155, 172, 192n1, 193n17
Espinal, Rosa, 114, 123
Espinoza, Leonor, 120

Federation of Autonomous Collective Kitchens of Lima and Callao (Federación de comedores autogestionarios de Lima y Callao), 113–25
Federation of Women from the District of Villa El Salvador (Federación de Mujeres Populares de Villa El Salvador), 108, 113, 123
Female Progress (Evolución Femenina), 67, 131

feminism
  and nongovernmental organizations, 71–78, 80, 89–91, 160, 163
  and party politics, 70–71, 131, 141–43, 168
  and political mobilization, 29, 73–77, 80, 131, 168
  and popular-sector movement(s), 29, 71–73, 115–17, 141
  and the State, 6, 75, 82–84, 87–92, 162, 164, 183n4
Feminist Movement Coordinating Collective (Colectivo de Coordinación del Movimiento Feminista), 71
FONCODES. *See* Social Development and Compensation Fund
food aid, 100, 108, 110, 118–23, 165
Food Aid Program for Grassroots Social Organizations (Programa de apoyo a la labor alimentaria de las organizaciones sociales de base), 110
FOVIDA, 115, 117
FREDEMO. *See* Democratic Front
Freedom Movement (Movimiento Libertad), 46, 47, 55
Fujimori, Alberto, 47, 83, 89, 121, 145, 147, 149–51, 155

Gallegos, Felicita, 123
García, Alan, 44–46, 108, 134, 184n2, 185n6, 185n7
Gender Coordinating Body (Mesa de Coordinación en Género), 79
Glass of Milk Coordinating Committee (Coordinadora del Vaso de Leche), 108, 112, 189n2
Green Plan (Plan Verde), 48, 49
Guzmán, Abimael, 55, 62, 150

Haya de la Torre, Víctor Raúl, 14, 184n1
Hermoza, Nicolás Bari de, 50

Higuchi, Susana, 83
Hilario, Emma, 112, 116
Hildebrant, Martha, 145

INDECOPI. *See* Consumers Protection Institute
IU. *See* United Left

Landavery, Rosa, 114, 191n24
LaRosa, Leonora, 74
Latin American and Caribbean Feminist Meeting (Encuentro Feminista Lationoamericano y del Caribe), 77
Law on the protection against family violence (Ley de protección frente a la violencia familiar), 89
Leguía, Augusto, 15
Llosa, Mario Vargas, 36, 46, 47, 59
López, Juana, 112
Lozada, Carmen, 138

MAM. *See* Women's Broad Movement
Manuela Ramos Movement (Movimiento Manuela Ramos), 69–72, 78, 80, 143–44, 152, 193n18, 194n32
MAS. *See* Movement Towards Socialism
Menem, Carlos, 21, 171, 172, 175
Merino, Beatriz, 137–38, 145–47, 193n13
MIBANCO. *See* Micro Credit Agency
Micro Credit Agency (Proyecto de Fomento al Crédito para la Micro Empresa), 85
Ministry for the Promotion of Women and Human Development, 63, 82–85, 90–92, 162
ML. *See* Freedom Movement
Montesinos, Vladimiro, 48, 57, 158, 187n21

Morales Bermúdez, Francisco, 41
Morales, Evo, 21
mother(s), 23, 101, 127, 165, 175
Mothers' Clubs (Clubes de madres), 101, 103, 109
Movement Towards Socialism (Movimiento al Socialismo), 21
Moyano, María Elena, 112–13
MRTA. *See* Tupac Amaru Revolutionary Movement
MUDE. *See* Women's Movement for Democracy
Municipal Elections Law (Ley de Elecciones Municipales), 139, 192n1

Nano, Lourdes Flores, 134, 145–46, 192n5
National Commission of Collective Kitchens (Comisión Nacional de Comedores), 97, 105–16, 121, 191n21
National Coordinating Commission on Family Planning and Reproductive Health Policies, 148
National Customs Agency (Superintendencia Nacional de Aduanas), 85
National Food Aid Program (Programa Nacional de Ayuda Alimentaria), 118, 119, 120–23, 151, 164
National Institute for Family Welfare (Instituto Nacional de Bienestar Familiar), 85
National Meeting of Collective Kitchens (Encuentro Nacional de Comedores), 105
National Office for Food Aid (Oficina Nacional de Apoyo Alimentario), 100, 119
National Social Mobilization Support System (Sistema Nacional de Apoyo a la Movilización Social), 40

National Working Group "Women for Real Equality" (Grupo Impulsor Nacional "Mujeres por la Igualdad Real"), 79, 80, 88
Nation's Conscience (Conciencia de Patria), 21
neighborhood organization (*organización vecinal*), 99, 100
neoliberalism
 and reforms, 19, 59–60, 159
neopopulism, 2–3, 16–22, 24, 30, 59–64, 159, 161, 173–78

Odria, Manuel, 131, 132
Office for the Promotion of Peru (Oficina de Promoción del Perú), 85
ONAA. *See* National Office for Food Aid

PAD. *See* Direct Assistance Program
PCP. *See* Peruvian Communist Party
People's Soup Kitchens (Comedores del Pueblo), 102, 105
Pérez de Cuellar, Javier, 49, 55
Permanent Commission on Women (Comisión de la Mujer), 137, 144, 148, 163
Permanent Commission on Women's Rights (Comisión Permanente de los Derechos de la Mujer), 80, 82, 84
Perón, Eva, 22–24
Perón, Juán, 22–23
Peronism, 22
Peruvian Communist Party (Partido Comunista Peruano), 40
Peruvian Feminism (Feminismo Peruano), 131
Peruvian Sports Institute (Instituto Peruano de Deporte), 85
Peruvian Women's Centre Flora Tristán (Centro de la Mujer Peruana Flora Tristán), 70–72, 80, 193n18

Popular Action Party (Acción Popular), 39, 41, 44, 132, 184n1
Popular Cooperation (Cooperación Popular), 85
populism, 2–3, 12–24, 45, 187n27
PPC. *See* Christian Popular Party
Project Pro-Woman (Promujer), 152–54, 156, 163, 194n32
PROMPERU. *See* Office for the Promotion of Peru
PROMUDEH. *See* Ministry for the Promotion of Women and Human Development
Promujer. *See* Project Pro-Woman
PRONAA. *See* National Food Aid Program
PSR. *See* Socialist Revolutionary Party
PUM. *See* Unified Mariategui Party

quota(s), 122, 133, 136, 139–40, 143, 152, 162, 171
 and law (Ley de Cuotas), 133, 145

Resettlement Support Program (Programa de Apoyo al Repoblamiento), 85

Salgado, Luz, 139, 140, 145
Sánchez Cerro, Luis, 14–15
Santistevan, Jorge, 82
Schenone, Miriam, 84
SEA. *See* Servicio de Educación El Agustino
SERNAM. *See* Servicio Nacional de la Mujer
Serrano, Benedicta, 115, 119, 123, 191n20, 191n33, 191n35
Servicio de Educación El Agustino (SEA), 115
Servicio Nacional de la Mujer (SERNAM), 171
Shining Path (Sendero Luminoso), 36, 43, 50, 55, 62, 111–13, 190n19

SINAMOS. *See* National Social Mobilization Support System
Social Development and Compensation Fund (Fondo de Compensación y Desarrollo Social), 118–19, 187n26
social programs
 and clientelism, 19, 63, 87, 121, 167
 and compensation, 85, 110, 118, 167
 and poverty reduction, 62, 118, 159
Socialist Front of Women, 70
Socialist Revolutionary Party (Partido Socialista Revolucionario), 40
Somos Perú, 122, 123
Sosa, Relinda, 114, 122
Soto, Hernando de, 46, 49
Soup Kitchens (*Ollas comunes*), 101, 102, 105
Specialized Women's Rights Section of the Ombudsman's Office (SWRS), 82–83, 86–87, 161, 189n19
State Taxation Agency, 75
SUNAD. *See* National Customs Agency
SUNAT. *See* State Taxation Agency
survival organizations (*organizaciones de superviviencia*), 99
SWRS. *See* Specialized Women's Rights Section of the Ombudsman's Office

TACIF, 107, 115
Toledo, Alejandro, 57, 134
Townsend, Ana-Elena, 146
Tripartite Follow-Up Working Group on the Population and Development Conference (Mesa Tripartita de Seguimiento a la Conferencia sobre Población y Desarrollo), 88–89, 91

Tupac Amaru Revolutionary Movement (Movimiento Revolucionario Túpac Amarú), 36, 43, 62

UCS. *See* Civic Unity Solidarity
unemployment, 59
Unified Mariategui Party (Partido Unificado Mariátegui), 43–44, 53
Unión por el Perú, 55
United Left (Izquierda Unida), 43, 45–46, 70, 106, 141–42, 194n19
United States Agency for International Development (USAID), 79, 119, 194n32
USAID. *See* United States Agency for International Development

Vamos Vecino, 122–23
Vargas, Virginia, 72, 80, 83–84, 93, 193n18
Vásquez, Roxana, 85
Villanueva, Rocío, 83, 86, 189n19
Villanueva, Victoria, 193n18
violence
 domestic, 83, 89–90, 144
 political, 50, 61–62, 64, 111–13, 176, 190n19
 sexual, 146

Woman's Forum (Foro-Mujer), 71, 142–43, 145, 193n13
Women in Struggle (Mujeres en Lucha), 70
Women's Broad Movement (Movimiento Amplio de Mujeres), 73–74, 89, 94, 155
Women's Movement for a Vote of Conscience (Movimiento de Mujeres por un Voto Consciente), 73
Women's Movement for Democracy (Movimiento de Mujeres por la Democracia), 73–74, 94, 152, 155

GPSR Compliance

The European Union's (EU) General Product Safety Regulation (GPSR) is a set of rules that requires consumer products to be safe and our obligations to ensure this.

If you have any concerns about our products, you can contact us on

ProductSafety@springernature.com

In case Publisher is established outside the EU, the EU authorized representative is:

Springer Nature Customer Service Center GmbH
Europaplatz 3
69115 Heidelberg, Germany

www.ingramcontent.com/pod-product-compliance
Lightning Source LLC
LaVergne TN
LVHW011816060526
838200LV00053B/3810